The Collected Poems of G.K. Chesterton

The Collected Poems of
G.K. Chesterton

WITH AN INTRODUCTION BY
Daniel B. Dodson

DODD, MEAD & COMPANY
NEW YORK

Library of Congress Cataloging in Publication Data

Chesterton, Gilbert Keith, 1874-1936.
   The collected poems of G. K. Chesterton.

   Includes index.
   CONTENTS: New Poems.—Ballad of St. Barbara.—
Poems.—[etc.]
PR4453.C4A17   1980   821'.912   80-16874
ISBN 0-396-07896-6 (pbk.)

ACKNOWLEDGMENT

The Publisher's grateful thanks are due to Messrs. Burns, Oates & Washbourne, Ltd., Messrs. J. M. Dent & Sons, Ltd., Messrs. Methuen & Co., Ltd., and G. P. Putnam's Sons, publishers of the "Ballad of St. Barbara," for their courteous and generous co-operation in the publication of the present Collected Edition of Mr. G. K. Chesterton's Poems.

CONTENTS

Introduction

Gilbert Keith Chesterton (1874–1936)

Gilbert Keith Chesterton began writing poetry as a child and continued to do so for over forty years, almost until his death. It was an avocation, a relief from other herculean literary activities. Indeed, the very magnitude of his accomplishments suggests an unpoetical discipline. Fleet Street was his habitat: the editorial offices, the printers' shops, and in between, the bars. He started an article on a scrap of paper, writing on his knee or any available wall, continuing over a bottle of claret, and finishing at the door of the periodical that had commissioned it.

It is impossible to determine accurately into what astronomical figures his collected works would run, since in 1933, after the death of his mother, Chesterton ordered several cartons of his papers destroyed before Dorothy Collins—his literary executrix, secretary, companion, and chauffeur—was able to intervene. The best guess runs to well over a hundred volumes, a performance that recalls the indefatigable labors of his revered Dickens, or for a broader analogy, the Spanish playwright Lope de Vega, who produced eighteen hundred comedies and four hundred *Auto Sacramentales.* For one popular journal alone, the *Illustrated London News,* he produced a fifteen-hundred-word article a week for thirty-one years, amounting to sixteen hundred articles, well over two million words. At the same time he engaged in a bewildering variety of other literary enterprises—biographies, novels, plays, short stories, political and social forensics, highly publicized lectures and public debates, the editing of his dead brother's paper, later his own, and in his final years, broadcasting over the BBC—while never neglecting a hyperactive social life.

When we think of the lives of poets we are likely to remember Wordsworth in the bucolic isolation of the Lake Country, or Shelley dreaming of Emilia Viviani in sun-splashed Tuscany, or Blake in his garden in Lambeth. Late in his life Chesterton added a garden to his house, Top Meadow, at Mrs. Chesterton's insistence, but he spent little time there. Like Dr. Johnson, for Chesterton London, twenty-five miles away, offered all a civilized man could conceivably desire.

Though not precisely luxurious, Chesterton's early family life was comfortable, with the conventional summers at the sea coast and attendance at the prestigious St. Paul's School. His grandfather had established Chesterton & Sons, House Agents (real estate to us), early in the nineteenth century, and the family business came down to Gilbert's father Edward and a brother. Edward married Marie Louise Grosjean, and from this union three children were born: Gilbert, Cecil, and a daughter, who died early. Gilbert and Cecil remained close spiritually and intellectually until Cecil's death of disease in World War I.

Persuaded on slender evidence of an artistic inclination in himself, Gilbert entered the famous Slade School where he spent three unproductive but informative years, convinced finally that he was not a painter. Following the itinerary of legions of writers before and after him, he was then turned out into the aggressively competitive world of the press to survive by his wit and verbal agility. His path, again traditional, led to a publishing company, Fisher Unwin, where he labored for several years at the conventional starvation salary, but simultaneously he began reviewing, that second-hand literary occupation that meagerly feeds and houses so many writers and aspiring writers.

An additional stimulus to succeed as a writer arrived in the person of one Frances Blogg whom, against maternal objections on both sides, he married in 1901. Under the economic duress of matrimony, he redoubled his literary efforts, writing for a wide variety of journals and papers, producing articles, novels, verse, and eventually beginning the famous Father Brown series of short stories, and inevitably engaging some of the best minds of the period in controversy, among them George Bernard Shaw. It is to the credit of both Shaw and Chesterton that, though they occupied diametrically opposed intellectual and spiritual postures, they remained personal friends and generous public enemies. For Chesterton's spiritual requirements led him ineluctably toward conservatism, and in his search for God, toward Catholicism, while Shaw remained the passionate advocate of creative evolution. In 1922 Chesterton was accepted into the Roman Catholic Church.

But long before this he had become a public figure, owing first to the apparently inexhaustible flow of his language, aphoristic, paradoxical, and though astute, gloriously careless of fact. Always too busy to correct proofs, he forgave the critics of his inaccuracies with genial concession. As a public figure he developed deliberate eccentricity. An immensely corpulent man—over six feet and three hundred pounds, the result of his heroic consumption of beer and wine—he assumed a Falstaffian role in the literary and political world. He was absentminded, unable to fathom the mysteries of tying his own tie, and baffled by geography, even the geography of London, but he strode through the Edwardian and Georgian worlds in an immense cape, a wide-brimmed hat, and carrying a sword-cane. Endearing admissions of an incorruptible romanticism sometimes broke through the dogmatic surface of his political, religious, and moral conservatism: He once confessed that the sword-cane served a quixotic dream that he might be called upon to defend not only the life, but the virtue of some endangered maiden.

It is no exaggeration to say that Chesterton "knew everyone" in the Edwardian and Georgian literary and political scene, from Henry James to T. S. Eliot, from Winston Churchill to the Webbs, but a particular friendship with Hillaire Belloc lasted from 1900 until Chesterton's death. And yet he insisted he was not at home in the twentieth century. In *The Victorian Age in Literature,* published in 1913, he wrote, "I was born a Victorian and sympathize not a little with the Victorian spirit." There is indeed a declared kinship with William Morris and Carlyle in his nostalgia for a world of lost assurances, the sacramental vision of the Middle Ages. Rejecting the languishing Pre-Raphaelite aestheticism of Wilde and Swinburne (who once invited him to Putney Hill) on the one side, the fate-directed tragedies of rural England in Hardy's tales on the other (he once described Hardy as "a sort of village atheist brooding and blaspheming over the village idiot"), and totally impervious to the modernist movement in poetry that emerged in the twenties with Pound and Eliot, Chesterton deliberately turned his back on the experiments of this alien world. In novels, literary studies, and in verse, his vision is didactic, personal, anachronistic, and utterly exempt from the complex ambiguities of symbolism, imagism, dadaism, and surrealism. And though he wrote literary studies on Chaucer, Dickens, Blake, Browning, R. L. Stevenson, and late in life plunged recklessly into theology with books on St. Francis of Assisi and St. Thomas Aquinas (the latter works highly praised by theologians), his perverse standards blinded him to the achievements of genius uncongenial to his own dogmatic tastes. Chesterton's place in anthologies of modern English verse is secure, but by no stretch of aesthetic canon can he be described as one of the major English poets.

The present volume contains all seven books of poetry published in Chesterton's lifetime, and though at first exposure it may impress the reader as a mixed bag, there are certain dominant strains that categorize his verse into two general types: satire in the school of Byron, or of Pope and the Augustans, including a wide range of occasional verse; and the serious verse and balladry on a variety of subjects mythological, legendary, historical, and religious.

What strikes the reader immediately, however, is the regularity of meter and rhyme scheme. Chesterton was locked into tradition;

he seems incapable of, or simply averse to, any kind of experimentation in free or even blank verse. He is given to old English prosody, rich in alliteration and assonance.

This is not to deny him skill of his craft. He handles the quatrain with dexterity; he exhibits extraordinary virtuosity in metrical effects, manipulating iambic tetrameters, pentameters, and, rather unusual in English verse, hexameters, and even heptameters, as in the jolly, widely anthologized "The Rolling English Road" (p. 188). He is able to emerge from the common iambic pattern into both dactyls and anapests, reflecting perhaps the wash of Swinburne's prosody over *fin de siècle* English verse. With few exceptions, however, his most accomplished lines are satire—satire on modern life, capitalist enterprise, and on prohibitionist movements, one of his *bêtes noires*. He has great fun providing the sea with an answer to Byron (p. 36), introducing a dog into Browning's Spanish Cloister (p. 38), and satirizing the form of modern poetry (p. 40).

Beneath the veneer of what may pass as casual animadversion against pet hates, there is often acidulous satire within satire. "The Song of Right and Wrong" (p. 201) is an example. It reads like any number of Chesterton's attacks on temperance beverages —until the third stanza.

> Tea, although an Oriental,
> Is a gentleman at least;
> Cocoa is a cad and coward,
> Cocoa is a vulgar beast,
> Cocoa is a dull, disloyal,
> Lying, crawling cad and clown,
> And may very well be grateful
> To the fool that takes him down.

For the unprepared reader this will pass as one more of Chesterton's genial displays of waspishness, until one learns that *The Daily News* was popularly known as the "Cocoa Press," and that

Chesterton had recently been fired from *The Daily News* on political grounds.

Of the serious verse, two examples must be mentioned, usually considered Chesterton's most successful and most popular poems. The first, "Lepanto," appeared in 1915 in the collection entitled *Poems*. Palpably owing some of its rhythmic effects to Browning's "Cavalier Tunes," "Lepanto" commemorates the crucial naval battle that took place in the Gulf of Corinth on October 7, 1571, in which the Holy League (Spain, Venice, and the papacy) under Don Juan of Austria, the Spanish monarch, annihilated the Turkish fleet, thus ending the domination of the Ottoman Empire in the Mediterranean. While the rest of Christendom is torn by internecine squabbles or lies in ruinous self-indulgence ignoring the Ottoman threat, Don Juan gathers his forces to meet the Turk, his progress tallied by the refrains: *"Don Juan of Austria is going to the war," "Don Juan of Austria is girt and going forth,"* and *"Don Juan of Austria is armed upon the deck."* (Emphasis in the original.)

A war poem (note the date of publication, 1915), and a successful work of this genre, it employs the long heptameter line to stirring effect, just this side of doggerel. The poem closes with a brief tableau of that other hero, Cervantes, who took part in the battle and was severely wounded in his left hand.

But Chesterton's serious readers almost unanimously agree that his most considerable accomplishment in verse is his long (almost one hundred pages) 1912 poem, "The Ballad of the White Horse." The subject is King Alred's heroic efforts to regroup his scattered army and prepare another assault on the marauding Danes who have defeated his forces on every earlier encounter. More than a celebration of the patriotic determination of the first of the English kings, however, it is also a witness to the triumph of Christianity over uncouth Nordic paganism, the forging of nationalism on the spiritual strength of the new religion. Crushed and humiliated, Alred manifests an enduring fidelity to a national and religious ideal, appealing to his scattered Wessex veterans for yet one more effort in the name of Our Lady.

Narrated in simple quatrains and five- and six-line stanzas, it achieves considerable power, particularly in the Fifth and Sixth Books, describing the triumphant battle of Ethandune.

There is no place or patience for the subtleties of modern verse in Chesterton's poetic aesthetics. What is quite evident in the poetry itself is reinforced by his comments on the role of the poet: He is "the man who can express himself; the poet means the man who can make himself understood." Designed obscurity is, by this definition, nonpoetic. Elsewhere he compares the poet to "the builder of the bridge," who crosses "the chasm between the world of unspoken ... truths to the world of spoken words. His triumph is when {sic} the bridge is completed and the word is spoken; above all when it is heard."

Quite clearly this is the expression of a very ancient poetic mission, primitive, indeed bardic, in its appeal.

DANIEL B. DODSON
Columbia University

Book One
New Poems

THE JUDGMENT OF ENGLAND

"Ill fares the land, to hastening ills a prey
Where Wealth accumulates and Men decay."
So rang of old the noble voice in vain
O'er the Last Peasants wandering on the plain,
Doom has reversed the riddle and the rhyme,
While sinks the commerce reared upon that crime,
The thriftless towns litter with lives undone,
To whom our madness left no joy but one;
And irony that glares like Judgment Day
Sees Men accumulate and Wealth decay.

THE MONSTER

"THE DEGENERATE GREEK INTELLECT WASTED ITSELF IN FUTILE DE-
BATES ABOUT THE DUAL NATURE OF CHRIST."—*Magazine Article.*

One with the golden eagle of the morning,
Flat and flung wide above the spinning plains,
It seemed my spirit sprang and wheeled and flew.
The world went under us like a river of light,
An ecstasy of order, where each life,
Rejoicing in its law, rushed to its end:
To break itself and breed; the embattled vines,
Grassland and grainland waved their thousand spears
In one wild rhythm as they swept along,
A map of marching armies, all one way;
And ploughmen on their uplands ribbed with gold,
Went forward happy, with their backs to heaven.

Only the sacred eagle up the stream
Strove back to his beginnings; left behind

The white archaic dawns on herbless hills,
The first cold hues of chaos; like a stair
Mounted the soundless cataracts of the sun,
Seeking the sun of suns; till suddenly
The last heavens opened; for one flash I saw
Something too large and calm for sight or reason,
The Urns of Evil and Good, vast as two worlds,
And over them a larger face than Fate's
Of that first Will that is when all was not.
But that unblinded burning eagle soared
And perched upon His thunderous right hand.
I cowered, and heard a cry torn out of me
In an unknown tongue older than all my race,
"O Father of Gods and Men"; and saw no more.

The vulture from his dark and hairy nest
Far down the low-browed cliffs of the abyss
Stood black against the sun; a shape of shame:
A plumed eclipse; and all the ways of men
Were paved with upturned faces; masks of hate:
For that hooked head was like a horrible tool,
An instrument of torture made alive
With creaking pinions; for what end they knew:
The vulture of the vengeance of the gods.

For a red under-light on all that land,
A hell that is the underside of heaven,
Glowed from men's struggling fires; and as I followed
That evil bird over lost battle-fields,
Where panoplied and like fallen palaces
The great and foolish kings who warred with doom
Lay sunken with their star; I saw far off,
Misshapen, against the dark red dome of sky,
A mountain on a mountain. As I gazed

The shape seemed changed: the upper mountain moved.
It heaved vast flanks ribbed like the red-ribbed hills,
Thrust down an uprooted forest with one heel
And stretched a Titan's arm to touch the sky.

"You slay for ever, but you slay too late;
A stolen secret turns not home again.
While I lie lifted high against your wrath,
Hanged on this gibbet of rock, far down below
The fire is spreading on the earth's dark plains
And my red stars come forth like flowers of night
And my red sun burns when your white sun dies.
See where man's watchfire dances and derides,
The sickly servile sunset crawling away:
Lo; my red banner thrashes through the air,
Nor dare your vulture peck it if he pass."

The vulture passed, a shadow on the fire,
And the dark hills were loud with dreadful cries.

I woke; the skies were empty of the eagle,
And empty of the vulture all the abyss:
And something in the yawning silence cried
Giants and gods were dying in new dawns:
Daylight itself had deepened; there opened in it
New depths or new dimensions; stone and tree
In that strange light grew solid; as does a statue
Or many-sided monument set beside
The flattened fables on a bas-relief.
Only in dark thin lines against the dawn
The last and lingering monsters limped away,
The boys with crooked legs and cries of goats
Ran as from one pursuing; amid the weeds
Wailed the strange women, neither fish nor flesh,

And from the hoary splendours of the sea
Rose Triton with the limbs that curled like whirlpools,
Stonily staring at some sign afar.

For a new light in a new silence shone
From some new nameless quarter of the sky
Behind us on the road; and all strange things
Looked back to something stranger than themselves
And, towering still and trampling, the Last Centaur
Cried in a roar that shook the shuddering trees,
"We rode our bodies without bridle at will,
We hurled our high breasts forward on flying hooves:
But these two bodies are a simple thing
Beside that Fear that comes upon the world.
A Monster walks behind." I dared not turn;
A shape lay like a shadow on the road.
I saw not but I heard; a sound more awful,
Then from the blackest cypress-close the call
Of some dark Janus shouting with two mouths:

"I am Prometheus. I am Jupiter.
In ravening obedience down from heaven,
Hailed of my hand and by this sign alone,
My eagle comes to tear me. Touch me not."

I lay there as one dead. But since I woke
This single world is double till I die.

THE MODERN MANICHEE

He sayeth there is no sin, and all his sin
Swells round him into a world made merciless;
The midnight of his universe of shame
Is the vast shadow of his shamelessness.

He blames all that begat him, gods or brutes,
And sires not sons he chides as with a rod.
The sins of the children visited on the fathers
Through all generations, back to a jealous God.

The fields that heal the humble, the happy forests
That sing to men confessed and men consoled,
To him are jungles only, greedy and groping,
Heartlessly new, unvenerably old.

Beyond the pride of his own cold compassion
Is only cruelty and imputed pain:
Matched with that mood, a boy's sport in the forest
Makes comrades of the slayer and the slain.

The innocent lust of the unfallen creatures
Moves him to hidden horror but no mirth;
Misplaced morality rots in the roots unconscious,
His stifled conscience stinks through the green earth.
The green things thrust like horrible huge snails,
Horns green and gross, each lifting a leering eye
He scarce can call a flower; it lolls obscene,
Its organs gaping to the sneering sky.

Dark with that dusk the old red god of gardens,
Still pagan but not merry any more,
Stirs up the dull adulteries of the dust,
Blind, frustrate, hopeless, hollow at the core;
The plants are brutes tied with green rope and roaring
Their terrible dark loves from tree to tree:
He shrinks as from a shaft, if by him singing,
A gilded pimp and pandar, goes the bee.

He sayeth, "I have no sin; I cast the stone,"
And throws his little pebble at the shrine,
Casts sin and stone away against the house
Whose health has turned earth's waters into wine.
The venom of that repudiated guilt
Poisons the sea and every natural flood
As once a wavering tyrant washed his hands,
And touching, turned the water black with blood.

THE PORT OF LONDON AUTHORITY

MR. BEN TILLETT IS REPORTED TO HAVE ONCE PRAYED IN PUBLIC
FOR THE DEATH OF LORD DEVONPORT.—*Daily Paper*

We whom great mercy holds in fear,
    Boast not the claim to cry,
Stricken of any mortal wrong,
    "Lord, let this live man die!"

But not incuriously we ask,
    Pondering on life and death,
What name befits that round of years,
    What name that span of breath.

That perfect dullness counting hands
    That have no man or woman,
That fullness of the commonplace
    That can despise the common.

That startling smallness that can stop
    The breath like an abyss,
As, staring at rows of noughts, we cry,
    "And men grow old for this!"

The thing that sniggers when it sneers,
  That never can forget,
The billycock outshines the cap,
  And then—the coronet!

O mighty to arise and smite,
  O mightier to forgive,
Sunburst that blasted Lazarus,
  Lord, let this dead man live!

BY A REACTIONARY

Smoke rolls in stinking, suffocating wrack
On Shakespeare's land, turning the green one black;
The crowds that once to harvest home would come
Hope for no harvest and possess no home,
While poor old tramps that liked a little ale,
In natural procession pass to gaol;
Because the world must, like the tramp, move on,
There does not seem much else that can be done.
As Lord Vangelt said in the House of Peers:
"None of us want Reaction." (Tory cheers).

So doubtful doctors punch and prod and prick
A man thought dead; and when there's not a kick
Left in the corpse, no twitch or faint contraction,
The doctors say: "See . . . there is no Reaction."

A BROAD MINDED BISHOP REBUKES THE VERMINOUS ST. FRANCIS

If Brother Francis pardoned Brother Flea,
There still seems need of such strange charity,
Seeing he is, for all his gay goodwill,
Bitten by funny little creatures still.

THE BATTLE OF THE STORIES (1915)

In the Caucasus.

They came uncounted like the stars that circle or are set,
They circled and they caught us as in a sparkling casting-
net
We burst it in the mountain gate where all the guns began,
When the snow stood up at Christmas on the hills of
Ardahan.
The guns—and not a bell to tell that God was made a man—
But we did all remember, though all the world forget.

Before Paris.

The kings came over the olden Rhine to break an ancient
debt,
We took their rush at the river of death in the fields where
first we met,
But we marked their millions swaying; then we marked a
standard fall;
And far beyond them, like a bird, Maunoury's bugle call:
And there were not kings or debts or doubts or anything
at all
But the People that remembers and the peoples that forget.

In Flanders.

Empty above your bleating hordes his throne abides the threat,
Who drew the sword of his despair to front your butcher's
bet:
You shall scan the empty scabbard; you shall search the
empty seat.
While he along the ruined skies rides royal with retreat,
In the judgment and the silence and the grass upon the street.
And the oath the heavens remember and you would fain
forget.

In Poland.

A cloud was on the face of God when three kings met,
What hour the worst of men were made the sun hath suffered
yet.
We knew them in their nibbling peace or ever they went to
war.
In petty school and pilfered field we know them what they
are.
And we drank the cup of anguish to the pardon of the Czar,
To the nations that remember and the empires that forget.

In the Dardanelles.

To the horned mount of the high Mahound of moon and of
minaret
Labouring go the sieging trains whose tracks are blood and
sweat.
The ships break in a sanguine sea; and far to the front a
boy
Fallen, and his face flung back to shout with the Son of God
for joy.
And the long land under the lifted smoke; and a great light
on Troy,
And all that men remember and madmen can forget.

In the Balkans.

They thrice on crags of death were dry and thrice in Dan-
ube wet
To prove an old man's empty heart was empty of regret,
For the Turks have taken his city's soul: his spurs of gold
are dross,
And the Crescent hangs upon him while we hang upon the
Cross.

But we heave our tower of pride upon Kossovo of the loss,
For a proof that we remember and the infidels forget.

In the Alps.

Master of Arts and mastery of arms, master of all things yet,
For the musket as for the mandolin the master fingers fret;
The news to the noise of the mandolin that all the world
 comes home,
And the young are young and the years return and the days of
 the kingdom come.
When the wars wearied, and the tribes turned; and the sun
 rose on Rome,
And all that Rome remembers when all her realms forget.

In the North Sea.

Though the seas were sown with the new dragons that knew
 not what they ate,
We broke St. George's banner out to the black wind and the
 wet,
He hath broken all the bridges we could fling, the world
 and we,
But the bridge of death in heaven that His people might
 be free,
That we straddled for the saddle of the riders of the sea.
For St. George that shall remember if the Dragon shall
 forget.

All the Voices.

Behold, we are men of many lands, in motley seasons set,
From Riga to the rock of Spain, from Orkney to Olivet,
Who stand up in the council in the turning of the year,
And, standing, give the judgment on the evil house of fear;
Knowing the End shall write again what we have written
 here,
On the day when God remembers and no man can forget.

TO THE UNKNOWN WARRIOR

You whom the kings saluted; who refused not
  The one great gesture of ignoble days,
Fame without name and glory without gossip,
  Whom no biographer befouls with praise.

Who said of you "Defeated"? In the darkness
  The dug-out where the limelight never comes,
Nor the big drum of Barnum's Show can shatter
  That vibrant stillness after all the drums.

Though the time come when every Yankee circus
  Can use our soldiers for its sandwich-men,
When those that pay the piper call the tune,
  You will not dance. You will not move again.

You will not march for Fatty Arbuckle,
  Though he have yet a favourable press,
Tender as San Francisco to St. Francis,
  Or all the Angels of Los Angeles.

They shall not storm the last unfallen fortress,
  The lonely castle where uncowed and free
Dwells the unknown and undefeated warrior
  That did alone defeat Publicity.

TO A LADY

Light of the young, before you have grown old
The world will have grown weary of its youth,
All its cheap charity and loose-lipped truth,
And passion that goes naked—and grows cold.

Tire of a pity so akin to hate,
Turn on a truth that is so near to treason,
When Time, the god of traitors, in their season
Marks down for dated all the up-to-date.

Then shall men know by the great grace you are,
How something better than blind fear or blunder
Bade us stand back, where we could watch with wonder,
Ladies like landscapes, very fair and far.

A crowd shall call your high estrangéd face,
A mask of blind reaction and resistance,
Because you have made large the world with distance,
As God made large the universe with space.

Yet beautiful your feet upon the mountains,
Moving in soundless music shall return,
And they that look into your eyes shall learn—
Having forced up the secret sea in fountains.

And having vulgarised infinity,
And splashed their brains against the starry steeps,
In what unfathomable inward deeps
Dwells the last mystery men call Liberty.

When they shall say we scorned and held in thrall
Spirits like yours; the mother of the tribe
Slandered, a slave, a butt for slur and gibe,
You shall confound the one great slur of all.

The one great slander answered long ago
By Her that hid all things within her heart,
One speaking when the veil was rent apart,
"Women alone can keep a secret so."

THE WORLD STATE

Oh, how I love Humanity,
  With love so pure and pringlish,
And how I hate the horrid French,
  Who never will be English!

The International Idea,
  The largest and the clearest,
Is welding all the nations now,
  Except the one that's nearest.

This compromise has long been known,
  This scheme of partial pardons,
In ethical societies
  And small suburban gardens—

The villas and the chapels where
  I learned with little labour
The way to love my fellow-man
  And hate my next-door neighbour.

THE OLD GENTLEMAN IN THE PARK

Beyond the trees like iron trees,
  The painted lamp-posts stand.
The old red road runs like the rust
  Upon this iron land.

Cars flat as fish and fleet as birds,
  Low-bodied and high speeded,
Go on their belly like the Snake,
  And eat the dust as he did.

But down the red dust never more
Her happy horse-hoofs go.
O, what a road of rust indeed!
O, what a Rotten Row!

THE BURIED CITY

You that go forth upon the buried cities,
    Whose witchcraft holds the withered kings together,
Seals up the very air of ancient seasons,
    Like secret skies walled up from the world's weather.
You that dig up dead towns—arise and strive:
Strike through the slums and save the towns alive!

Dig London out of London; pierce the cavern
    Where Manchester lies lost in Manchester.
You that re-chart the choked-up squares and markets,
    Retrace the plan our blindness made a blur:
Until a name no more, but wide and tall,
Arise and shine the shield of London Wall.

Strike you the stones of these most desert places,
    Huge warehouses the lonely watchmen tread,
Where ringed in noise the hollow heart of London
    Lies all night long a city of the dead.
Or does One watch high o'er this maze that sprawls,
High on the varnished spire of Old St. Paul's?

Lift up your heads, ye gates of our remembrance,
    Be lifted up, ye everlasting walls,
The gates revolve upon their giant hinges,
    The guilds return unto their ancient halls.
Tell Bishopsgate a Bishop rides to town,
Not only come to pull the churches down.

You that let light into the sunken cities,
  Let life into the void where light is vain
Ere vandals wreck the temples, porch and pillar,
  Bring back the people to the porch again,
Who find in tombs strange flowers, flattened and dried,
Quicken the incredible seed of London Pride.

If our vain haste has smothered home in houses
  As our vain creeds have smothered man in men,
Though in that rock-tomb sleeps the King less deeply
  Than in this brick-tomb sleeps the Citizen,
What will not God achieve if Man awake,
Since a rock-tomb was rended for our sake?

NAMESAKE

  Mary of Holyrood may smile indeed,
    Knowing what grim historic shade it shocks
  To see wit, laughter and the Popish creed,
    Cluster and sparkle in the name of Knox.

OUTLINE OF HISTORY

A fishbone pattern of flint arrows flattened
  A fossil vision of the Age of Stone—
And sages in war-weary empires quarrel
  With those quaint quarrels and forget their own.
What riddle is of the elf-darts or the elves
But the strange stony riddle of ourselves?

As by long worms the hills are pierced with holes,
  Where long day's journeyings without light of day
Lead to a painted cave, a buried sky,
  Whose clouds are creatures sprawling in coloured clay;
And men ask how and why such things were done
Darkly, with dyes that never saw the sun.

I have seen a statue in a London square.
    One whose long-winded lies are long forgot
Gleams with the rain above the twinkling bushes,
    And birds perch on him in that unroofed plot.
Unriddle that dark image; and I will show
The secret of your pictured rocks below.

As green volcanic skies bury dark sunsets,
    Green rust like snakes crawled, and their work concealed
The men who were red shadows in copper mirrors,
    When groaned the golden and the brazen shield.
And the slaves worked the copper for their lords,
Stiff swarthy kings holding their yellow swords.

We have written the names of hucksters on the heavens
    And tied our pigmy slaves to giant tools,
And chosen our nobles from the mart; and never
    Stank to the sky the praise of prouder fools.
And 'mid the blare, the doctors and the dons,
In the Age of Brass brood on the Age of Bronze.

We clothe the dead in their theatric raiment
    To hide their nakedness of normality;
Disguise by gilded mask or horned mitre
    The accusing faces of such men as we:
Till the last brotherhood of men brings down
Us with the troglodytes in their twilight town.

ON A PROHIBITIONIST POEM

Though Shakespeare's Mermaid, ocean's mightiest daughter,
With vintage could the seas incarnadine:
And Keats's name that was not writ in water
                Was often writ in wine.

Though wine that seeks the loftiest habitation
Went to the heads of Villon and Verlaine,
Yet Hiram Hopper needs no inspiration
  But water on the brain.

THE MODERN MAGIC

Prester John on his lands looked down
He bore in one mystery mitre and crown,
And the scaly webs of the strange attire
Stripped from the dragon that feeds on fire,
And high over luminous rocks and trees
And the purple fish of his secret seas
And the whole sprawled map of the magical place,
A crystal mirror before his face
For ever stood; in whose circle shone
The world and all that is done thereon.

And the Seven Kings by his throne that stand
Cried, "Tell us the news from the Holy Land."

"Richard the King, of the scarlet ships,
Sweeps over Acre, but swerves and slips
From Godfrey's gate and from God's own crown,
And is shot in the ditch of a small French town.
Such is the news of the world," he said;
"But the signs of the world will never be read
In a glass darkly, by anyone;
We must wait for the sunrise," said Prester John.

Nigh on a thousand years were past:
To the strange priest's paradise pierced at last,
The men of the west, with the wondrous things
Of western wizards and western kings,

And high on their staggering engines borne
A marvel of marvels, the mighty Horn
Within whose cave, like a giant's ear,
Might all men speak and might all men hear
The noise of a battle, the noise of a bird,
Even all the sounds of the earth were heard.

And the Seven Kings said "It is ended then,
The demon of distance, rending men,
Deafness of deserts and random deeds,
When everyone knows what everyone needs,
Seeing that words like winds can come,
All will be Bethlehem, all will be Rome,
And all men answer and understand,
Tell us the news from the Holy Land."

"No battle-noise and no battle-news,
But shaking of shekels and laughter of Jews,
And a rattle of golden balls they toss
High o'er the ruin of Crescent and Cross,
And a usurer's voice in cold command,
These are the sounds from the Holy Land.

O, horns may call us from far away,
But men hear only what men can say,
And words may go as the wide wind blows,
But what everyone wants is what nobody knows:
And the Horn will not tell it to anyone,
We must wait for the Trumpet," said Prester John.

LINES TO AN OLD PRO-BOER WHO ASKED FOR A CONTRIBUTION TO A PEACE PERIODICAL

You cannot think my heart so tough
  To shrieks that ring or shards that rend;

You cannot think me bad enough
　　Nor good enough for tortures, friend.

Nor do I lightly talk of tears
　　Through some vague pageant of the past;
The shriek of shafts, the shock of spears,
　　The bursting of the arbelast.

Do you recall in that base fight,
　　When men were crushed with clubs of gold,
The meek and murderous flag of white
　　Of which our English lies were told,

Till white had washed away the red
　　And a calmed country found release?
Look forth to-day, and count the dead
　　Under your leprous flag of peace.

Rather than peace's pearl to pray,
　　When cast before us by such swine,
I would again your friends and mine
　　Were riding to Pretoria.

THE APOLOGY OF BOTTOM THE WEAVER

Once when an honest weaver slept,
　　And Puck passed by, a kindly traitor,
And on his shoulders set the head
　　Of a Shakespearean commentator,

The man had walked proverbial ways,
　　Fair Science frowned not on his birth,
Nor lost in long and tangled dreams,
　　The mother-wit of mother-earth.

Elaborate surgeons had not found
  The cobweb made the cure too brief,
Nor vegetarians taught the rule
  Of eating mustard without beef.

Only in that green night of growth
  Came to him, splendid, without scorn,
The lady of the dreams of men;
  The rival of all women born.

And he, for all his after weaving,
  Drew up from that abysmal dream
Immortal art, that proves by seeming
  All things more real than they seem.

The dancing moth was in his shuttle,
  The pea's pink blossom in his woof,
Your driving schools, your dying hamlets,
  Go through them all and find the proof—

That you, where'er the old crafts linger,
  Draw in their webs like nets of gold,
Hang up like banners for a pattern,
  The leavings of the looms of old.

And even as this home-made rhyme
  Drags but the speech of Shakespeare down,
These home-made patterns but repeat
  The traceries of an ancient clown.

And while the modern fashions fade,
  And while the ancient standards stream,
No psycho-analyst has knocked
  The bottom out of Bottom's dream.

THE NEW OMAR

A book of verses underneath the bough,
  Provided that the verses do not scan,
A loaf of bread, a jug of wine and Thou,
  Short-haired, all angles, looking like a man.

But let the wine be unfermented, pale,
  Of chemicals compounded, God knows how—
This were indeed the Prophet's Paradise,
  O Paradise were Wilderness enow.

AMERICANISATION

Britannia needs no Boulevards,
  No spaces wide and gay:
Her march was through the crooked streets
  Along the narrow way.
Nor looks she where, New York's seduction,
The Broadway leadeth to destruction.

Britannia needs no Cafés:
  If Coffee needs must be,
Its place should be the Coffee-house
  Where Johnson growled for Tea;
But who can hear that human mountain
Growl for an ice-cream soda-fountain?

She needs no Russian Theatre,
  Where Father strangles Mother,
In scenes where all the characters
  And colours kill each other:
Her boast is freedom had by halves,
And Britons never shall be Slavs.

But if not hers the Dance of Death,
    Great Dostoievsky's dance,
And if the things most finely French
    Are better done in France—
Might not Americanisation
Be best applied to its own nation?

Ere every shop shall be a store
    And every Trade a Trust . . .
Lo, many men in many lands
    Know when their cause is just.
There will be quite a large attendance
When *we* Declare our Independence.

ALLITERATIVISM (1914)

(THE LATEST SCHOOL)

(FRENCH AIRMEN HAVE BEEN FLYING OVER BADEN AND BAVARIA, VIOLATING BELGIAN NEUTRALITY. *Stated on German authority in the "Westminster Gazette."*)

See the flying French depart
Like the bees of Bonaparte,
Swarming up with a most venomous vitality.
Over Baden and Bavaria,
And Brighton and Bulgaria,
Thus violating Belgian neutrality.

And the injured Prussian may
Not unreasonably say
"Why, it cannot be so small a nationality!
Since Brixton and Batavia,
Bolivia and Belgravia,
Are bursting with the Belgian neutrality.

By pure Alliteration
You may trace this curious nation,
And respect this somewhat scattered principality;
When you see a B in Both
You may take your Bible oath
You are violating Belgian neutrality.

RACE-MEMORY

(BY A DAZED DARWINIAN)

I remember, I remember,
  Long before I was born,
The tree-tops where my racial self
  Went dancing round at morn.

Green wavering archipelagos,
  Great gusty bursts of blue,
In my race-memory I recall
  (Or I am told I do).

In that green-turreted Monkeyville
  (So I have often heard)
It seemed as if a Blue Baboon
  Might soar like a Blue Bird.

Low crawling Fundamentalists
  Glared up through the green mist,
I hung upon my tail in heaven
  A Firmamentalist.

*　　*　　*　　*　　*　　*　　*　　*

I am too fat to climb a tree,
  There are no trees to climb;
Instead, the factory chimneys rise,
  Unscaleable, sublime.

The past was bestial ignorance:
    But I feel a little funky,
To think I'm further off from heaven
    Than when I was a monkey.

A PATRIOTIC SONG

The Golden Hind went bowling
Nor'westward of the Main,
And Drake drank deep of Spanish wine
And spat the lees at Spain.
Till northward on the colder coasts
The savages came out
To hail the ship with tossing spear
And tomahawk and shout:
For the red gods and the witch-doctors
Had cursed the golden grape
Bidding him yield up Malvoisie
And wine in every shape.

  And need I say that Drake complied
  And poured the wine over the side,
  Invited all the Reds inside
  And let them ransack far and wide
  The ship that was his sinful pride
  For anything his men might hide,
  That so he might escape.

The top-sails of the Victory
Turned westward on a day
Great Nelson saw his sunrise land
Like a sunset fade away.
And pledged immortal beauty
And the isle beyond the foam

In the dark wine of Oporto
That his father drank at home.
His hand and glass were lifted
When they reached the rebel shore
And Hiram Hugginburg came forth
And bade him drink no more.

And naturally Nelson ran
To do his bidding and began
To empty every cup and can
And snatch the rum from every man
Who (ignorant of Hiram's ban)
Had broken with him the battle-van
From the Nile to Elsinore.

Lo, of that leaping pennant learn,
Of those world-wandering graves,
In what more modest modern style
Britannia rules the waves.

If, loyal to some foreign cause,
We still are careful, clause by clause,
Obeying other countries' laws.
We never shall be slaves.

SOME WISHES AT XMAS

Mince-Pies grant Wishes: let each name his Prize,
But as for us, we wish for more Mince-Pies.

MR. EPSTEIN

What wish has Epstein's art portrayed?
Toward what does Rima rise?

Those little hands were never made
 To tear out eagles' eyes:
She for Green Mansions yearns; but not
So green a mansion as she got.

DEAN INGE

What deep desires inspire the Gloomy Dean,
While Rima chants The Wearing of the Green?
Does he have childlike hopes at Christmas time
And sing a carol or a nursery rhyme?
Does he hang up a stocking—or a gaiter—
Or ask for gifts from any Alma Mater?
(Tell me, do Matthew, Mark, and Luke and John
Bless beds the Higher Critics lie upon?
Or if, while the Fourth Gospel is re-read,
"Synoptists" sleep on a three-cornered bed).
Or, like the Deutero-Job, who far away
On his interpolated ash-heap lay,
Damns he the day whereon his body and soul
Escaped the vigilance of Birth-Control?
Or, softened while the herald angel sings,
Does he more mildly wish for lesser things
That warning cracks, marking the house that falls,
Should decorate St. Peter's, not St. Paul's;
Or wish in all good faith to friends held dear
A Gloomy Christmas and a Glum New Year?
A Merry Christmas to a Merrier Dean!
Whatever he may want, whatever mean,
He won't be happy till he gets it; when
He does, perhaps he won't be happy then.

*   *   *   *   *   *   *   *

A LADY M.P.

She wants a new England, more bright and more clean,
Where foul tap-room revelries never are seen.
And after the quarter-staff flies the quart-pot,
For she wants a new England where these things are not,
And our love of old England is vain in her sight,
As the noise of blind drunkards that strive in the night,
As if our old England like fable could fade,
And a Puritan purge through the ages had made
A Shaker of Shakespeare, a grave man of Gay,
And a Pussyfoot Johnson with Boswell to play.
For she wants a new England, where censors and prigs
Can browbeat our jokes and can bridle our jigs.
The title is apt, and the tale is soon told,
She wants a New England, three hundred years old.

*   *   *   *   *   *   *   *

THE COMMUNISTS

There are two normal nuisances
  That stir us late or soon:
One is the man who wants the earth,
  The other wants the moon.
Choosing between these last and Jix,
  We much prefer the lunatics.

*   *   *   *   *   *   *   *

JIX

Since Christmas time brings charity
  For Jix and for the Kaiser,
We wish that they were wise enough
  To wish that they were wiser.

COMMERCIAL CANDOUR

(ON THE OUTSIDE OF A SENSATIONAL NOVEL IS PRINTED THE STATE-
MENT: "THE BACK OF THE COVER WILL TELL YOU THE PLOT.")

Our fathers to creed and tradition were tied,
They opened a book to see what was inside,
And of various methods they deemed not the worst
Was to find the first chapter and look at it first.
And so from the first to the second they passed,
Till in servile routine they arrived at the last.
But a literate age, unbenighted by creed,
Can find on two boards all it wishes to read;
For the front of the cover shows somebody shot
And the back of the cover will tell you the plot.

Between, that the book may be handily padded,
Some pages of mere printed matter are added,
Expanding the theme, which in case of great need
The curious reader might very well read
With the zest that is lent to a game worth the winning,
By knowing the end when you start the beginning;
While our barbarous sires, who would read every word
With a morbid desire to find out what occurred,
Went drearily drudging through Dickens and Scott.
But the back of the cover will tell you the plot.

The wild village folk in earth's earliest prime
Could often sit still for an hour at a time
And hear a blind beggar, nor did the tale pall
Because Hector must fight before Hector could fall:
Nor was Scheherazade required, at the worst,
To tell her tales backwards and finish them first;
And the minstrels who sang about battle and banners

Found the rude camp-fire crowd had some notion of manners.
Till Forster (who pelted the people like crooks,
The Irish with buckshot, the English with books),
Established the great educational scheme
Of compulsory schooling, that glorious theme.
Some learnt how to read, and the others forgot,
And the back of the cover will tell you the plot.

O Genius of Business! O marvellous brain,
Come in place of the priests and the warriors to reign!
O Will to Get On that makes everything go—
O Hustle! O Pep! O Publicity! O!
Shall I spend three-and-sixpence to purchase the book,
Which we all can pick up on the bookstall and look?
Well, it may appear strange, but I think I shall not,
For the back of the cover will tell you the plot.

HUMAN NATURE: OR MARCONI MEMORIES

(FROM OUR "SIMPLIFIED PSYCHOLOGY FOR STATESMEN" SERIES)

Human nature is a bird
Whose complaint is often heard,
And will make demands of any legislature;
And you need not claim to be
Giving seven pence for three;
It exceeds the wildest hopes of Human Nature.

Human Nature is a thing
It is difficult to sing,
And very much more difficult to deal with:
But you need not call it "function"—
You can own without compunction
That your brother is a man you take a meal with.

Human Nature it prefers
To be told of what occurs
Without suppressing any vital feature;
And when statesmen hold their peace
Until searched by the police,
It rasps the finer edge of Human Nature.

Human Nature, it is said,
Thinks investment should be made
By someone who has cash enough to pay it;
And that one who pouched the pay,
And had nothing more to say.
Need not go to South America to say it.

Human Nature is not keen
On the words "corrupt" or "clean"
Or any other shades of nomenclature;
But, when what the Party cost
Is discovered when it's lost,
A shade of doubt is merely Human Nature.

Human Nature it is prone
To be soft about the Throne,
And even make the Peerage paramounter;
But it startles it to drop
Into Mr. Pearson's shop,
And find a Scottish Lord behind the counter.

So till all men learn the truth
(And not only Handel Booth)
And the Gospel has been preached to every creature,
Even rotten things may fail,
Even thieves may go to gaol,
And all through not observing Human Nature.

THE PEACE OF PETROL

(TO BE SUNG TO THE AIR OF "KABUL RIVER" ON THE CONCLUSION
OF AN ENGLISH PEACE BROUGHT ABOUT BY AMERICAN INTER-
VENTION)

He has many a car and chuffer
  (Still the bugle, sheathe the sword),
So I left my mates to suffer
  All because of Mr. Ford.
Ford, Ford, Ford of many millions,
  Ford of many motors in the Park;
And our lord will laugh like thunder at the Good Cause going
    under
  When we stab it, to oblige him, in the dark.

We'll give up the blasted place
  (Drop the bugle, break the sword)
For one smile upon his face,
  O, the shiny face of Ford!
Ford, Ford, Ford; the French are falling,
  And the Serbians on the mountains lying stark,
All their eyes on us, disdaining, and it ain't no use explaining
  That a millionaire has bought us for a lark.

O the motors he can make!
  (Sell the bugle, pawn the sword)
We'll be humbled for his sake,
  Break our faith and keep our Ford.
Ford, Ford, Ford—till death remove him
  To a place on which it's needless to remark,
And the rich whose minds are muddy, who consider honour
    bloody,
  Go down to their damnation in the dark.

TO A HOLY ROLLER

(THE SECT OF THE HOLY ROLLERS DEMONSTRATED AGAINST EVOLU-
TION AT DAYTON)

"Roll on," said Gilbert to the earth:
"Roll on," said Byron to the sea:
Accepting natural features thus,
Freely I say "Roll on" to thee.

Time like an ever rolling stream
Bears his most rolling sons away
Bryanite saint, Darwinian sage,
And even Dayton has its day.

Earth changes; sings another bard,
"There rolls the deep where grew the tree";
Convulsions viewed with equal calm
By Tennyson and Tennessee.

But ere you roll down history's slope,
A moment you may set us thinking
How Prohibition suits their mood,
Who get so drunk by never drinking.

What rows of bottles, blends of liquor,
We need to reach in one wild leap
Those reels and rolls you get for nothing,
Great Bacchic Maenads on the cheap!

I blame you not that, writhing prone,
You flout the grave Darwinian's view,
Of his extremely Missing Link,
For he is quite amusing too.

Marking the human ape evolve
  (He puts his rolling into Latin),
Through epochs barely large enough
  To swing an old Egyptian cat in.

Since you believe Man truly tilled
  The Garden for the great Controller,
You back your Garden party up,
  Like a consistent Garden Roller.

We, too, may deem on Adam's birth
  Some more mysterious splendour shone,
Than prigs can pick off monkey's bones,
  Never you mind! Roll on! Roll on!

Grovel and gambol on all fours
  Till you have proved beyond dispute,
That human dignity is freed
  From all connection with the brute.

THE NEW FICTION

("LEAVE THEM ALONE," WE SEEM TO HEAR MR. GALSWORTHY SAY
OF HIS YOUNG PEOPLE.—*From a Review by Mr. Bettany*)

Little Blue-Fits has lost his wits,
  And doesn't know where to find them;
Leave them alone and they'll come home,
  And leave their tales behind them.

The remarkable tales, with remarkable sales,
  And Bonnets and Bees in disorder;
For the Bonnets we view are exceedingly Blue,
  And decidedly over the Border.

ANSWERS TO THE POETS

The Skylark Replies to Wordsworth

(As it might have appeared to Byron)

Ephemeral minstrel, staring at the sky,
　Dost thou despise the earth where wrongs abound,
Or, eyeing me, hast thou the other eye
　Still on the Court, with pay-day coming round,
That pension that could bring thee down at will
Those rebel wings composed, that protest still?

Past the last trace of meaning and beyond
　Mount, daring babbler, that pay-prompted strain
'Twixt thee and Kings a never-failing bond
　Swells not the less their carnage o'er the plain.
Type of the wise, who drill but never fight,
True to the kindred points of Might and Right.

*　　*　　*　　*　　*　　*　　*　　*

The Sea Replies to Byron

(As it might have appeared to Wordsworth)

Stroll on, thou dark not deep "blue" dandy, stroll,
　Ten thousand duns call after thee in vain.
Thy tailor's marked with ruin; his control
　Stops with my shore; beyond he doth retain
No shadow of a chance of what's his own,
But sinks above his bills with bubbling groan,
"Absconded; gone; abroad; address unknown."

Thy songs are speeches, void of all save Thee,
　Childe Harold, Lara, Manfred, what care I?

My water washed them down—you got it free,
  And many a wine-cup since when you were dry,
Till nature blows the man-hater sky-high,
Howling against his gods in stark D.T.,
And dashes him against the Truth. There let him *lie*.

THE FAT WHITE WOMAN SPEAKS

Why do you rush through the field in trains,
Guessing so much and so much.
Why do you flash through the flowery meads,
Fat-head poet that nobody reads;
And why do you know such a frightful lot
About people in gloves as such?

And how the devil can you be sure,
Guessing so much and so much,
How do you know but what someone who loves
Always to see me in nice white gloves
At the end of the field you are rushing by,
Is waiting for his Old Dutch?

*   *   *   *   *   *   *   *

LUCASTA REPLIES TO LOVELACE

Tell me not, friend, you are unkind,
  If ink and books laid by,
You turn up in a uniform
  Looking all smart and spry.

I thought your ink one horrid smudge,
  Your books one pile of trash,
And with less fear of smear embrace
  A sword, a belt, a sash.

Yet this inconstancy forgive,
 Though gold lace I adore,
I could not love the lace so much
 Loved I not Lovelace more.

* * * * * * * *

By a Captain, or Perhaps a Colonel, or Possibly a Knight-at-Arms

Poet or pamphleteer, or what you please,
Who chance behind this space of wall to dwell,
Upon my soul I cannot very well
Correct my fire for arguments like these,
The great Emathian conqueror be blowed!
I have not got a spear or you a bower.
London is packed with poets; temple and tower
Swarm with them; where the devil should we be
Storming a town, if the repeated plea
Of Puritanic poets had the power
To stop a piece of ordnance with an ode?

* * * * * * * *

From the Spanish Cloister

Grrrr—what's that? A dog? A poet?
 Uttering his damnations thus—
If hate killed things, Brother Browning,
 God's Word, would not hate kill us?

If we'd ever meet together,
 Salve tibi! I might hear
How you know poor monks are really
 So much worse than they appear.

There's a great text in Corinthians
   Hinting that our faith entails
Something else, that never faileth,
   Yet in you, perhaps, it fails.

But if *plena gratia* chokes you,
   You at least can teach us how
To converse in wordless noises,
   Hy, zi; hullo!—Grrrr—Bow-wow!

*   *   *   *   *   *   *   *

DOLORES REPLIES TO SWINBURNE

Cold passions, and perfectly cruel,
   Long odes that go on for an hour,
With a most economical jewel
   And a quite metaphorical flower.
I implore you to stop it and stow it,
   I adjure you, relent and refrain,
Oh, pagan Priapean poet,
                         You give me a pain.

I am sorry, old dear, if I hurt you,
   No doubt it is all very nice
With the lilies and languors of virtue
   And the raptures and roses of vice.
But the notion impels me to anger,
   That vice is all rapture for me,
And if you think virtue is languor
                         Just try it and see.

We shall know when the critics discover
   If your poems were shallow or deep;
Who read you from cover to cover,

Will know if they sleep not or sleep.
But you say I've endured through the ages
  (Which is rude) as Our Lady of Pain,
You have said it for several pages,
            So say it again.

  *   *   *   *   *   *   *   *

To a Modern Poet

Well,
What
about it?

I am sorry
  if you have
    a green pain
gnawing your brain away.
      I suppose
quite a lot of it is
  gnawed away
    by this time.

I did not give you
    a green pain
    or even
    a grey powder.
It is rather you, so winged, so vortical,
  Who give me a pain.

When I have a pain
    I never notice
      the colour.

But I am very unobservant.
I cannot say
I ever noticed that the pillar-box
was like a baby
skinned alive and screaming.
I have not
a Poet's
Eye
which can see Beauty
everywhere.

Now you mention it,
Of course, the sky
is like a large mouth
shown to a dentist,
and I never noticed
a little thing
like that.

But I can't help wishing
You got more fun out of it;
you seem to have taken
quite a dislike
to things
They seem to make you jump
And double up unexpectedly—

And when you write
like other poets,
on subjects
not entirely
novel,
such as, for instance,
the Sea,

it is mostly about
    Sea-sickness.
As you say—
It is the New Movement,
    The Emetic Ecstasy.

*   *   *   *   *   *   *   *

POST-RECESSIONAL

God of your fathers, known of old,
  For patience with man's swaggering line,
He did not answer you when told
  About you and your palm and pine,
Though you deployed your far-flung host
And boasted that you did not boast.

Though drunk with sight of power and blind,
  Even as you bowed your head in awe,
You kicked up both your heels behind
  At lesser breeds without the law;
Lest they forget, lest they forget,
That yours was the exclusive set.

We fancied heaven preferring much,
  Your rowdiest song, your slangiest sentence,
Your honest banjo banged, to such
  Very recessional repentance;
Now if your native land be dear,
Whisper (or shout) and we shall hear.

Cut down, our navies melt away.
  From ode and war-song fades the fire,
We are a jolly sight to-day
  Too near to Sidon and to Tyre

To make it sound so very nice
To offer ancient sacrifice.

Rise up and bid the trumpets blow
    When it is gallant to be gay,
Tell the wide world it shall not know
    Our face until we turn to bay.
Bless you, you shall be blameless yet,
For God forgives and men forget.

VARIATIONS ON AN AIR

Composed on Having to Appear in a Pageant as Old King Cole

Old King Cole was a merry old soul,
And a merry old soul was he;
He called for his pipe,
He called for his bowl,
And he called for his fiddlers three.

After Lord Tennyson.

Cole, that unwearied prince of Colchester,
Growing more gay with age and with long days
Deeper in laughter and desire of life,
As that Virginian climber on our walls
Flames scarlet with the fading of the year;
Called for his wassail and that other weed
Virginian also, from the western woods
Where English Raleigh checked the boast of Spain,
And lighting joy with joy, and piling up
Pleasure as crown for pleasure, bade men bring
Those three, the minstrels whose emblazoned coats
Shone with the oyster-shells of Colchester;

And these three played, and playing grew more fain
Of mirth and music; till the heathen came,
And the King slept beside the northern sea.

After W. B. Yeats.

Of an old King in a story
   From the grey sea-folk I have heard,
Whose heart was no more broken
   Than the wings of a bird.

As soon as the moon was silver
   And the thin stars began,
He took his pipe and his tankard,
   Like an old peasant man.

And three tall shadows were with him
   And came at his command;
And played before him for ever
   The fiddles of fairyland.

And he died in the young summer
   Of the world's desire;
Before our hearts were broken
   Like sticks in a fire.

After Robert Browning.

Who smoke-snorts toasts o' My Lady Nicotine,
Kicks stuffing out of Pussyfoot, bids his trio
Stick up their Stradivarii (that's the plural
Or near enough, my fatheads; *nimium*
Vicina Cremonæ; that's a bit too near.)
Is there some stockfish fails to understand?
Catch hold o' the notion, bellow and blurt back "Cole"?

Must I bawl lessons from a horn-book, howl,
Cat-call the cat-gut "fiddles"? Fiddlesticks!

After Walt Whitman.

Me clairvoyant,
Me conscious of you, old camarado,
Needing no telescope, lorgnette, field-glass, opera-glass, myopic
    pince-nez,
Me piercing two thousand years with eye naked and not
    ashamed;
The crown cannot hide you from me;
Musty old feudal-heraldic trappings cannot hide you from me,
I perceive that you drink.
(I am drinking with you. I am as drunk as you are).
I see you are inhaling tobacco, puffing, smoking, spitting
(I do not object to your spitting),
You prophetic of American largeness,
You anticipating the broad masculine manners of these States;
I see in you also there are movements, tremors, tears, desire
    for the melodious,
I salute your three violinists, endlessly making vibrations,
Rigid, relentless, capable of going on for ever;
They play my accompaniment; but I shall take no notice of
    any accompaniment;
I myself am a complete orchestra.
So long.

After Swinburne.

In the time of old sin without sadness
    And golden with wastage of gold
Like the gods that grow old in their gladness
    Was the king that was glad, growing old:
And with sound of loud lyres from his palace

The voice of his oracles spoke,
And the lips that were red from his chalice
Were splendid with smoke.

When the weed was as flame for a token
And the wine was as blood for a sign;
And upheld in his hands and unbroken
The fountains of fire and of wine.
And a song without speech, without singer,
Stung the soul of a thousand in three
As the flesh of the earth has to sting her,
The soul of the sea.

A BALLAD OF ABBREVIATIONS

The American's a hustler, for he says so,
And surely the American must know.
He will prove to you with figures why it pays so
Beginning with his boyhood long ago.
When the slow-maturing anecdote is ripest,
He'll dictate it like a Board of Trade Report,
And because he has no time to call a typist,
He calls her a Stenographer for short.

He is never known to loiter or malinger,
He rushes, for he knows he has "a date";
He is always on the spot and full of ginger,
Which is why he is invariably late.
When he guesses that it's getting even later,
His vocabulary's vehement and swift,
And he yells for what he calls the Elevator,
A slang abbreviation for a lift.

Then nothing can be nattier or nicer
For those who like a light and rapid style,

Than to trifle with a work of Mr. Dreiser
    As it comes along in waggons by the mile.
He has taught us what a swift selective art meant
    By description of his dinners and all that,
And his dwelling, which he says is an Apartment,
    Because he cannot stop to say a flat.

We may whisper of his wild precipitation,
    That its speed is rather longer than a span,
But there really is a definite occasion
    When he does not use the longest word he can.
When he substitutes, I freely make admission,
    One shorter and much easier to spell;
If you ask him what he thinks of Prohibition
    He may tell you quite succinctly it is Hell.

JEALOUSY

THE ROMAN CATHOLIC CHURCH HAS NEVER FORGIVEN US FOR
CONVERTING SIR ARTHUR CONAN DOYLE FROM HIS AGNOSTICISM;
WHEN MEN LIKE MR. DENNIS BRADLEY CAN NO LONGER BE
CONTENT WITH THE OLD FAITH, A SPIRIT OF JEALOUSY IS NATURALLY
ROUSED.— *A Spiritualist Paper.*

She sat upon her Seven Hills
She rent the scarlet robes about her
Nor yet in her two thousand years
Had even grieved that men should doubt her
But what new horror shakes the mind
Making her moan and mutter madly
Lo! Rome's high heart is broken at last
Her foes have borrowed Dennis Bradley.

If she must lean on lesser props
Of earthly fame or ancient art

Make shift with Raphael and Racine
Put up with Dante and Descartes
Not wholly can she mask her grief
But touch the wound and murmur sadly
"These lesser things are theirs to love
Who lose the love of Mr. Bradley."

She saw great Origen depart
And Photius rend the world asunder
Her cry to all the East rolled back
In Islam its ironic thunder
She lost Jerusalem and the North
Accepting these arrangements gladly
Until it came to be a case
Of Conan Doyle and Dennis Bradley.

O fond and foolish hopes that still
In broken hearts unbroken burn
What if grown weary of new ways
The precious wanderer should return
The Trumpet whose uncertain sound
Has just been cracking rather badly
May yet within her courts remain
His Trumpet—blown by Dennis Bradley.

His and her Trumpet blown before
The battle where the good cause wins
Louder than all the Irish harps
Or the Italian violins
When, armed and mounted like St. Joan
She meets the mad world riding madly
Under the Oriflamme of old
Crying "Montjoie St. Dennis Bradley!"

But in this hour she sorrows still,
Though all anew the generations
Rise up and call her blessèd, claim
Her name upon the new-born nations
But still she mourns the only thing
She ever really wanted badly
The sympathy of Conan Doyle
'The patronage of Dennis Bradley.

Book Two
Ballad of St. Barbara

THE BALLAD OF ST. BARBARA

(ST. BARBARA IS THE PATRON SAINT OF ARTILLERY AND OF
THOSE IN DANGER OF SUDDEN DEATH)

When the long grey lines came flooding upon Paris in the
    plain,
We stood and drank of the last free air we never could taste
    again:
They had led us back from the lost battle, to halt we knew
    not where
And stilled us; and our gaping guns were dumb with our
    despair.
The grey tribes flowed for ever from the infinite lifeless lands
And a Norman to a Breton spoke, his chin upon his hands.

"There was an end of Ilium; and an end came to Rome:
And a man plays on a painted stage in the land that he calls
    home;
Arch after arch of triumph, but floor beyond falling floor,
That lead to a low door at last; and beyond there is no door."

And the Breton to the Norman spoke, like a small child
    spoke he,
And his sea-blue eyes were empty as his home beside the sea:
"There are more windows in one house than there are eyes
    to see,
There are more doors in a man's house, but God has hid the
    key:
Ruin is a builder of windows; her legend witnesseth
Barbara, the saint of gunners, and a stay in sudden death."

It seemed the wheel of the world stood still an instant in its
  turning,
More than the kings of the earth that turned with the turning
  of Valmy mill:
While trickled the idle tale and the sea-blue eyes were
  burning,
Still as the heart of a whirlwind the heart of the world stood
  still.

"Barbara the beautiful
Had praise of lute and pen:
Her hair was like a summer night
Dark and desired of men.

Her feet like birds from far away
That linger and light in doubt;
And her face was like a window
Where a man's first love looked out.

Her sire was master of many slaves
A hard man of his hands;
They built a tower about her
In the desolate golden lands,

Sealed as the tyrants sealed their tombs,
Planned with an ancient plan,
And set two windows in the tower,
Like the two eyes of a man."

Our guns were set toward the foe; we had no word, for
  firing.
Grey in the gateway of St. Gond the Guard of the tyrant
  shone;
Dark with the fate of a falling star, retiring and retiring,
The Breton line went backward and the Breton tale went on.

"Her father had sailed across the sea
From the harbour of Africa
When all the slaves took up their tools
For the bidding of Barbara.

She smote the bare wall with her hand
And bade them smite again;
She poured them wealth of wine and meat
To stay them in their pain.

And cried through the lifted thunder
Of thronging hammer and hod
'Throw open the third window
In the third name of God.'

Then the hearts failed and the tools fell,
And far towards the foam,
Men saw a shadow on the sands
And her father coming home."

Speak low and low, along the line the whispered word is
      flying
Before the touch, before the time, we may not loose a breath:
Their guns must mash us to the mire and there be no replying,
Till the hand is raised to fling us for the final dice to death.

"There were two windows in your tower,
Barbara, Barbara,
For all between the sun and moon
In the lands of Africa.

Hath a man three eyes, Barbara,
A bird three wings,
That you have riven roof and wall
To look upon vain things?"

Her voice was like a wandering thing
That falters yet is free,
Whose soul has drunk in a distant land
Of the rivers of liberty.

" 'There are more wings than the wind knows
Or eyes than see the sun
In the light of the lost window
And the wind of the doors undone.

For out of the first lattice
Are the red lands that break
And out of the second lattice
Sea like a green snake,

But out of the third lattice
Under low eaves like wings
Is a new corner of the sky
And the other side of things.' "

It opened in the inmost place an instant beyond uttering,
A casement and a chasm and a thunder of doors undone,
A seraph's strong wing shaken out the shock of its unshut-
    tering,
That split the shattered sunlight from a light behind the sun.

"Then he drew sword and drave her
Where the judges sat and said
'Caesar sits above the gods,
Barbara the maid.

Caesar hath made a treaty
With the moon and with the sun,
All the gods that men can praise
Praise him every one.

There is peace with the anointed
Of the scarlet oils of Bel,
With the Fish God, where the whirlpool
Is a winding stair to hell,

With the pathless pyramids of slime,
Where the mitred negro lifts
To his black cherub in the cloud
Abominable gifts,

With the leprous silver cities
Where the dumb priests dance and nod,
But not with the three windows
And the last name of God.' "

They are firing, we are falling, and the red skies rend and
　　shiver us,
Barbara, Barbara, we may not loose a breath—
Be at the bursting doors of doom, and in the dark deliver us,
Who loosen the last window on the sun of sudden death.

"Barbara the beautiful
Stood up as queen set free,
Whose mouth is set to a terrible cup
And the trumpet of liberty.

'I have looked forth from a window
That no man now shall bar,
Caesar's toppling battle-towers
Shall never stretch so far.

The slaves are dancing in their chains,
The child laughs at the rod,
Because of the bird of the three wings,
And the third face of God.'

The sword upon his shoulder
Shifted and shone and fell,
And Barbara lay very small
And crumpled like a shell."

What wall upon what hinges turned stands open like a door?
Too simple for the sight of faith, too huge for human eyes,
What light upon what ancient way shines to a far-off floor,
The line of the lost land of France or the plains of Paradise?

"Caesar smiled above the gods
His lip of stone was curled,
His iron armies wound like chains
Round and round the world,

And the strong slayer of his own
That cut down flesh for grass,
Smiled too, and went to his own tower
Like a walking tower of brass,

And the songs ceased and the slaves were dumb;
And far towards the foam
Men saw a shadow on the sands;
And her father coming home. . .

Blood of his blood upon the sword
Stood red but never dry.
He wiped it slowly, till the blade
Was blue as the blue sky.

But the blue sky split with a thunder-crack,
Spat down a blinding brand,
And all of him lay back and flat
As his shadow on the sand."

The touch and the tornado; all our guns give tongue to-
    gether
St. Barbara for the gunnery and God defend the right,
They are stopped and gapped and battered as we blast away
    the weather,
Building window upon window to our lady of the light.
For the light is come on Liberty, her foes are falling, falling,
They are reeling, they are running, as the shameful years
    have run,
She is risen for all the humble, she has heard the conquered
    calling,
St. Barbara of the Gunners, with her hand upon the gun.
They are burst asunder in the midst that eat of their own
    flatteries,
Whose lip is curled to order as its barbered hair is curled. . . .
Blast of the beauty of sudden death, St. Barbara of the bat-
    teries!
That blow the new white window in the wall of all the
    world.

For the hand is raised behind us, and the bolt smites hard
Through the rending of the doorways, through the death-gap
    of the Guard,
For the cry of the Three Colours is in Condé and beyond
And the Guard is flung for carrion in the graveyard of St.
    Gond,
Through Mondemont and out of it, through Morin marsh
    and on
With earthquake of salutation the impossible thing is gone,
Gaul, charioted and charging, great Gaul upon a gun,
Tip-toe on all her thousand years and trumpeting to the sun:
As day returns, as death returns, swung backwards and swung
    home,

Back on the barbarous reign returns the battering-ram of
    Rome;
While that that the east held hard and hot like pincers in a
    forge,
Came like the west wind roaring up the cannon of St. George,
Where the hunt is up and racing over stream and swamp
    and tarn
And their batteries, black with battle, hold the bridgeheads
    of the Marne,
And across the carnage of the Guard, by Paris in the plain,
The Normans to the Bretons cried and the Bretons cheered
    again. . .
But he that told the tale went home to his house beside the
    sea
And burned before St. Barbara, the light of the windows
    three,
Three candles for an unknown thing, never to come again,
That opened like the eye of God on Paris in the plain.

ELEGY IN A COUNTRY CHURCHYARD

The men that worked for England
They have their graves at home:
And bees and birds of England
About the cross can roam.

But they that fought for England,
Following a falling star,
Alas, alas for England
They have their graves afar.

And they that rule in England,
In stately conclave met,
Alas, alas for England
They have no graves as yet.

THE SWORD OF SURPRISE

Sunder me from my bones, O sword of God,
Till they stand stark and strange as do the trees;
That I whose heart goes up with the soaring woods
May marvel as much at these.

Sunder me from my blood that in the dark
I hear that red ancestral river run,
Like branching buried floods that find the sea
But never see the sun.

Give me miraculous eyes to see my eyes,
Those rolling mirrors made alive in me,
Terrible crystal more incredible
Than all the things they see.

Sunder me from my soul, that I may see
The sins like streaming wounds, the life's brave beat;
Till I shall save myself, as I would save
A stranger in the street.

A WEDDING IN WAR-TIME

Our God who made two lovers in a garden,
And smote them separate and set them free,
Their four eyes wild for wonder and wrath and pardon
And their kiss thunder as lips of land and sea:
Each rapt unendingly beyond the other,
Two starry worlds of unknown gods at war,
Wife and not mate, a man and not a brother,
We thank thee thou hast made us what we are.

Make not the grey slime of infinity
To swamp these flowers thou madest one by one;

Let not the night that was thine enemy
Mix a mad twilight of the moon and sun;
Waken again to thunderclap and clamour
The wonder of our sundering and the song,
Or break our hearts with thine hell-shattering hammer
But leave a shade between us all day long.

Shade of high shame and honourable blindness
When youth, in storm of dizzy and distant things,
Finds the wild windfall of a little kindness
And shakes to think that all the world has wings.
When the one head that turns the heavens in turning
Moves yet as lightly as a lingering bird,
And red and random, blown astray but burning,
Like a lost spark goes by the glorious word.

Make not this sex, this other side of things,
A thing less distant than the world's desire;
What colour to the end of evening clings
And what far cry of frontiers and what fire
Fallen too far beyond the sun for seeking,
Let it divide us though our kingdom come;
With a far signal in our secret speaking
To hang the proud horizon in our home.

Once we were one, a shapeless cloud that lingers
Loading the seas and shutting out the skies,
One with the woods, a monster of myriad fingers,
You laid on me no finger of surprise.
One with the stars, a god with myriad eyes,
I saw you nowhere and was blind for scorn:
One till the world was riven and the rise
Of the white days when you and I were born.

Darkens the world: the world-old fetters rattle;
And these that have no hope behind the sun
May feed like bondmen and may breed like cattle,
One in the darkness as the dead are one;
Us if the rended grave give up its glory
Trumpets shall summon asunder and face to face:
We will be strangers in so strange a story
And wonder, meeting in so wild a place.

Ah, not in vain or utterly for loss
Come even the black flag and the battle-hordes,
If these grey devils flee the sign of the cross
Even in the symbol of the crossing swords.
Nor shall death doubt Who made our souls alive
Swords meeting and not stakes set side by side,
Bade us in the sunburst and the thunder thrive
Earthquake and Dawn; the bridegroom and the bride.

Death and not dreams or doubt of things undying,
Of whose the holy hearth or whose the sword;
Though sacred spirits dissever in strong crying
Into Thy hands, but Thy two hands, O Lord,
Though not in Earth as once in Eden standing,
So plain again we see Thee what thou art,
As in this blaze, the blasting and the branding
Of this wild wedding where we meet and part.

THE MYSTERY

If sunset clouds could grow on trees
It would but match the may in flower;
And skies be underneath the seas
No topsyturvier than a shower.

If mountains rose on wings to wander
They were no wilder than a cloud;
Yet all my praise is mean as slander,
Mean as these mean words spoken aloud.

And never more than now I know
That man's first heaven is far behind;
Unless the blazing seraph's blow
Has left him in the garden blind.

Witness, O Sun that blinds our eyes,
Unthinkable and unthankable King,
That though all other wonder dies
I wonder at not wondering.

"THE MYTH OF ARTHUR"

O learned man who never learned to learn,
Save to deduce, by timid steps and small,
From towering smoke that fire can never burn
And from tall tales that men were never tall.
Say, have you thought what manner of man it is
Of whom men say 'He could strike giants down'?
Or what strong memories over time's abyss
Bore up the pomp of Camelot and the crown.
And why one banner all the background fills,
Beyond the pageants of so many spears,
And by what witchery in the western hills
A throne stands empty for a thousand years.
Who hold, unheeding this immense impact,
Immortal story for a mortal sin;
Lest human fable touch historic fact,
Chase myths like moths, and fight them with a pin.
Take comfort; rest—there needs not this ado.
You shall not be a myth, I promise you.

THE OLD SONG

(ON THE EMBANKMENT IN STORMY WEATHER)

A livid sky on London
And like the iron steeds that rear
A shock of engines halted,
And I knew the end was near:
And something said that far away, over the hills and far away,
There came a crawling thunder and the end of all things here.
For London Bridge is broken down, broken down, broken
    down,
As digging lets the daylight on the sunken streets of yore,
The lightning looked on London town, the broken bridge of
    London town,
The ending of a broken road where men shall go no more.

I saw the kings of London town,
The kings that buy and sell,
That built it up with penny loaves
And penny lies as well:

And where the streets were paved with gold the shrivelled
    paper shone for gold,
The scorching light of promises that pave the streets of hell.
For penny loaves will melt away, melt away, melt away,
Mock the mean that haggled in the grain they did not grow;
With hungry faces in the gate, a hundred thousand in the
    gate,
A thunder-flash on London and the finding of the foe.

I heard the hundred pin-makers
Slow down their racking din,
Till in the stillness men could hear

The dropping of the pin:
And somewhere men without the wall, beneath the wood,
without the wall,
Had found the place where London ends and England can
begin.
For pins and needles bend and break, bend and break, bend
and break,
Faster than the breaking spears or the bending of the bow,
Of pageants pale in thunder-light, 'twixt thunder-load and
thunder-light,
The Hundreds marching on the hills in the wars of long ago.

I saw great Cobbett riding,
The horseman of the shires;
And his face was red with judgment
And a light of Luddite fires:
And south to Sussex and the sea the lights leapt up for
liberty,
The trumpet of the yeomanry, the hammer of the squires;
For bars of iron rust away, rust away, rust away,
Rend before the hammer and the horseman riding in,
Crying that all men at the last, and at the worst and at the
last,
Have found the place where England ends and England can
begin.

His horse-hoofs go before you,
Far beyond your bursting tyres;
And time is bridged behind him
And our sons are with our sires.

A trailing meteor on the Downs he rides above the rotting
towns,
The Horseman of Apocalypse, the Rider of the Shires.

For London Bridge is broken down, broken down, broken
down;
Blow the horn of Huntingdon from Scotland to the sea—
. . . Only a flash of thunder-light, a flying dream of thunder-
light,
Had shown under the shattered sky a people that were free.

THE TRINKETS

A wandering world of rivers,
A wavering world of trees,
If the world grow dim and dizzy
With all changes and degrees,
It is but Our Lady's mirror
Hung dreaming in its place,
Shining with only shadows
Till she wakes it with her face.

The standing whirlpool of the stars,
The wheel of all the world,
Is a ring on Our Lady's finger
With the suns and moons empearled
With stars for stones to please her
Who sits playing with her rings
With the great heart that a woman has
And the love of little things.

Wings of the whirlwind of the world
From here to Ispahan,
Spurning the flying forests,
Are light as Our Lady's fan:
For all things violent here and vain
Lie open and all at ease
Where God has girded heaven to guard
Her holy vanities.

THE PHILANTHROPIST

(*With Apologies to a Beautiful Poem*)

Abou Ben Adhem (may his tribe decrease
By cautious birth-control and die in peace)
Mellow with learning lightly took the word
That marked him not with them that love the Lord,
And told the angel of the book and pen
"Write me as one that loves his fellow-men:
For them alone I labour; to reclaim
The ragged roaming Bedouin and to tame
To ordered service; to uproot their vine
Who mock the Prophet, being mad with wine;
Let daylight through their tents and through their lives,
Number their camels, even count their wives;
Plot out the desert into streets and squares,
And count it a more fruitful work than theirs
Who lift a vain and visionary love
To your vague Allah in the skies above."

Gently replied the angel of the pen:
"Labour in peace and love your fellow-men:
And love not God, since men alone are dear,
Only fear God; for you have cause to fear."

ON THE DOWNS

When you came over the top of the world
In the great day on the Downs,
The air was crisp and the clouds were curled,
When you came over the top of the world,
And under your feet were spire and street
And seven English towns.

And I could not think that the pride was perished
As you came over the down;
Liberty, chivalry, all we cherished,
Lost in a rattle of pelf and perished;
Or the land we love that you walked above
Withering town by town.

For you came out on the dome of the earth
Like a vision of victory,
Out on the great green dome of the earth
As the great blue dome of the sky for girth,
And under your feet the shires could meet
And your eyes went out to sea.

Under your feet the towns were seven,
Alive and alone on high,
Your back to the broad white wall of heaven;
You were one and the towns were seven,
Single and one as the soaring sun
And your head upheld the sky.

And I thought of a thundering flag unfurled
And the roar of the burghers' bell:
Beacons crackled and bolts were hurled
As you came over the top of the world;
And under your feet were chance and cheat
And the slime of the slopes of hell.

It has not been as the great wind spoke
On the great green down that day:
We have seen, wherever the wide wind spoke,
Slavery slaying the English folk:
The robbers of land we have seen command;
The rulers of land obey.

We have seen the gigantic golden worms
In the garden of paradise:
We have seen the great and the wise make terms
With the peace of snakes and the pride of worms,
And them that plant make covenant
With the locust and the lice.

And the wind blows and the world goes on
And the world can say that we,
Who stood on the cliffs where the quarries shone,
Stood upon clouds that the sun shone on:
And the clouds dissunder and drown in thunder
The news that will never be.

Lady of all that have loved the people,
Light over roads astray,
Maze of steading and street and steeple,
Great as a heart that has loved the people:
Stand on the crown of the soaring down,
Lift up your arms and pray.

Only you I have not forgotten
For wreck of the world's renown,
Rending and ending of things gone rotten,
Only the face of you unforgotten:
And your head upthrown in the skies alone
As you came over the down.

THE RED SEA

Our souls shall be Leviathans
In purple seas of wine

When drunkenness is dead with death,
And drink is all divine;
Learning in those immortal vats
What mortal vineyards mean;
For only in heaven we shall know
How happy we have been.

Like clouds that wallow in the wind
Be free to drift and drink;
Tower without insolence when we rise,
Without surrender sink:
Dreams dizzy and crazy we shall know
And have no need to write
Our blameless blasphemies of praise,
Our nightmares of delight.

For so in such misshapen shape
The vision came to me,
Where such titanic dolphins dark
Roll in a sunset sea:
Dark with dense colours, strange and strong
As terrible true love,
Haloed like fish in phosphor light
The holy monsters move.

Measure is here and law, to learn,
When honour rules it so,
To lift the glass and lay it down
Or break the glass and go.
But when the world's New Deluge boils
From the New Noah's vine,
Our souls shall be Leviathans
In sanguine seas of wine.

FOR A WAR MEMORIAL

(Suggested Inscription Probably not Selected by the Committee)

The hucksters haggle in the mart
The cars and carts go by;
Senates and schools go droning on;
For dead things cannot die.

A storm stooped on the place of tombs
With bolts to blast and rive;
But these be names of many men
The lightning found alive.

If usurers rule and rights decay
And visions view once more
Great Carthage like a golden shell
Gape hollow on the shore,

Still to the last of crumbling time
Upon this stone be read
How many men of England died
To prove they were not dead.

MEMORY

If I ever go back to Baltimore,
The City of Maryland,
I shall miss again as I missed before
A thousand things of the world in store,
The story standing in every door
That beckons on every hand.

I shall not know where the bonds were riven,
And a hundred faiths set free,

Where a wandering cavalier had given
Her hundredth name to the Queen of Heaven,
And made oblation of feuds forgiven
To Our Lady of Liberty.

I shall not travel the tracks of fame
Where the war was not to the strong;
Where Lee the last of the heroes came
With the Men of the South and a flag like flame,
And called the land by its lovely name
In the unforgotten song.

If ever I cross the sea and stray
To the city of Maryland,
I will sit on a stone and watch or pray
For a stranger's child that was there one day:
And the child will never come back to play,
And no one will understand.

THE ENGLISH GRAVES

Were I that wandering citizen whose city is the world,
I would not weep for all that fell before the flags were furled;
I would not let one murmur mar the trumpets volleying forth
How God grew weary of the kings, and the cold hell in the
north.
But we whose hearts are homing birds have heavier thoughts
of home,
Though the great eagles burn with gold on Paris or on Rome,
Who stand beside our dead and stare, like seers at an eclipse,
At the riddle of the island tale and the twilight of the ships.

For these were simple men that loved with hands and feet and
eyes,

Whose souls were humbled to the hills and narrowed to the
    skies,
The hundred little lands within one little land that lie,
Where Severn seeks the sunset isles or Sussex scales the sky.

And what is theirs, though banners blow on Warsaw risen
    again,
Or ancient laughter walks in gold through the vineyards of
    Lorraine,
Their dead are marked on English stones, their loves on Eng-
    lish trees,
How little is the prize they win, how mean a coin for these—
How small a shrivelled laurel-leaf lies crumpled here and
    curled:
They died to save their country and they only saved the world.

NIGHTMARE

The silver and violet leopard of the night
Spotted with stars and smooth with silence sprang;
And though three doors stood open, the end of light
Closed like a trap; and stillness was a clang.

Under the leopard sky of lurid stars
I strove with evil sleep the hot night long,
Dreams dumb and swollen of triumphs without wars,
Of tongueless trumpet and unanswering gong.

I saw a pale imperial pomp go by,
Helmet and hornèd mitre and heavy wreath;
Their high strange ensigns hung upon the sky
And their great shields were like the doors of death.

Their mitres were as moving pyramids
And all their crowns as marching towers were tall;
Their eyes were cold under their carven lids
And the same carven smile was on them all.

Over a paven plain that seemed unending
They passed unfaltering till it found an end
In one long shallow step; and these descending
Fared forth anew as long away to wend.

I thought they travelled for a thousand years;
And at the end was nothing for them all,
For all that splendour of sceptres and of spears,
But a new step, another easy fall.

The smile of stone seemed but a little less,
The load of silver but a little more:
And ever was that terraced wilderness
And falling plain paved like a palace floor.

Rust red as gore crawled on their arms of might
And on their faces wrinkles and not scars:
Till the dream suddenly ended; noise and light
Loosened the tyranny of the tropic stars.

But over them like a subterranean sun
I saw the sign of all the fiends that fell;
And a wild voice cried "Hasten and be done,
Is there no steepness in the stairs of hell?"

He that returns, He that remains the same,
Turned the round real world, His iron vice;
Down the grey garden paths a bird called twice,
And through three doors mysterious daylight came.

A SECOND CHILDHOOD

When all my days are ending
And I have no song to sing,
I think I shall not be too old
To stare at everything;
As I stared once at a nursery door
Or a tall tree and a swing.

Wherein God's ponderous mercy hangs
On all my sins and me,
Because He does not take away
The terror from the tree
And stones still shine along the road
That are and cannot be.

Men grow too old for love, my love,
Men grow too old for wine,
But I shall not grow too old to see
Unearthly daylight shine,
Changing my chamber's dust to snow
Till I doubt if it be mine.

Behold, the crowning mercies melt,
The first surprises stay;
And in my dross is dropped a gift
For which I dare not pray:
That a man grow used to grief and joy
But not to night and day.

Men grow too old for love, my love,
Men grow too old for lies;
But I shall not grow too old to see
Enormous night arise,

A cloud that is larger than the world
And a monster made of eyes.

Nor am I worthy to unloose
The latchet of my shoe;
Or shake the dust from off my feet
Or the staff that bears me through
On ground that is too good to last,
Too solid to be true.

Men grow too old to woo, my love,
Men grow too old to wed:
But I shall not grow too old to see
Hung crazily overhead
Incredible rafters when I wake
And find I am not dead.

A thrill of thunder in my hair:
Though blackening clouds be plain,
Still I am stung and startled
By the first drop of the rain:
Romance and pride and passion pass
And these are what remain.

Strange crawling carpets of the grass,
Wide windows of the sky:
So in this perilous grace of God
With all my sins go I:
And things grow new though I grow old,
Though I grow old and die.

"MEDIÆVALISM"

If men should rise and return to the noise and time of the
tourney,

The name and fame of the tabard, the tangle of gules and gold,
Would these things stand and suffice for the bourne of a back-
    ward journey,
A light on our days returning, as it was in the days of old?

Nay, there is none rides back to pick up a glove or a feather,
Though the gauntlet rang with honour or the plume was more
    than a crown:
And hushed is the holy trumpet that called the nations together
And under the Horns of Hattin the hope of the world went
    down.

Ah, not in remembrance stored, but out of oblivion starting,
Because you have sought new homes and all that you sought
    is so,
Because you had trodden the fire and barred the door in de-
    parting,
Returns in your chosen exile the glory of long ago.

Not then when you barred the door, not then when you trod
    the embers,
But now, at your new road's end, you have seen the face of a
    fate,
That not as a child looks back, and not as a fool remembers,
All that men took too lightly and all that they love too late.

It is you that have made no rubric for saints, no raiment for
    lovers
Your caps that cry for a feather, your roofs that sigh for a
    spire:
Is it a dream from the dead if your own decay discovers
Alive in your rotting graveyard the worm of the world's
    desire?

Therefore the old trees tower, that the green trees grow and are
    stunted:
Therefore these dead men mock you, that you the living are
    dead:
Since ever you battered the saints and the tools of your crafts
    were blunted,
Or shattered the glass in its glory and loaded yourselves with
    the lead.

When the usurer hunts the squire as the squire has hunted the
    peasant,
As sheep that are eaten of worms where men were eaten of
    sheep:
Now is the judgment of earth, and the weighing of past and
    present,
Who scorn to weep over ruins, behold your ruin and weep.

Have ye not known, ye fools, that have made the present a
    prison,
That thirst can remember water and hunger remember bread?
We went not gathering ghosts; but the shriek of your shame is
    arisen
Out of your own black Babel too loud; and it woke the dead.

POLAND

Augurs that watched archaic birds
Such plumèd prodigies might read,
The eagles that were double-faced,
The eagle that was black indeed;
And when the battle-birds went down
And in their track the vultures come,
We know what pardon and what peace
Will keep our little masters dumb.

The men that sell what others make,
As vultures eat what others slay,
Will prove in matching plume with plume
That naught is black and all is grey;
Grey as those dingy doves that once,
By money-changers palmed and priced,
Amid the crash of tables flapped
And huddled from the wrath of Christ.

But raised for ever for a sign
Since God made anger glorious,
Where eagles black and vultures grey
Flocked back about the heroic house,
Where war is holier than peace,
Where hate is holier than love,
Shone terrible as the Holy Ghost
An eagle whiter than a dove.

THE HUNTING OF THE DRAGON

When we went hunting the Dragon
In the days when we were young,
We tossed the bright world over our shoulder
As bugle and baldrick slung;
Never was world so wild and fair
As what went by on the wind,
Never such fields of paradise
As the fields we left behind:
For this is the best of a rest for men
That men should rise and ride
Making a flying fairyland
Of market and country-side,
Wings on the cottage, wings on the wood,
Wings upon pot and pan,

For the hunting of the Dragon
That is the life of a man.

For men grow weary of fairyland
When the Dragon is a dream,
And tire of the talking bird in the tree,
The singing fish in the stream;
And the wandering stars grow stale, grow stale,
And the wonder is stiff with scorn;
For this is the honour of fairyland
And the following of the horn;

Beauty on beauty called us back
When we could rise and ride,
And a woman looked out of every window
As wonderful as a bride:
And the tavern-sign as a tabard blazed,
And the children cheered and ran,
For the love of the hate of the Dragon
That is the pride of a man.

The sages called him a shadow
And the light went out of the sun:
And the wise men told us that all was well
And all was weary and one:
And then, and then, in the quiet garden,
With never a weed to kill,
We knew that his shining tail had shone
In the white road over the hill:
We knew that the clouds were flakes of flame,
We knew that the sunset fire
Was red with the blood of the Dragon
Whose death is the world's desire.

For the horn was blown in the heart of the night
That men should rise and ride,

Keeping the tryst of a terrible jest
Never for long untried;
Drinking a dreadful blood for wine,
Never in cup or can,
The death of a deathless Dragon,
That is the life of a man.

SONNET

High on the wall that holds Jerusalem
I saw one stand under the stars like stone.
And when I perish it shall not be known
Whether he lived, some strolling son of Shem,
Or was some great ghost wearing the diadem
Of Solomon or Saladin on a throne:
I only know, the features being unshown,
I did not dare draw near and look on them.

Did ye not guess . . . the diadem might be
Plaited in stranger style by hands of hate . . .
But when I looked, the wall was desolate
And the grey starlight powdered tower and tree:
And vast and vague beyond the Golden Gate
Heaved Moab of the mountains like a sea.

FANTASIA

The happy men that lose their heads
They find their heads in heaven
As cherub heads with cherub wings,
And cherub haloes even:
Out of the infinite evening lands
Along the sunset sea,
Leaving the purple fields behind,

The cherub wings beat down the wind
Back to the groping body and blind
As the bird back to the tree.

Whether the plumes be passion-red
For him that truly dies
By headsman's blade or battle-axe,
Or blue like butterflies,
For him that lost it in a lane
In April's fits and starts,
His folly is forgiven then:
But higher, and far beyond our ken,
Is the healing of the unhappy men,
The men that lost their hearts.

Is there not pardon for the brave
And broad release above,
Who lost their heads for liberty
Or lost their hearts for love?
Or is the wise man wise indeed
Whom larger thoughts keep whole?
Who sees life equal like a chart,
Made strong to play the saner part,
And keep his head and keep his heart,
And only lose his soul.

A CHRISTMAS CAROL

(THE CHIEF CONSTABLE HAS ISSUED A STATEMENT DECLARING
THAT CAROL SINGING IN THE STREETS BY CHILDREN IS ILLEGAL, AND
MORALLY AND PHYSICALLY INJURIOUS. HE APPEALS TO THE PUBLIC
TO DISCOURAGE THE PRACTICE.—*Daily Paper*)

God rest you merry gentlemen,
Let nothing you dismay;

The Herald Angels cannot sing,
The cops arrest them on the wing,
And warn them of the docketing
Of anything they say.

God rest you merry gentlemen,
May nothing you dismay:
On your reposeful cities lie
Deep silence, broken only by
The motor horn's melodious cry,
The hooter's happy bray.

So, when the song of children ceased
And Herod was obeyed,
In his high hall Corinthian
With purple and with peacock fan,
Rested that merry gentleman;
And nothing him dismayed.

TO CAPTAIN FRYATT

Trampled yet red is the last of the embers,
Red the last cloud of a sun that has set;
What of your sleeping though Flanders remembers,
What of your waking, if England forget?

Why should you share in the hearts that we harden,
In the shame of our nature, who see it and live?
How more than the godly the greedy can pardon,
How well and how quickly the hungry forgive.

Ah, well if the soil of the stranger had wrapped you,
While the lords that you served and the friends that you knew
Hawk in the marts of the tyrants that trapped you,
Tout in the shops of the butchers that slew.

Why should you wake for a realm that is rotten,
Stuffed with their bribes and as dead to their debts?
Sleep and forget us, as we have forgotten;
For Flanders remembers and England forgets.

FOR FOUR GUILDS:

I. THE GLASS-STAINERS

To every Man his Mystery,
A trade and only one:
The masons make the hives of men,
The domes of grey or dun,
But we have wrought in rose and gold
The houses of the sun.

The shipwrights build the houses high,
Whose green foundations sway
Alive with fish like little flames,
When the wind goes out to slay.
But we abide with painted sails
The cyclone of the day.

The weavers make the clothes of men
And coats for everyone;
They walk the streets like sunset clouds;
But we have woven and spun
In scarlet or in golden-green
The gay coats of the sun.

You whom the usurers and the lords
With insolent liveries trod,
Deep in dark church behold, above
Their lance-lengths by a rod,
Where we have blazed the tabard
Of the trumpeter of God.

FOR FOUR GUILDS:

II. THE BRIDGE-BUILDERS

In the world's whitest morning
As hoary with hope,
The Builder of Bridges
Was priest and was pope:
And the mitre of mystery
And the canopy his,
Who darkened the chasms
And doomed the abyss.

To eastward and westward
Spread wings at his word
The arch with the key-stone
That stoops like a bird;
That rides the wild air
And the daylight cast under;
The highway of danger,
The gateway of wonder.

Of his throne were the thunders
That rivet and fix
Wild weddings of strangers,
That meet and not mix;
The town and the cornland;
The bride and the groom;
In the breaking of bridges
Is treason and doom.

But he bade us, who fashion
The road that can fly,
That we build not too heavy
And build not too high:

Seeing alway that under
The dark arch's bend
Shine death and white daylight
Unchanged to the end.

Who walk on his mercy
Walk light, as he saith,
Seeing that our life
Is a bridge above death;
And the world and its gardens
And hills, as ye heard,
Are born above space
On the wings of a bird.

Not high and not heavy
Is building of his:
When ye seal up the flood
And forget the abyss,
When your towers are uplifted,
Your banners unfurled,
In the breaking of bridges
Is the end of the world.

FOR FOUR GUILDS:

III. THE STONE-MASONS

We have graven the mountain of God with hands,
As our hands were graven of God, they say,
Where the seraphs burn in the sun like brands
And the devils carry the rains away;
Making a thrift of the throats of hell,
Our gargoyles gather the roaring rain,
Whose yawn is more than a frozen yell
And their very vomiting not in vain.

Wilder than all that a tongue can utter,
Wiser than all that is told in words,
The wings of stone of the soaring gutter
Fly out and follow the flight of the birds;
The rush and rout of the angel wars
Stand out above the astounded street,
Where we flung our gutters against the stars
For a sign that the first and the last shall meet.

We have graven the forest of heaven with hands,
Being great with a mirth too gross for pride,
In the stone that battered him Stephen stands
And Peter himself is petrified:
Such hands as have grubbed in the glebe for bread
Have bidden the blank rock blossom and thrive,
Such hands as have stricken a live man dead
Have struck, and stricken the dead alive.

Fold your hands before heaven in praying,
Lift up your hands into heaven and cry;
But look where our dizziest spires are saying
What the hands of a man did up in the sky:
Drenched before you have heard the thunder,
White before you have felt the snow;
For the giants lift up their hands to wonder
How high the hands of a man could go.

FOR FOUR GUILDS:

IV. The Bell-Ringers

The angels are singing like birds in a tree
In the organ of good St. Cecily:

And the parson reads with his hand upon
The graven eagle of great St. John:
But never the fluted pipes shall go
Like the fifes of an army all a-row,
Merrily marching down the street
To the marts where the busy and idle meet;
And never the brazen bird shall fly
Out of the window and into the sky,
Till men in cities and shires and ships
Look up at the living Apocalypse.

But all can hark at the dark of even
The bells that bay like the hounds of heaven,
Tolling and telling that over and under,
In the ways of the air like a wandering thunder,
The hunt is up over hills untrod:
For the wind is the way of the dogs of God:
From the tyrant's tower to the outlaw's den
Hunting the souls of the sons of men.
Ruler and robber and pedlar and peer,
Who will not hearken and yet will hear;
Filling men's heads with the hurry and hum
Making them welcome before they come.

And we poor men stand under the steeple
Drawing the cords that can draw the people,
And in our leash like the leaping dogs
Are God's most deafening demagogues:
And we are but little, like dwarfs underground,
While hang up in heaven the houses of sound,
Moving like mountains that faith sets free,
Yawning like caverns that roar with the sea,
As awfully loaded, as airily buoyed,

Armoured archangels that trample the void:
Wild as with dancing and weighty with dooms,
Heavy as their panoply, light as their plumes.

Neither preacher nor priest are we:
Each man mount to his own degree:
Only remember that just such a cord
Tosses in heaven the trumpet and sword;
Souls on their terraces, saints on their towers,
Rise up in arms at alarum like ours:
Glow like great watchfires that redden the skies
Titans whose wings are a glory of eyes,
Crowned constellations by twelves and by sevens,
Domed dominations more old than the heavens,
Virtues that thunder and thrones that endure
Sway like a bell to the prayers of the poor.

THE CONVERT

After one moment when I bowed my head
And the whole world turned over and came upright,
And I came out where the old road shone white,
I walked the ways and heard what all men said,
Forests of tongues, like autumn leaves unshed,
Being not unlovable but strange and light;
Old riddles and new creeds, not in despite
But softly, as men smile about the dead.

The sages have a hundred maps to give
That trace their crawling cosmos like a tree,
They rattle reason out through many a sieve
That stores the sand and lets the gold go free:
And all these things are less than dust to me
Because my name is Lazarus and I live.

SONGS OF EDUCATION:

I. HISTORY

Form 991785, *Sub-Section D*

The Roman threw us a road, a road,
And sighed and strolled away:
The Saxon gave us a raid, a raid,
A raid that came to stay;
The Dane went west, but the Dane confessed
That he went a bit too far;
And we all became, by another name,
The Imperial race we are.

Chorus.
The Imperial race, the inscrutable race,
The invincible race we are.

Though Sussex hills are bare, are bare,
And Sussex weald is wide,
From Chichester to Chester
Men saw the Norman ride;
He threw his sword in the air and sang
To a sort of a light guitar;
It was all the same, for we all became
The identical nobs we are.

Chorus.
The identical nobs, individual nobs,
Unmistakable nobs we are.

The people lived on the land, the land,
They pottered about and prayed;
They built a cathedral here and there

Or went on a small crusade:
Till the bones of Becket were bundled out
For the fun of a fat White Czar,
And we all became, in spoil and flame,
The intelligent lot we are.

Chorus.

The intelligent lot, the intuitive lot,
The infallible lot we are.

O Warwick woods are green, are green,
But Warwick trees can fall:
And Birmingham grew so big, so big,
And Stratford stayed so small.
Till the hooter howled to the morning lark
That sang to the morning star;
And we all became, in freedom's name,
The fortunate chaps we are.

Chorus.

The fortunate chaps, felicitous chaps,
The fairy-like chaps we are.

The people they left the land, the land,
But they went on working hard;
And the village green that had got mislaid
Turned up in the squire's back-yard:
But twenty men of us all got work
On a bit of his motor car;
And we all became, with the world's acclaim,
The marvellous mugs we are:

Chorus.

The marvellous mugs, miraculous mugs,
The mystical mugs we are.

SONGS OF EDUCATION:

II. GEOGRAPHY.

Form 17955301, *Sub-Section Z*

The earth is a place on which England is found,
And you find it however you twirl the globe round;
For the spots are all red and the rest is all grey;
And that is the meaning of Empire Day.

Gibraltar's a rock that you see very plain,
And attached to its base is the district of Spain.
And the island of Malta is marked further on,
Where some natives were known as the Knights of St. John.
Then Cyprus, and east to the Suez Canal,
That was conquered by Dizzy and Rothschild his pal
With the Sword of the Lord in the old English way;
And that is the meaning of Empire Day.

Our principal imports come far as Cape Horn;
For necessities, cocoa; for luxuries, corn;
Thus Brahmins are born for the rice-field, and thus,
The Gods made the Greeks to grow currants for us;
Of earth's other tributes are plenty to choose,
Tobacco and petrol and Jazzing and Jews:
The Jazzing will pass but the Jews they will stay;
And that is the meaning of Empire Day.

Our principal exports, all labelled and packed,
At the ends of the earth are delivered intact: ·
Our soap or our salmon can travel in tins
Between the two poles and as like as two pins;
So that Lancashire merchants whenever they like
Can water the beer of a man in Klondike

Or poison the meat of a man in Bombay;
And that is the meaning of Empire Day.

The day of St. George is a musty affair
Which Russians and Greeks are permitted to share;
The day of Trafalgar is Spanish in name
And the Spaniards refuse to pronounce it the same;
But the day of the Empire from Canada came
With Morden and Borden and Beaverbrook's fame
And saintly seraphical souls such as they:
And that is the meaning of Empire Day.

SONGS OF EDUCATION:

III. For the Crêche

Form 8277059, Sub-Section K

I remember my mother, the day that we met,
A thing I shall never entirely forget;
And I toy with the fancy that, young as I am,
I should know her again if we met in a tram.
　　But mother is happy in turning a crank
　　That increases the balance at somebody's bank;
　　And I feel satisfaction that mother is free
　　From the sinister task of attending to me.

They have brightened our room, that is spacious and cool,
With diagrams used in the Idiot School,
And Books for the Blind that will teach us to see;
But mother is happy, for mother is free.
　　For mother is dancing up forty-eight floors,
　　For love of the Leeds International Stores,
　　And the flame of that faith might perhaps have grown cold,
　　With the care of a baby of seven weeks old.

For mother is happy in greasing a wheel
For somebody else, who is cornering Steel;
And though our one meeting was not very long,
She took the occasion to sing me this song:
  "O, hush thee, my baby, the time will soon come
  When thy sleep will be broken with hooting and hum;
  There are handles want turning and turning all day,
  And knobs to be pressed in the usual way;

O, hush thee, my baby, take rest while I croon,
For Progress comes early, and Freedom too soon."

SONGS OF EDUCATION:

IV. CITIZENSHIP.

Form 8889512, *Sub-Section Q*

How slowly learns the child at school
The names of all the nobs that rule
From Ponsonby to Pennant;
Ere his bewildered mind find rest,
Knowing his host can be a Guest,
His landlord is a Tennant.

He knew not, at the age of three
What Lord St. Leger next will be
Or what he was before;
A Primrose in the social swim
A Mr. Primrose is to him,
And he is nothing more.

But soon, about the age of ten,
He finds he is a Citizen,
And knows his way about;

Can pause within, or just beyond,
The line 'twixt Mond and Demi-Mond,
'Twixt Getting On—or Out.

The Citizen will take his share
(In every sense) as bull and bear;
Nor need this oral ditty
Invoke the philologic pen
To show you that a Citizen
Means Something in the City.

Thus gains he, with the virile gown,
The fasces and the civic crown,
The forum of the free;
Not more to Rome's high law allied
Is Devonport in all his pride
Or Lipton's self than he.

For he will learn, if he will try,
The deep interior truths whereby
We rule the Commonwealth;
What is the Food-Controller's fee
And whether the Health Ministry
Are in it for their health.

SONGS OF EDUCATION:

V. THE HIGHER MATHEMATICS

Form 339125, Sub-Section M

Twice one is two,
Twice two is four,
But twice two is ninety-six if you know the way to
score.

Half of two is one,
Half of four is two,
But half of four is forty per cent. if your name is
Montagu:
For everything else is on the square
If done by the best quadratics;
And nothing is low in High Finance
Or the Higher Mathematics.

A straight line is straight
And a square mile is flat:
But you learn in trigonometrics a trick worth two
of that.
Two straight lines
Can't enclose a Space,
But they can enclose a Corner to support the
Chosen Race:
For you never know what Dynamics do
With the lower truths of Statics;
And half of two is a touring car
In the Higher Mathematics.

There is a place apart
Beyond the solar ray,
Where parallel straight lines can meet in an un-
official way.
There is a room that holds
The examiner or his clerks,
Where you can square the circle or the man that
gives the marks.
Where you hide in the cellar and then look down
On the poets that live in the attics;
For the whole of the house is upside down
In the Higher Mathematics.

SONGS OF EDUCATION:

VI. HYGIENE

Form 394411102, Sub-Section X

"ALL PRACTICAL EUGENISTS ARE AGREED ON THE IMPORTANCE OF SLEEP."—*The Eugenic Congress.*

When Science taught mankind to breathe
A little while ago,
Only a wise and thoughtful few
Were really in the know:
Nor could the Youth his features wreathe,
Puffing from all the lungs beneath:
When Duty whispered softly "Breathe!"
The Youth would answer "Blow!"

When Science proved with lucid care
The need of Exercise,
Our thoughtless Youth was climbing trees
Or lightly blacking eyes:
To reckless idlers breaking bounds
For football or for hare-and-hounds,
Or fighting hard for fourteen rounds,
It came as a surprise.

But when she boldly counsels Sleep
To persons when in bed,
Then, then indeed men blush to see
The daybreak blushing red:
The early risers whom we term
Healthy, grow sickly and infirm;
The Early Bird who caught the Worm
Will catch the Germ instead.

For this at least be Science praised
If all the rest be rot,
That now she snubs the priggish child
That quits too soon his cot:
The pharisaic pachyderm
Of spiritual pride shall squirm:
The Early Bird catches the worm,
The Worm that dieth not.

Book Three
Poems

PREFATORY NOTE.

This collection was made a long time ago and includes items written a very long time before that: things that are indeed merely juvenile. But I have decided that it is very difficult to disentangle the threads in a patchwork which may already be thought threadbare: and I have let these schoolboy verses remain side by side with some that I wrote at least in maturer years and on more momentous occasions.

G. K. C.

TO EDMUND CLERIHEW BENTLEY

THE DEDICATION OF THE MAN WHO WAS THURSDAY

A cloud was on the mind of men, and wailing went the weather,
Yea, a sick cloud upon the soul when we were boys together.
Science announced nonentity and art admired decay;
The world was old and ended: but you and I were gay.
Round us in antic order their crippled vices came—
Lust that had lost its laughter, fear that had lost its shame.
Like the white lock of Whistler, that lit our aimless gloom,
Men showed their own white feather as proudly as a plume.
Life was a fly that faded, and death a drone that stung;
The world was very old indeed when you and I were young.
They twisted even decent sin to shapes not to be named:
Men were ashamed of honour; but we were not ashamed.

Weak if we were and foolish, not thus we failed, not thus;
When that black Baal blocked the heavens he had no hymns
    from us.
Children we were—our forts of sand were even as weak as we,
High as they went we piled them up to break that bitter sea.
Fools as we were in motley, all jangling and absurd,
When all church bells were silent our cap and bells were heard.

Not all unhelped we held the fort, our tiny flags unfurled;
Some giants laboured in that cloud to lift it from the world.
I find again the book we found, I feel the hour that flings
Far out of fish-shaped Paumanok some cry of cleaner things;
And the Green Carnation withered, as in forest fires that pass,
Roared in the wind of all the world ten million leaves of grass;
Or sane and sweet and sudden as a bird sings in the rain—
Truth out of Tusitala spoke and pleasure out of pain.

Yea, cool and clear and sudden as a bird sings in the grey,
Dunedin to Samoa spoke, and darkness unto day.
But we were young; we lived to see God break their bitter
    charms,
God and the good Republic come riding back in arms:
We have seen the city of Mansoul, even as it rocked, relieved—
Blessed are they who did not see, but being blind, believed.

This is a tale of those old fears, even of those emptied hells,
And none but you shall understand the true thing that it tells—
Of what colossal gods of shame could cow men and yet crash,
Of what huge devils hid the stars, yet fell at a pistol flash.
The doubts that were so plain to chase, so dreadful to with-
    stand—
Oh, who shall understand but you; yea, who shall understand?
The doubts that drove us through the night as we two talked
    amain,
And day had broken on the streets e'er it broke upon the brain.
Between us, by the peace of God, such truth can now be told;
Yea, there is strength in striking root, and good in growing old.
We have found common things at last, and marriage and a
    creed,
And I may safely write it now, and you may safely read.

TO HILAIRE BELLOC

THE DEDICATION OF *The Napoleon of Notting Hill.*

For every tiny town or place
    God made the stars especially;
Babies look up with owlish face
    And see them tangled in a tree:
You saw a moon from Sussex Downs,
    A Sussex moon, untravelled still,

I saw a moon that was the town's,
 The largest lamp on Campden Hill.

Yea, Heaven is everywhere at home,
 'The big blue cap that always fits,
And so it is (be calm; they come
 To goal at last, my wandering wits),
So is it with the heroic thing;
 This shall not end for the world's end,
And though the sullen engines swing,
 Be you not much afraid, my friend.

This did not end by Nelson's urn
 Where an immortal England sits—
Nor where our tall young men in turn
 Drank death like wine at Austerlitz.
And when the pedants bade us mark
 What cold mechanic happenings
Must come; our souls said in the dark,
 "Belike; but there are likelier things."

Likelier across these flats afar,
 These sulky levels smooth and free,
The drums shall crash a waltz of war
 And Death shall dance with Liberty;
Likelier the barricades shall blare
 Slaughter below and smoke above,
And death and hate and hell declare
 That men have found a thing to love.

Far from your sunny uplands set
 I saw the dream; the streets I trod,
The lit straight streets shot out and met
 The starry streets that point to God;

The legend of an epic hour
    A child I dreamed, and dream it still,
Under the great grey water tower
    That strikes the stars on Campden Hill.

TO *M.E.W.*

Words, for alas my trade is words, a barren burst of rhymes,
    Rubbed by a hundred rhymesters, battered a thousand times,
Take them, you, that smile on strings, those nobler sounds than
        mine,
    The words that never lie, or brag, or flatter, or malign.

I give a hand to my lady, another to my friend,
    To whom you too have given a hand; and so before the end
We four may pray, for all the years, whatever suns be set,
    The sole two prayers worth praying—to live and not forget.

The pale leaf falls in pallor, but the green leaf turns to gold;
    We that have found it good to be young shall find it good to
        be old;
Life that bringeth the marriage bell, the cradle and the grave,
    Life that is mean to the mean of heart, and only brave to the
        brave.

In the calm of the last white winter, when all the past is ours,
    Old tears are frozen as jewels, old storms frosted as flowers.
Dear Lady, may we meet again, stand up again, we four,
    Beneath the burden of the years, and praise the earth once
        more.

LEPANTO

White founts falling in the courts of the sun,
And the Soldan of Byzantium is smiling as they run;

There is laughter like the fountains in that face of all men
    feared,
It stirs the forest darkness, the darkness of his beard,
It curls the blood-red crescent, the crescent of his lips,
For the inmost sea of all the earth is shaken with his ships.
They have dared the white republics up the capes of Italy,
They have dashed the Adriatic round the Lion of the Sea,
And the Pope has cast his arms abroad for agony and loss,
And called the kings of Christendom for swords about the
    Cross,
The cold queen of England is looking in the glass;
The shadow of the Valois is yawning at the Mass;
From evening isles fantastical rings faint the Spanish gun,
And the Lord upon the Golden Horn is laughing in the sun.

Dim drums throbbing, in the hills half heard,
Where only on a nameless throne a crownless prince has stirred,
Where, risen from a doubtful seat and half-attainted stall,
The last knight of Europe takes weapons from the wall,
The last and lingering troubadour to whom the bird has sung,
That once went singing southward when all the world was
    young,
In that enormous silence, tiny and unafraid,
Comes up along a winding road the noise of the Crusade.
Strong gongs groaning as the guns boom far,
Don John of Austria is going to the war,
Stiff flags straining in the night-blasts cold
In the gloom black-purple, in the glint old-gold,
Torchlight crimson on the copper kettle-drums,
Then the tuckets, then the trumpets, then the cannon, and he
    comes.
Don John laughing in the brave beard curled,
Spurning of his stirrups like the thrones of all the world,
Holding his head up for a flag of all the free.

Love-light of Spain—hurrah!
Death-light of Africa!
Don John of Austria
Is riding to the sea.

Mahound is in his paradise above the evening star,
(*Don John of Austria is going to the war.*)
He moves a mighty turban on the timeless houri's knees,
His turban that is woven of the sunset and the seas.
He shakes the peacock gardens as he rises from his ease,
And he strides among the tree-tops and is taller than the trees,
And his voice through all the garden is a thunder sent to bring
Black Azrael and Ariel and Ammon on the wing.
Giants and the Genii,
Multiplex of wing and eye,
Whose strong obedience broke the sky
When Solomon was king.

They rush in red and purple from the red clouds of the morn,
From temples where the yellow gods shut up their eyes in
        scorn;
They rise in green robes roaring from the green hells of the sea
Where fallen skies and evil hues and eyeless creatures be;
On them the sea-valves cluster and the grey sea-forests curl,
Splashed with a splendid sickness, the sickness of the pearl;
They swell in sapphire smoke out of the blue cracks of the
        ground,—
They gather and they wonder and give worship to Mahound.
And he saith, "Break up the mountains where the hermit-folk
        may hide,
And sift the red and silver sands lest bone of saint abide,
And chase the Giaours flying night and day, not giving rest,
For that which was our trouble comes again out of the west.
We have set the seal of Solomon on all things under sun,

Of knowledge and of sorrow and endurance of things done,
But a noise is in the mountains, in the mountains, and I know
The voice that shook our palaces—four hundred years ago:
It is he that saith not 'Kismet'; it is he that knows not Fate;
It is Richard, it is Raymond, it is Godfrey in the gate!
It is he whose loss is laughter when he counts the wager worth,
Put down your feet upon him, that our peace be on the earth."
For he heard drums groaning and he heard guns jar,
(*Don John of Austria is going to the war.*)
Sudden and still—hurrah!
Bolt from Iberia!
Don John of Austria
Is gone by Alcalar.

St. Michael's on his Mountain in the sea-roads of the north
(*Don John of Austria is girt and going forth.*)
Where the grey seas glitter and the sharp tides shift
And the sea folk labour and the red sails lift.
He shakes his lance of iron and he claps his wings of stone;
The noise is gone through Normandy; the noise is gone alone;
The North is full of tangled things and texts and aching eyes
And dead is all the innocence of anger and surprise,
And Christian killeth Christian in a narrow dusty room,
And Christian dreadeth Christ that hath a newer face of doom,
And Christian hateth Mary that God kissed in Galilee,
But Don John of Austria is riding to the sea.
Don John calling through the blast and the eclipse
Crying with the trumpet, with the trumpet of his lips,
Trumpet that sayeth ha!
   Domino gloria!
Don John of Austria
Is shouting to the ships.

King Philip's in his closet with the Fleece about his neck
(*Don John of Austria is armed upon the deck.*)

The walls are hung with velvet that is black and soft as sin,
And little dwarfs creep out of it and little dwarfs creep in.
He holds a crystal phial that has colours like the moon,
He touches, and it tingles, and he trembles very soon,
And his face is as a fungus of a leprous white and grey
Like plants in the high houses that are shuttered from the day,
And death is in the phial, and the end of noble work,
But Don John of Austria has fired upon the Turk.
Don John's hunting, and his hounds have bayed—
Booms away past Italy the rumour of his raid.
Gun upon gun, ha! ha!
Gun upon gun, hurrah!
Don John of Austria
Has loosed the cannonade.

The Pope was in his chapel before day or battle broke,
(*Don John of Austria is hidden in the smoke.*)
The hidden room in a man's house where God sits all the year,
The secret window whence the world looks small and very
    dear.
He sees as in a mirror on the monstrous twilight sea
The crescent of his cruel ships whose name is mystery;
They fling great shadows foe-wards, making Cross and Castle
    dark,
They veil the plumèd lions on the galleys of St. Mark;
And above the ships are palaces of brown, black-bearded chiefs,
And below the ships are prisons, where with multitudinous
    griefs,
Christian captives sick and sunless, all a labouring race repines
Like a race in sunken cities, like a nation in the mines.
They are lost like slaves that swat, and in the skies of morning
    hung
The stairways of the tallest gods when tyranny was young.

They are countless, voiceless, hopeless as those fallen or flee-
     ing on
Before the high Kings' horses in the granite of Babylon.
And many a one grows witless in his quiet room in hell
Where a yellow face looks inward through the lattice of his cell,
And he finds his God forgotten, and he seeks no more a sign—
(But Don John of Austria has burst the battle-line!)
Don John pounding from the slaughter-painted poop,
Purpling all the ocean like a bloody pirate's sloop,
Scarlet running over on the silvers and the golds,
Breaking of the hatches up and bursting of the holds,
Thronging of the thousands up that labour under sea
White for bliss and blind for sun and stunned for liberty.
Vivat Hispania!
Domino Gloria!
Don John of Austria
Has set his people free!

Cervantes on his galley sets the sword back in the sheath
(Don John of Austria rides homeward with a wreath.)
And he sees across a weary land a straggling road in Spain,
Up which a lean and foolish knight forever rides in vain,
And he smiles, but not as Sultans smile, and settles back the
     blade. . . .
(But Don John of Austria rides home from the Crusade.)

MARCH OF THE BLACK MOUNTAIN

1913

What will there be to remember
     Of us in the days to be?
Whose faith was a trodden ember
     And even our doubts not free;

Parliaments built of paper,
  And the soft swords of gold
That twist like a waxen taper
  In the weak aggressor's hold;
A hush around Hunger, slaying
  A city of serfs unfed;
What shall we leave for a saying
  To praise us when we are dead?
But men shall remember the Mountain
  That broke its forest chains,
And men shall remember the Mountain
  When it arches against the plains:
And christen their children from it
  And season and ship and street,
When the Mountain came to Mahomet
  And looked small before his feet.

His head was as high as the crescent
  Of the moon that seemed his crown,
And on glory of past and present
  The light of his eyes looked down;
One hand went out to the morning
  Over Brahmin and Buddhist slain,
And one to the west in scorning
  To point at the scars of Spain:
One foot on the hills for warden
  By the little Mountain trod;
And one was in a garden
  And stood on the grave of God.
But men shall remember the Mountain,
  Though it fall down like a tree,
They shall see the sign of the Mountain
  Faith cast into the sea;

Though the crooked swords overcome it
    And the Crooked Moon ride free,
When the Mountain comes to Mahomet
    It has more life than he.

But what will there be to remember
    Or what will there be to see—
Though our towns through a long November
    Abide to the end and be?
Strength of slave and mechanic
    Whose iron is ruled by gold,
Peace of immortal panic,
    Love that is hate grown cold—
Are these a bribe or a warning
    That we turn not to the sun,
Nor look on the lands of morning
    Where deeds at last are done?
Where men shall remember the Mountain
    When truth forgets the plain—
And walk in the way of the Mountain
    That did not fail in vain;
Death and eclipse and comet,
    Thunder and seals that rend:
When the Mountain came to Mahomet;
    Because it was the end.

BLESSED ARE THE PEACEMAKERS

Of old with a divided heart
    I saw my people's pride expand,
Since a man's soul is torn apart
By mother earth and fatherland.

I knew, through many a tangled tale,
    Glory and truth not one but two:

        King, Constable, and Amirail
            Took me like trumpets: but I knew

    A blacker thing than blood's own dye
        Weighed down great Hawkins on the sea;
    And Nelson turned his blindest eye
        On Naples and on liberty.

    Therefore to you my thanks, O throne,
        O thousandfold and frozen folk;
    For whose cold frenzies all your own
        The Battle of the Rivers broke;

    Who have no faith a man could mourn,
        Nor freedom any man desires;
    But in a new clean light of scorn
        Close up my quarrel with my sires;

    Who bring my English heart to me,
        Who mend me like a broken toy;
    Till I can see you fight and flee,
        And laugh as if I were a boy.

THE WIFE OF FLANDERS

Low and brown barns thatched and repatched and tattered
    Where I had seven sons until to-day,
A little hill of hay your spur has scattered. . . .
    This is not Paris. You have lost the way.

You, staring at your sword to find it brittle,
    Surprised at the surprise that was your plan,
Who shaking and breaking barriers not a little
    Find never more the death-door of Sedan.

Must I for more than carnage call you claimant,
  Paying you a penny for each son you slay?
Man, the whole globe in gold were no repayment
  For what *you* have lost. And how shall I repay?

What is the price of that red spark that caught me
  From a kind farm that never had a name?
What is the price of that dead man they brought me?
  For other dead men do not look the same.

How should I pay for one poor graven steeple
  Whereon you shattered what you shall not know,
How should I pay you, miserable people?
  How should I pay you everything you owe?

Unhappy, can I give you back your honour?
  Though I forgave would any man forget?
While all the great green land has trampled on her
  The treason and terror of the night we met.

Not any more in vengeance or in pardon
  An old wife bargains for a bean that's hers.
You have no word to break: no heart to harden.
  Ride on and prosper. You have lost your spurs.

THE CRUSADER RETURNS FROM CAPTIVITY

I have come forth alive from the land of purple and poison and
      glamour,
  Where the charm is strong as the torture, being chosen to
      change the mind;
Torture of wordless dance and wineless feast without clamour,
  Palace hidden in palace, garden with garden behind;

Women veiled in the sun, or bare as brass in the shadows,
    And the endless eyeless patterns where each thing seems an
        eye. . . .
And my stride is on Caesar's sand where it slides to the English
    meadows,
    To the last low woods of Sussex and the road that goes to
      Rye.

In the cool and careless woods the eyes of the eunuchs burned
    not,
    But the wild hawk went before me, being free to return or
      roam,
The hills had broad unconscious backs; and the tree-tops turned
    not,
    And the huts were heedless of me; and I knew I was at home.

And I saw my lady afar and her holy freedom upon her,
    A head, without veil, averted, and not to be turned with
      charms,
And I heard above bannerets blown the intolerant trumpets of
    honour,
    That usher with iron laughter the coming of Christian arms.

My shield hangs stainless still; but I shall not go where they
    praise it,
    A sword is still at my side, but I shall not ride with the King.
Only to walk and to walk and to stun my soul and amaze it,
    A day with the stone and the sparrow and every marvellous
      thing.

I have trod the curves of the Crescent, in the maze of them that
    adore it,
    Curved around doorless chambers and unbeholden abodes,

But I walk in the maze no more; on the sign of the cross I
  swore it,
 The wild white cross of freedom, the sign of the white cross-
  roads.

And the land shall leave me or take, and the Woman take me
  or leave me,
 There shall be no more night, or nightmares seen in a glass;
But Life shall hold me alive, and Death shall never deceive me
 As long as I walk in England in the lanes that let me pass.

GLENCOE

The star-crowned cliffs seem hinged upon the sky,
The clouds are floating rags across them curled,
They open to us like the gates of God
Cloven in the last great wall of all the world.

I looked, and saw the valley of my soul
Where naked crests fight to achieve the skies,
Where no grain grows nor wine, no fruitful thing,
Only big words and starry blasphemies.

But you have clothed with mercy like a moss
The barren violence of its primal wars,
Sterile although they be and void of rule,
You know my shapeless crags have loved the stars.

How shall I thank you, O courageous heart,
That of this wasteful world you had no fear;
But bade it blossom in clear faith and sent
Your fair flower-feeding rivers: even as here

The peat burns brimming from their cups of stone
Glow brown and blood-red down the vast decline

As if Christ stood on yonder clouded peak
And turned its thousand waters into wine.

LOVE'S TRAPPIST

There is a place where lute and lyre are broken,
Where scrolls are torn and on a wild wind go,
Where tablets stand wiped naked for a token,
Where laurels wither and the daisies grow.

Lo: I too join the brotherhood of silence,
I am Love's trappist and you ask in vain,
For man through Love's gate, even as through Death's gate,
Goeth alone and comes not back again.

Yet here I pause, look back across the threshold,
Cry to my brethren, though the world be old,
Prophets and sages, questioners and doubters,
O world, old world, the best hath ne'er been told!

CONFESSIONAL

Now that I kneel at the throne, O Queen,
Pity and pardon me.
Much have I striven to sing the same,
Brother of beast and tree;
Yet when the stars catch me alone
Never a linnet sings—
And the blood of a man is a bitter voice
And cries for foolish things.

Not for me be the vaunt of woe;
Was not I from a boy
Vowed with the helmet and spear and spur
To the blood-red banner of joy?

A man may sing his psalms to a stone,
Pour his blood for a weed,
But the tears of a man are a sudden thing,
And come not of his creed.

Nay, but the earth is kind to me,
Though I cry for a star,
Leaves and grasses, feather and flower,
Cover the foolish scar,
Prophets and saints and seraphim
Lighten the load with song,
And the heart of a man is a heavy load
For a man to bear along.

MUSIC

Sounding brass and tinkling cymbal,
    He that made me sealed my ears,
And the pomp of gorgeous noises,
    Waves of triumph, waves of tears,

Thundered empty round and past me,
    Shattered, lost for evermore,
Ancient gold of pride and passion,
    Wrecked like treasure on a shore.

But I saw her cheek and forehead
    Change, as at a spoken word,
And I saw her head uplifted
    Like a lily to the Lord.

Nought is lost, but all transmuted,
    Ears are sealed, yet eyes have seen;
Saw her smiles (O soul be worthy!),
    Saw her tears (O heart be clean!).

THE DELUGE

Though giant rains put out the sun,
    Here stand I for a sign.
Though Earth be filled with waters dark,
    My cup is filled with wine.
Tell to the trembling priests that here
    Under the deluge rod,
One nameless, tattered, broken man
    Stood up and drank to God.

Sun has been where the rain is now,
    Bees in the heat to hum,
Haply a humming maiden came,
    Now let the deluge come:
Brown of aureole, green of garb,
    Straight as a golden rod,
Drink to the throne of thunder now!
    Drink to the wrath of God.

High in the wreck I held the cup,
    I clutched my rusty sword,
I cocked my tattered feather
    To the glory of the Lord.
Not undone were the heaven and earth,
    This hollow world thrown up,
Before one man had stood up straight,
    And drained it like a cup.

THE STRANGE MUSIC

Other loves may sink and settle, other loves may loose and slack,
But I wander like a minstrel with a harp upon his back,
Though the harp be on my bosom, though I finger and I fret,
Still, my hope is all before me: for I cannot play it yet.

In your strings is hid a music that no hand hath e'er let fall,
In your soul is sealed a pleasure that you have not known at all;
Pleasure subtle as your spirit, strange and slender as your frame,
Fiercer than the pain that folds you, softer than your sorrow's
　　name.

Not as mine, my soul's anointed, not as mine the rude and light
Easy mirth of many faces, swaggering pride of song and fight;
Something stranger, something sweeter, something waiting you
　　afar,
Secret as your stricken senses, magic as your sorrows are.

But on this, God's harp supernal, stretched but to be stricken
　　once,
Hoary time is a beginner, Life a bungler, Death a dunce.
But I will not fear to match them—no, by God, I will not fear,
I will learn you, I will play you and the stars stand still to hear.

THE GREAT MINIMUM

It is something to have wept as we have wept,
It is something to have done as we have done,
It is something to have watched when all men slept,
And seen the stars which never see the sun.

It is something to have smelt the mystic rose,
Although it break and leave the thorny rods,
It is something to have hungered once as those
Must hunger who have ate the bread of gods.

To have seen you and your unforgotten face,
Brave as a blast of trumpets for the fray,
Pure as white lilies in a watery space,
It were something, though you went from me to-day.

To have known the things that from the weak are furled,
Perilous ancient passions, strange and high;
It is something to be wiser than the world,
It is something to be older than the sky.

In a time of sceptic moths and cynic rusts,
And fatted lives that of their sweetness tire,
In a world of flying loves and fading lusts,
It is something to be sure of a desire.

Lo, blessed are our ears for they have heard;
Yea, blessed are our eyes for they have seen:
Let thunder break on man and beast and bird
And the lightning. It is something to have been.

THE MORTAL ANSWERS

. . . COME AWAY—
WITH THE FAIRIES, HAND IN HAND,
FOR THE WORLD IS MORE FULL OF WEEPING
THAN YOU CAN UNDERSTAND.

W. B. Yeats.

From the Wood of the Old Wives' Fables
    They glittered out of the grey,
And with all the armies of Elf-land
    I strove like a beast at bay;

With only a right arm wearied,
    Only a red sword worn,
And the pride of the house of Adam
    That holdeth the stars in scorn.

For they came with chains of flowers
  And lilies' lances free,
There in the quiet greenwood
  To take my grief from me.

And I said, "Now all is shaken
  When heavily hangs the brow,
When the hope of the years is taken,
  The last star sunken. Now—

"Hear, you chattering cricket,
  Hear, you spawn of the sod,
The strange strong cry in the darkness
  Of one man praising God,

"That out of the night and nothing
  With travail of birth he came
To stand one hour in the sunlight
  Only to say her name.

"Falls through her hair the sunshine
  In showers; it touches, see,
Her high bright cheeks in turning;
  Ah, Elfin Company,

"The world is hot and cruel,
  We are weary of heart and hand,
But the world is more full of glory
  Than you can understand."

A MARRIAGE SONG

Why should we reck of hours that rend
  While we two ride together?

The heavens rent from end to end
    Would be but windy weather,
The strong stars shaken down in spate
    Would be a shower of spring,
And we should list the trump of fate
    And hear a linnet sing.

We break the line with stroke and luck,
    The arrows run like rain,
If you be struck, or I be struck,
    There's one to strike again.
If you befriend, or I befriend,
    The strength is in us twain,
And good things end and bad things end,
    And you and I remain.

Why should we reck of ill or well
    While we two ride together?
The fires that over Sodom fell
    Would be but sultry weather.
Beyond all ends to all men given
    Our race is far and fell,
We shall but wash our feet in heaven,
    And warm our hands in hell.

Battles unborn and vast shall view
    Our faltered standards stream,
New friends shall come and frenzies new,
    New troubles toil and teem;
New friends shall pass and still renew
    One truth that does not seem,
That I am I, and you are you,
    And Death a morning dream.

Why should we reck of scorn or praise
  While we two ride together?
The icy air of godless days
  Shall be but wintry weather.
If hell were highest, if the heaven
  Were blue with devils blue,
I should have guessed that all was even,
  If I had dreamed of you.

Little I reck of empty prides,
  Of creeds more cold than clay;
To nobler ends and longer rides,
  My lady rides to-day.
To swing our swords and take our sides
  In that all-ending fray
When stars fall down and darkness hides,
  When God shall turn to bay.

Why should we reck of grin and groan
  While we two ride together?
The triple thunders of the throne
  Would be but stormy weather.
For us the last great fight shall roar,
  Upon the ultimate plains,
And we shall turn and tell once more
  Our love in English lanes.

BAY COMBE

With leaves below and leaves above,
And groping under tree and tree,
I found the home of my true love,
Who is a wandering home for me.

Who, lost in ruined worlds aloof,
Bore the dread dove wings like a roof;
Who, past the last lost stars of space,
Carried the fire-light on her face.

Who, passing as in idle hours,
Tamed the wild weeds to garden flowers;
Stroked the strange whirlwind's whirring wings,
And made the comets homely things.

Where she went by upon her way
The dark was dearer than the day;
Where she paused in heaven or hell,
The whole world's tale had ended well.

With leaves below and leaves above,
And groping under tree and tree,
I found the home of my true love,
Who is a wandering home for me.

Where she was flung, above, beneath,
By the rude dance of life and death,
Grow she at Gotham—die at Rome,
Between the pine trees is her home.

In some strange town, some silver morn,
She may have wandered to be born;
Stopped at some motley crowd impressed,
And called them kinsfolk for a jest.

If we again in goodness thrive,
And the dead saints become alive,
Then pedants bald and parchments brown
May claim her blood for London town.

But leaves below and leaves above,
And groping under tree and tree,
I found the home of my true love,
Who is a wandering home for me.

The great gravestone she may pass by,
And without noticing, may die;
The streets of silver Heaven may tread,
With her grey awful eyes unfed.

The city of great peace in pain
May pass, until she find again
This little house of holm and fir
God built before the stars for her.

Here in the fallen leaves is furled
Her secret centre of the world.
We sit and feel in dusk and dun
The stars swing round us like a sun.

For leaves below and leaves above,
And groping under tree and tree,
I found the home of my true love,
Who is a wandering home for me.

THE WISE MEN

Step softly, under snow or rain,
    To find the place where men can pray;
The way is all so very plain
    That we may lose the way.

Oh, we have learnt to peer and pore
    On tortured puzzles from our youth,

We know all labyrinthine lore,
We are the three wise men of yore,
   And we know all things but the truth.

We have gone round and round the hill
   And lost the wood among the trees,
And learnt long names for every ill,
And served the mad gods, naming still
   The furies the Eumenides.

The gods of violence took the veil
   Of vision and philosophy,
The Serpent that brought all men bale,
He bites his own accursed tail,
   And calls himself Eternity.

Go humbly . . . it has hailed and snowed . . .
   With voices low and lanterns lit;
So very simple is the road,
   That we may stray from it.

The world grows terrible and white,
   And blinding white the breaking day;
We walk bewildered in the light,
For something is too large for sight,
   And something much too plain to say.

The Child that was ere worlds begun
   (. . . We need but walk a little way,
We need but see a latch undone . . .)
The Child that played with moon and sun
   Is playing with a little hay.

The house from which the heavens are fed,
   The old strange house that is our own,

Where tricks of words are never said,
And Mercy is as plain as bread,
  And Honour is as hard as stone.

Go humbly, humble are the skies,
  And low and large and fierce the Star;
So very near the Manger lies
  That we may travel far.

Hark! Laughter like a lion wakes
  To roar to the resounding plain,
And the whole heaven shouts and shakes,
For God Himself is born again,
And we are little children walking
  Through the snow and rain.

THE HOUSE OF CHRISTMAS

There fared a mother driven forth
Out of an inn to roam;
In the place where she was homeless
All men are at home.
The crazy stable close at hand,
With shaking timber and shifting sand,
Grew a stronger thing to abide and stand
Than the square stones of Rome.

For men are homesick in their homes,
And strangers under the sun,
And they lay their heads in a foreign land
Whenever the day is done.
Here we have battle and blazing eyes,
And chance and honour and high surprise,
But our homes are under miraculous skies
Where the yule tale was begun.

A Child in a foul stable,
Where the beasts feed and foam;
Only where He was homeless
Are you and I at home;
We have hands that fashion and heads that know,
But our hearts we lost—how long ago!
In a place no chart nor ship can show
Under the sky's dome.

This world is wild as an old wives' tale,
And strange the plain things are,
The earth is enough and the air is enough
For our wonder and our war;
But our rest is as far as the fire-drake swings
And our peace is put in impossible things
Where clashed and thundered unthinkable wings
Round an incredible star.

To an open house in the evening
Home shall men come,
To an older place than Eden
And a taller town than Rome.
To the end of the way of the wandering star,
To the things that cannot be and that are,
To the place where God was homeless
And all men are at home.

A SONG OF GIFTS TO GOD

When the first Christmas presents came, the straw where
    Christ was rolled
Smelt sweeter than their frankincense, burnt brighter than
    their gold,
And a wise man said, "We will not give; the thanks would be
    but cold."

"Nay," said the next. "To all new gifts, to this gift or another,
Bends the high gratitude of God; even as He now, my brother,
Who had a Father for all time, yet thanks Him for a Mother.

"Yet scarce for Him this yellow stone or prickly smells and
    sparse,
Who holds the gold heart of the sun that fed these timber bars,
Nor any scentless lily lives for One that smells the stars."

Then spake the third of the Wise Men, the wisest of the three:
"We may not with the widest lives enlarge His liberty,
Whose wings are wider than the world. It is not He, but we.

"We say not He has more to gain, but we have less to lose.
Less gold shall go astray, we say, less gold, if thus we choose,
Go to make harlots of the Greeks and hucksters of the Jews.

"Less clouds before colossal feet redden in the underlight,
To the blind gods from Babylon less incense burn to-night,
To the high beasts of Babylon, whose mouths make mock of
    right."

Babe of the thousand birthdays, we that are young yet grey,
White with the centuries, still can find no better thing to say,
We that with sects and whims and wars have wasted Christmas
    Day.

Light Thou Thy censer to Thyself, for all our fires are dim,
Stamp Thou Thine image on our coins, for Cæsar's face grows
    grim,
And a dumb devil of pride and greed has taken hold of him.

We bring Thee back great Christendom, churches and towns
    and towers.

And if our hands are glad, O God, to cast them down like
  flowers,
'Tis not that they enrich Thine hands, but they are saved from
  ours.

THE KINGDOM OF HEAVEN

Said the Lord God, "Build a house,
  Build it in the gorge of death,
Found it in the throats of hell.
  Where the lost sea muttereth,
Fires and whirlwinds, build it well."

Laboured sternly flame and wind,
  But a little, and they cry,
"Lord, we doubt of this Thy will,
  We are blind and murmur why,"
And the winds are murmuring still.

Said the Lord God, "Build a house,
  Cleave its treasure from the earth,
With the jarring powers of hell
  Strive with formless might and mirth,
Tribes and war-men, build it well."

Then the raw red sons of men
  Brake the soil, and lopped the wood,
But a little and they shrill,
  "Lord, we cannot view Thy good,"
And the wild men clamour still.

Said the Lord God, "Build a house,
  Smoke and iron, spark and steam,

Speak and vote and buy and sell;
 Let a new world throb and stream,
Seers and makers, build it well."

Strove the cunning men and strong,
 But a little and they cry,
"Lord, mayhap we are but clay,
 And we cannot know the why,"
And the wise men doubt to-day.

Yet though worn and deaf and blind,
 Force and savage, king and seer,
Labour still, they know not why;
 At the dim foundation here,
Knead and plough and think and ply.

Till at last, mayhap, hereon,
 Fused of passion and accord,
Love its crown and peace its stay,
 Rise the city of the Lord
That we darkly build to-day.

A HYMN FOR THE CHURCH MILITANT

Great God, that bowest sky and star,
 Bow down our towering thoughts to thee,
And grant us in a faltering war
 The firm feet of humility.

Lord, we that snatch the swords of flame,
 Lord, we that cry about Thy car,
We too are weak with pride and shame,
 We too are as our foemen are.

Yea, we are mad as they are mad,
  Yea, we are blind as they are blind,
Yea, we are very sick and sad
  Who bring good news to all mankind.

The dreadful joy Thy Son has sent
  Is heavier than any care;
We find, as Cain his punishment,
  Our pardon more than we can bear.

Lord, when we cry Thee far and near
  And thunder through all lands unknown
The gospel into every ear,
  Lord, let us not forget our own.

Cleanse us from ire of creed or class,
  The anger of the idle kings;
Sow in our souls, like living grass,
  The laughter of all lowly things.

FRAGMENT FROM DANTE

Then Bernard smiled at me, that I should gaze
  But I had gazed already; caught the view,
Faced the unfathomable ray of rays
  Which to itself and by itself is true.

Then was my vision mightier than man's speech;
  Speech snapt before it like a flying spell;
And memory and all that time can teach
  Before that splendid outrage failed and fell.

As when one dreameth and remembereth not
  Waking, what were his pleasures or his pains,

With every feature of the dream forgot,
    The printed passion of the dream remains:—

Even such am I; within whose thoughts resides
    No picture of that sight nor any part,
Nor any memory: in whom abides
    Only a happiness within the heart,

A secret happiness that soaks the heart
    As hills are soaked by slow unsealing snow,
Or secret as that wind without a chart
    Whereon did the wild leaves of Sibyl go.

O light uplifted from all mortal knowing,
    Send back a little of that glimpse of thee,
That of its glory I may kindle glowing
    One tiny spark for all men yet to be.

THE TRUCE OF CHRISTMAS

Passionate peace is in the sky—
And in the snow in silver sealed
The beasts are perfect in the field,
And men seem men so suddenly—
    (But take ten swords and ten times ten
    And blow the bugle in praising men;
    For we are for all men under the sun;
    And they are against us every one;
    And misers haggle and madmen clutch,
    And there is peril in praising much,
    And we have the terrible tongues uncurled
    That praise the world to the sons of the world.)

The idle humble hill and wood
Are bowed upon the sacred birth,

And for one little hour the earth
Is lazy with the love of good—
   (But ready are you, and ready am I,
   If the battle blow and the guns go by;
   For we are for all men under the sun,
   And they are against us every one;
   And the men that hate herd all together,
   To pride and gold, and the great white feather,
   And the thing is graven in star and stone
   That the men who love are all alone.)

Hunger is hard and time is tough,
But bless the beggars and kiss the kings;
For hope has broken the heart of things,
And nothing was ever praised enough.
   (But hold the shield for a sudden swing
   And point the sword when you praise a thing,
   For we are for all men under the sun,
   And they are against us every one;
   And mime and merchant, thane and thrall
   Hate us because we love them all;
   Only till Christmastide go by
   Passionate peace is in the sky.)

A HYMN

O God of earth and altar,
   Bow down and hear our cry,
Our earthly rulers falter,
   Our people drift and die;
The walls of gold entomb us,
   The swords of scorn divide,
Take not thy thunder from us,
   But take away our pride.

From all that terror teaches,
  From lies of tongue and pen,
From all the easy speeches
  That comfort cruel men,
For sale and profanation
  Of honour and the sword,
From sleep and from damnation,
  Deliver us, good Lord.

Tie in a living tether
  The prince and priest and thrall,
Bind all our lives together,
  Smite us and save us all;
In ire and exultation
  Aflame with faith, and free,
Lift up a living nation,
  A single sword to thee.

A CHRISTMAS SONG FOR THREE GUILDS

TO BE SUNG A LONG TIME AGO—OR HENCE

The Carpenters.

St. Joseph to the Carpenters said on a Christmas Day:
"The master shall have patience and the 'prentice shall obey;
And your word unto your women shall be nowise hard or
  wild:
For the sake of me, your master, who have worshipped Wife
  and Child.
But softly you shall frame the fence, and softly carve the door,
And softly plane the table—as to spread it for the poor,
And all your thoughts be soft and white as the wood of the
  white tree.

But if they tear the Charter, let the toscin speak for me!
Let the wooden sign above your shop be prouder to be
    scarred
Than the lion-shield of Lancelot that hung at Joyous Garde."

The Shoemakers.

St. Crispin to the shoemakers said on a Christmastide:
"Who fashions at another's feet will get no good of pride.
They were bleeding on the Mountain, the feet that brought
    good news,
The latchet of whose shoes we were not worthy to unloose.
See that your feet offend not, nor lightly lift your head,
Tread softly on the sunlit roads the bright dust of the dead.
Let your own feet be shod with peace; be lowly all your lives.
But if they touch the Charter, ye shall nail it with your knives.
And the bill-blades of the commons drive in all as dense array
As once a crash of arrows came, upon St. Crispin's Day."

The Painters.

St. Luke unto the painters on Christmas Day he said:
"See that the robes are white you dare to dip in gold and red;
For only gold the kings can give, and only blood the saints;
And his high task grows perilous that mixes them in paints.
Keep you the ancient order; follow the men that knew
The labyrinth of black and white, the maze of green and
    blue;
Paint mighty things, paint paltry things, paint silly things or
    sweet,
But if men break the Charter, you may slay them in the
    street.
And if you paint one post for them, then . . . but you know
    it well,
You paint a harlot's face to drag all heroes down to hell.

All together.

Almighty God to all mankind on Christmas Day said he:
"I rent you from the old red hills and, rending made you free.
There was charter, there was challenge; in a blast of breath
    I gave;
You can be all things other; you cannot be a slave.
You shall be tired and tolerant of fancies as they fade,
But if men doubt the Charter, ye shall call on the Crusade—
Trumpet and torch and catapult, cannon and bow and blade,
Because it was My challenge to all the things I made."

THE NATIVITY

The thatch on the roof was as golden,
  Though dusty the straw was and old,
The wind had a peal as of trumpets,
  Though blowing and barren and cold,
The mother's hair was a glory
  Though loosened and torn,
For under the eaves in the gloaming
  A child was born.

Have a myriad children been quickened,
  Have a myriad children grown old,
Grown gross and unloved and embittered,
  Grown cunning and savage and cold?
God abides in a terrible patience,
  Unangered, unworn,
And again for the child that was squandered
  A child is born.

What know we of aeons behind us,
  Dim dynasties lost long ago,

Huge empires, like dreams unremembered,
  Huge cities for ages laid low?
This at least—that with blight and with blessing,
  With flower and with thorn,
Love was there, and his cry was among them,
  "A child is born."

Though the darkness be noisy with systems,
  Dark fancies that fret and disprove,
Still the plumes stir around us, above us
  The wings of the shadow of love:
Oh! princes and priests, have ye seen it
  Grow pale through your scorn;
Huge dawns sleep before us, deep changes,
  A child is born.

And the rafters of toil still are gilded
  With the dawn of the stars of the heart,
And the wise men draw near in the twilight,
  Who are weary of learning and art,
And the face of the tyrant is darkened,
  His spirit is torn,
For a new king is enthroned; yea, the sternest,
  A child is born.

And the mother still joys for the whispered
  First stir of unspeakable things,
Still feels that high moment unfurling
  Red glory of Gabriel's wings.
Still the babe of an hour is a master
  Whom angels adorn,
Emmanuel, prophet, anointed,
  A child is born.

And thou, that art still in thy cradle,
  The sun being crown for thy brow,
Make answer, our flesh, make an answer,
  Say, whence art thou come—who art thou?
Art thou come back on earth for our teaching
  To train or to warn—?
Hush—how may we know?—knowing only
  A child is born.

A CHILD OF THE SNOWS

There is heard a hymn when the panes are dim,
  And never before or again,
When the nights are strong with a darkness long,
  And the dark is alive with rain.

Never we know but in sleet and in snow,
  The place where the great fires are,
That the midst of the earth is a raging mirth
  And the heart of the earth a star.

And at night we win to the ancient inn
  Where the child in the frost is furled,
We follow the feet where all souls meet
  At the inn at the end of the world.

The gods lie dead where the leaves lie red,
  For the flame of the sun is flown,
The gods lie cold where the leaves lie gold,
  And a Child comes forth alone.

A WORD

A word came forth in Galilee, a word like to a star;
It climbed and rang and blessed and burnt wherever brave
    hearts are;
A word of sudden secret hope, of trial and increase
Of wrath and pity fused in fire, and passion kissing peace.
A star that o'er the citied world beckoned, a sword of flame;
A star with myriad thunders tongued: a mighty word there
    came.

The wedge's dart passed into it, the groan of timber wains,
The ringing of the rivet nails, the shrieking of the planes;
The hammering on the roofs at morn, the busy workshop
    roar;
The hiss of shavings drifted deep along the windy floor;
The heat-browned toiler's crooning song, the hum of human
    worth
Mingled of all the noise of crafts, the ringing word went
    forth.

The splash of nets passed into it, the grind of sand and
    shell,
The boat-hook's clash, the boat-oars' jar, the cries to buy and
    sell,
The flapping of the landed shoals, the canvas crackling free,
And through all varied notes and cries, the roaring of the
    sea,
The noise of little lives and brave, of needy lives and high;
In gathering all the throes of earth, the living word went by.

Earth's giants bowed down to it, in Empire's huge eclipse,
When darkness sat above the thrones, seven thunders on her
    lips,
The woes of cities entered it, the clang of idols' falls,

The scream of filthy Caesars stabbed high in their brazen
    halls,
The dim hoarse floods of naked men, the world-realms' snap-
    ping girth,
The trumpets of Apocalypse, the darkness of the earth:

The wrath that brake the eternal lamp and hid the eternal
    hill,
A world's destruction loading, the word went onward still—
The blaze of creeds passed into it, the hiss of horrid fires,
The headlong spear, the scarlet cross, the hair-shirt and the
    briars,
The cloistered brethren's thunderous chaunt, the errant cham-
    pion's song,
The shifting of the crowns and thrones, the tangle of the
    strong.

The shattering fall of crest and crown and shield and cross
    and cope,
The tearing of the gauds of time, the blight of prince and
    pope,
The reign of ragged millions leagued to wrench a loaded
    debt,
Loud with the many throated roar, the word went forward
    yet.
The song of wheels passed into it, the roaring and the smoke,
The riddle of the want and wage, the fogs that burn and
    choke.

The breaking of the girths of gold, the needs that creep and
    swell,
The strengthening hope, the dazing light, the deafening
    evangel,
Through kingdoms dead and empires damned, through
    changes without cease,

With earthquake, chaos, born and fed, rose,—and the word
was "Peace."

ANTICHRIST, OR THE REUNION OF CHRISTEN-
DOM: AN ODE

"A BILL WHICH HAS SHOCKED THE CONSCIENCE OF EVERY
CHRISTIAN COMMUNITY IN EUROPE."—*Mr. F. E. Smith,*
ON THE WELSH DISESTABLISHMENT BILL.

Are they clinging to their crosses,
   F. E. Smith,
Where the Breton boat-fleet tosses,
   Are they, Smith?
Do they, fasting, trembling, bleeding,
  Wait the news from this our city?
Groaning "That's the Second Reading!"
  Hissing "There is still Committee!"
If the voice of Cecil falters,
  If McKenna's point has pith,
Do they tremble for their altars?
   Do they, Smith?

Russian peasants round their pope
   Huddled, Smith,
Hear about it all, I hope,
   Don't they, Smith?
In the mountain hamlets clothing
  Peaks beyond Caucasian pales,
Where Establishment means nothing
  And they never heard of Wales,
Do they read it all in Hansard
  With a crib to read it with—
"Welsh Tithes: Dr. Clifford Answered."
   Really, Smith?

In the lands where Christians were,
    F. E. Smith,
In the little lands laid bare,
    Smith, O Smith!
Where the Turkish bands are busy,
  And the Tory name is blessed
Since they hailed the Cross of Dizzy
  On the banners from the West!
Men don't think it half so hard if
  Islam burns their kin and kith,
Since a curate lives in Cardiff
    Saved by Smith.

It would greatly, I must own,
    Soothe me, Smith!
If you left this theme alone,
    Holy Smith!
For your legal cause or civil
  You fight well and get your fee;
For your God or dream or devil
  You will answer, not to me.
Talk about the pews and steeples
  And the Cash that goes therewith!
But the souls of Christian peoples . . .
    Chuck it, Smith!

THE REVOLUTIONIST: OR LINES TO A
STATESMAN

"I WAS NEVER STANDING BY WHILE A REVOLUTION WAS GOING
ON."—*Speech by the Rt. Hon. Walter Long.*

When Death was on thy drums, Democracy,
And with one rush of slaves the world was free,

In that high dawn that Kings shall not forget,
A void there was and Walter was not yet.
Through sacked Versailles, at Valmy in the fray,
They did without him in some kind of way;
Red Christendom all Walterless they cross,
And in their fury hardly feel their loss . . .
Fades the Republic; faint as Roland's horn,
Her trumpets taunt us with a sacred scorn . . .
Then silence fell: and Mr. Long was born.

From his first hours in his expensive cot
He never saw the tiniest viscount shot.
In deference to his wealthy parents' whim
The mildest massacres were kept from him.
The wars that dyed Pall Mall and Brompton red
Passed harmless o'er that one unconscious head:
For all that little Long could understand
The rich might still be rulers of the land.
Vain are the pious arts of parenthood,
Foiled Revolution bubbled in his blood;
Until one day (the babe unborn shall rue it)
The Constitution bored him and he slew it.

If I were wise and good and rich and strong—
Fond, impious thought, if I were Walter Long—
If I could water sell like molten gold,
And make grown people do as they were told,
If over private fields and wastes as wide
As a Greek city for which heroes died,
I owned the houses and the men inside—
If all this hung on one thin thread of habit
I would not revolutionize a rabbit.

I would sit tight with all my gifts and glories,
And even preach to unconverted Tories,

That the fixed system that our land inherits,
Viewed from a certain standpoint, has its merits.
I'd guard the laws like any Radical,
And keep each precedent, however small,
However subtle, misty, dusty, dreamy,
Lest man by chance should look at me and see me;
Lest men should ask what madman made me lord
Of English ploughshares and the English sword;
Lest men should mark how sleepy is the nod
That drills the dreadful images of God!

Walter, be wise! avoid the wild and new!
The Constitution is the game for you.
Walter, beware! scorn not the gathering throng,
It suffers, yet it may not suffer wrong,
It suffers, yet it cannot suffer Long.
And if you goad it these grey rules to break,
For a few pence, see that you do not wake
Death and the splendour of the scarlet cap,
Boston and Valmy, Yorktown and Jemmappes,
Freedom in arms, the riding and the routing,
The thunder of the captains and the shouting,
All that lost riot that you did not share—
And when that riot comes—you *will* be there.

THE SHAKESPEARE MEMORIAL

Lord Lilac thought it rather rotten
That Shakespeare should be quite forgotten,
And therefore got on a Committee
With several chaps out of the City,
And Shorter and Sir Herbert Tree,
Lord Rothschild and Lord Rosebery,
And F.C.G. and Comyns Carr,

Two dukes and a dramatic star,
Also a clergyman now dead;
And while the vain world careless sped
Unheeding the heroic name—
The souls most fed with Shakespeare's flame
Still sat unconquered in a ring,
Remembering him like anything.

Lord Lilac did not long remain,
Lord Lilac did not come again.
He softly lit a cigarette
And sought some other social set
Where, in some other knots or rings,
People were doing cultured things,
—Miss Zwilt's Humane Vivarium
—The little men that paint on gum
—The exquisite Gorilla Girl. . . .
He sometimes, in this giddy whirl
(Not being really bad at heart),
Remembered Shakespeare with a start—
But not with that grand constancy
Of Clement Shorter, Herbert Tree,
Lord Rosebery and Comyns Carr
And all the other names there are;
Who stuck like limpets to the spot,
Lest they forgot, lest they forgot.

Lord Lilac was of slighter stuff;
Lord Lilac had had quite enough.

THE HORRIBLE HISTORY OF JONES

Jones had a dog; it had a chain;
Not often worn, not causing pain;

But, as the I.K.L. had passed
Their "Unleashed Cousins Act" at last,
Inspectors took the chain away;
Whereat the canine barked "hurray!"
At which, of course, the S.P.U.
(Whose Nervous Motorists' Bill was through)
Were forced to give the dog in charge
For being Audibly at Large.
None, you will say, were now annoyed,
Save haply Jones—the yard was void.
But something being in the lease
About "alarms to aid police,"
The U.S.U. annexed the yard
For having no sufficient guard;
Now if there's one condition
The C.C.P. are strong upon
It is that every house one buys
Must have a yard for exercise;
So Jones, as tenant, was unfit,
His state of health was proof of it.
Two doctors of the T.T.U.'s
Told him his legs, from long disuse,
Were atrophied; and saying "So
From step to higher step we go
Till everything is New and True,"
They cut his legs off and withdrew.
You know the E.T.S.T.'s views
Are stronger than the T.T.U.'s:
And soon (as one may say) took wing
The Arms, though not the Man, I sing.
To see him sitting limbless there
Was more than the K.K. could bear.
"In mercy silence with all speed
That mouth there are no hands to feed;

What cruel sentimentalist,
O Jones, would doom thee to exist—
Clinging to selfish Selfhood yet?
Weak one! Such reasoning might upset
The Pump Act, and the accumulation
Of all constructive legislation;
Let us construct you up a bit—"
The head fell off when it was hit:
Then words did rise and honest doubt,
And four Commissioners sat about
Whether the slash that left him dead
Cut off his body or his head.

An author in the Isle of Wight
Observed with unconcealed delight
A land of old and just renown
Where Freedom slowly broadened down
From Precedent to Precedent . . .
And this, I think, was what he meant.

THE NEW FREETHINKER

John Grubby, who was short and stout
And troubled with religious doubt,
Refused about the age of three
To sit upon the curate's knee;
(For so the eternal strife must rage
Between the spirit of the age
And Dogma, which, as is well known,
Does simply hate to be outgrown).
Grubby, the young idea that shoots,
Outgrew the ages like old boots;
While still, to all appearance, small,
Would have no Miracles at all;

And just before the age of ten
Firmly refused Free Will to men.
The altars reeled, the heavens shook,
Just as he read of in the book;
Flung from his house went forth the youth
Alone with tempests and the Truth,
Up to the distant city and dim
Where his papa had bought for him
A partnership in Chepe and Deer
Worth, say, twelve hundred pounds a year.
But he was resolute. Lord Brute
Had found him useful; and Lord Loot,
With whom few other men would act,
Valued his promptitude and tact;
Never did even philanthropy
Enrich a man more rapidly:
'Twas he that stopped the Strike in Coal,
For hungry children racked his soul;
To end their misery there and then
He filled the mines with Chinamen,
Sat in that House that broke the Kings,
And voted for all sorts of things—
And rose from Under-Sec. to Sec.
With scarce a murmur or a check.
Some grumbled. Growlers who gave less
Than generous worship to success,
The little printers in Dundee,
Who got ten years for blasphemy,
(Although he let them off with seven)
Respect him rather less than heaven.
No matter. This can still be said:
Never to supernatural dread,
Never to unseen deity,
Did Sir John Grubby bend the knee;

Never did dream of hell or wrath
Turn Viscount Grubby from his path;
Nor was he bribed by fabled bliss
To kneel to any world but this.
The curate lives in Camden Town,
His lap still empty of renown,
And still across the waste of years
John Grubby, in the House of Peers,
Faces that curate, proud and free,
And never sits upon his knee.

IN MEMORIAM P.D.

NICE, JANUARY 30, 1914

If any in an island cradle curled
Of comfort, may make offering to you,
Who in the day of all denial blew
A bugle through the blackness of the world,

An English hand would touch your shroud, in trust
That truth again be told in English speech,
And we too yet may practice what we preach,
Though it were practising the bayonet thrust,

Cutting that giant neck from sand to sand,
From sea to sea; it was a little thing
Beside your sudden shout and sabre swing
That cut the throat of thieves in every land.

Heed not if half-wits mock your broken blade:
Mammon our master doeth all things ill.
You are the Fool that charged a windmill. Still,
The Miller is a knave; and was afraid.

Lay down your sword. Ruin will know her own.
Let each small statesman sow his weak wild oat,
Or turn his coat to decorate his coat,
Or take the throne and perish by the throne.

Lay down your sword. And let the White Flag fade
To grey; and let the Red Flag fade to pink,
For these that climb and climb; and cannot sink
So deep as death and honour, Déroulède.

SONNET WITH THE COMPLIMENTS OF THE SEASON

TO A POPULAR LEADER MUCH TO BE CONGRATULATED ON THE
AVOIDANCE OF A STRIKE AT CHRISTMAS

I know you. You will hail the huge release,
Saying the sheathing of a thousand swords,
In silence and injustice, well accords
With Christmas bells. And you will gild with grease
The papers, the employers, the police,
And vomit up the void your windy words
To your New Christ; who bears no whip of cords
For them that traffic in the doves of peace.

The feast of friends, the candle-fruited tree,
I have not failed to honour. And I say
It would be better for such men as we,
And we be nearer Bethlehem, if we lay
Shot dead on scarlet snows for liberty,
Dead in the daylight upon Christmas Day.

A SONG OF SWORDS

"A DROVE OF CATTLE CAME INTO A VILLAGE CALLED SWORDS, AND
WAS STOPPED BY THE RIOTERS."—*Daily Paper*.

In the place called Swords on the Irish road
It is told for a new renown
How we held the horns of the cattle, and how
We will hold the horns of the devil now
Ere the lord of hell, with the horn on his brow,
    Is crowned in Dublin town

Light in the East and light in the West,
And light on the cruel lords,
On the souls that suddenly all men knew,
And the green flag flew and the red flag flew,
And many a wheel of the world stopped, too,
    When the cattle were stopped at Swords.

Be they sinners or less than saints
That smite in the street for rage,
We know where the shame shines bright; we know
You that they smite at, you their foe,
Lords of the lawless wage and low,
    This is your lawful wage.

You pinched a child to a torture price
That you dared not name in words;
So black a jest was the silver bit
That your own speech shook for the shame of it,
And the coward was plain as a cow they hit
    When the cattle have strayed at Swords.

The wheel of the torment of wives went round
To break men's brotherhood;

You gave the good Irish blood to grease
The clubs of your country's enemies;
You saw the brave man beat to the knees:
    And you saw that it was good.

The rope of the rich is long and long—
The longest of hangmen's cords;
But the kings and crowds are holding their breath,
In a giant shadow o'er all beneath
Where God stands holding the scales of Death
    Between the cattle and Swords.

Haply the lords that hire and lend,
The lowest of all men's lords,
Who sell their kind like kine at a fair,
Will find no head of their cattle there;
But faces of men where cattle were:
    Faces of men—and Swords.

And the name shining and terrible,
The sternest of all man's words,
Still mark that place to seek or shun,
In the streets where the struggling cattle run—
Grass and a silence of judgment done
    In the place that is called Swords.

A SONG OF DEFEAT

The line breaks and the guns go under,
    The lords and the lackeys ride the plain;
I draw deep breaths of the dawn and thunder,
    And the whole of my heart grows young again.
For our chiefs said "Done," and I did not deem it;
    Our seers said "Peace," and it was not peace;

Earth will grow worse till men redeem it,
　And wars more evil, ere all wars cease.
But the old flags reel and the old drums rattle,
　As once in my life they throbbed and reeled;
I have found my youth in the lost battle,
　I have found my heart on the battlefield.
　　For we that fight till the world is free,
　　We are not easy in victory:
　　We have known each other too long, my brother,
　　And fought each other, the world and we.

And I dream of the days when work was scrappy,
　And rare in our pockets the mark of the mint,
When we were angry and poor and happy,
　And proud of seeing our names in print.
For so they conquered and so we scattered,
　When the Devil rode and his dogs smelt gold,
And the peace of a harmless folk was shattered;
　When I was twenty and odd years old.
When the mongrel men that the market classes
　Had slimy hands upon England's rod,
And sword in hand upon Afric's passes
　Her last Republic cried to God.
　　For the men no lords can buy or sell,
　　They sit not easy when all goes well,
　　They have said to each other what naught can smother,
　　They have seen each other, our souls and hell.

It is all as of old; the empty clangour,
　The Nothing scrawled on a five-foot page,
The huckster who, mocking holy anger,
　Painfully paints his face with rage.
And the faith of the poor is faint and partial,
　And the pride of the rich is all for sale,

And the chosen heralds of England's Marshal
  Are the sandwich-men of the *Daily Mail*.
And the niggards that dare not give are glutted,
  And the feeble that dare not fail are strong,
So while the City of Toil is gutted,
  I sit in the saddle and sing my song.
    For we that fight till the world is free,
    We have no comfort in victory;
    We have read each other as Cain his brother,
    We know each other, these slaves and we.

SONNET

ON HEARING A LANDLORD ACCUSED (FALSELY, FOR ALL THE BARD
CAN SAY) OF NEGLECTING ONE OF THE NUMEROUS WHITE
HORSES THAT WERE OR WERE NOT CONNECTED WITH
ALFRED THE GREAT

If you have picked your lawn of leaves and snails,
If you have told your valet, even with oaths,
Once a week or so, to brush your clothes,
If you have dared to clean your teeth, or nails,
While the Horse upon the holy mountain fails—
Then God that Alfred to his earth betrothes
Send on you screaming all that honour loathes,
Horsewhipping, Houndsditch, debts, and *Daily Mails*.

Can you not even conserve? For if indeed
The White Horse fades; then closer creeps the fight
When we shall scour the face of England white,
Plucking such men as you up like a weed,
And fling them far beyond a shaft shot right
When Wessex went to battle for the Creed.

AFRICA

A sleepy people, without priests or kings,
Dreamed here, men say, to drive us to the sea:
  O let us drive ourselves! For it is free
And smells of honour and of English things.
How came we brawling by these bitter springs,
  We of the North?—two kindly nations—we?
Though the dice rattles and the clear coin rings,
  Hear is no place for living men to be.
Leave them the gold that worked and whined for it,
  Let them that have no nation anywhere
Be native here, and fat and full of bread;
But we, whose sins were human, we will quit
  The land of blood, and leave these vultures there,
Noiselessly happy, feeding on the dead.

THE DEAD HERO

We never saw you, like our sires,
    For whom your face was Freedom's face,
Nor know what office-tapes and wires
    With such strong cords may interlace;
We know not if the statesmen then
    Were fashioned as the sort we see,
We know that not under your ken
    Did England laugh at Liberty.

Yea; this one thing is known of you,
    We know that not till you were dumb,
Not till your course was thundered through,
    Did Mammon see his kingdom come.
The songs of theft, the swords of hire,
    The clerks that raved, the troops that ran.

The empire of the world's desire,
  The dance of all the dirt began.

The happy jewelled alien men
  Worked then but as a little leaven;
From some more modest palace then
  The Soul of Dives stank to Heaven.
But when they planned with lisp and leer
  Their careful war upon the weak,
They smote your body on its bier,
  For surety that you could not speak.

A hero in the desert died;
  Men cried that saints should bury him,
And round the grave should guard and ride,
  A chivalry of Cherubim.
God said: "There is a better place,
  A nobler trophy and more tall;
The beasts that fled before his face
  Shall come to make his funeral.

"The mighty vermin of the void
  That hid them from his bended bow,
Shall crawl from caverns overjoyed,
  Jackal and snake and carrion crow.
And perched above the vulture's eggs,
  Reversed upon its hideous head,
A blue-faced ape shall wave its legs
  To tell the world that he is dead."

AN ELECTION ECHO

1906

This is their trumpet ripe and rounded,
They have burnt the wheat and gathered the chaff,

And we that have fought them, we that have watched them,
Have we at least not cause to laugh?

Never so low at least we stumbled—
Dead we have been but not so dead
As these that live on the life they squandered,
As these that drink of the blood they shed.

We never boasted the thing we blundered,
We never flaunted the thing that fails,
We never quailed from the living laughter,
To howl to the dead who tell no tales.

'Twas another finger at least that pointed
Our wasted men or our emptied bags,
It was not we that sounded the trumpet
In front of the triumph of wrecks and rags.

Fear not these, they have made their bargain,
They have counted the cost of the last of raids,
They have staked their lives on the things that live not,
They have burnt their house for a fire that fades.

Five years ago and we might have feared them,
Been drubbed by the coward and taught by the dunce;
Truth may endure and be told and re-echoed,
But a lie can never be young but once.

Five years ago and we might have feared them;
Now, when they lift the laurelled brow,
There shall naught go up from our hosts assembled
But a laugh like thunder. We know them now.

THE SONG OF THE WHEELS

WRITTEN DURING A FRIDAY AND SATURDAY IN AUGUST, 1911

King Dives he was walking in his garden all alone,
Where his flowers are made of iron and his trees are made of
    stone,
And his hives are full of thunder and the lightning leaps
    and kills,
For the mills of God grind slowly; and he works with other
    mills.
Dives found a mighty silence; and he missed the throb and
    leap,
The noise of all the sleepless creatures singing him to sleep.
And he said: "A screw has fallen—or a bolt has slipped aside—
Some little thing has shifted": and the little things replied:

"Call upon the wheels, master, call upon the wheels;
We are taking rest, master, finding how it feels,
Strict the law of thine and mine: theft we ever shun—
All the wheels are thine, master—tell the wheels to run!
Yea, the Wheels are mighty gods—set them going then!
We are only men, master, have you heard of men?

"O, they live on earth like fishes, and a gasp is all their
    breath.
God for empty honours only gave them death and scorn of
    death,
And you walk the worms for carpet and you tread a stone
    that squeals
Only, God that made them worms did not make them wheels.
Man shall shut his heart against you and you shall not find
    the spring.
Man who wills the thing he wants not, the intolerable thing—

Once he likes his empty belly better than your empty head
Earth and heaven are dumb before him: he is stronger than
the dead.

"Call upon the wheels, master, call upon the wheels,
Steel is beneath your hand, stone beneath your heels,
Steel will never laugh aloud, hearing what we heard,
Stone will never break its heart, mad with hope deferred—
Men of tact that arbitrate, slow reform that heals—
Save the stinking grease, master, save it for the wheels.

"King Dives in the garden, we have naught to give or hold—
(Even while the baby came alive the rotten sticks were sold.)
The savage knows a cavern and the peasants keep a plot,
Of all the things that men have had—lo! we have them
not.
Not a scrap of earth where ants could lay their eggs—
Only this poor lump of earth that walks about on legs—
Only this poor wandering mansion, only these two walking
trees,
Only hands and hearts and stomachs—what have you to do
with these?
You have engines big and burnished, tall beyond our fathers'
ken,
Why should you make peace and traffic with such feeble folk
as men?

"Call upon the wheels, master, call upon the wheels,
They are deaf to demagogues, deaf to crude appeals;
Are our hands our own, master?—how the doctors doubt!
Are our legs our own, master? wheels can run without—
Prove the points are delicate—they will understand.
All the wheels are loyal; see how still they stand!"

King Dives he was walking in his garden in the sun,
He shook his hand at heaven, and he called the wheels to
  run,
And the eyes of him were hateful eyes, the lips of him were
  curled,
And he called upon his father that is lord below the world,
Sitting in the Gate of Treason, in the gate of broken seals,
"Bend and bind them, bend and bind them, bend and bind
  them into wheels,
Then once more in all my garden there may swing and sound
  and sweep—
The noise of all the sleepless things that sing the soul to
  sleep."

Call upon the wheels, master, call upon the wheels,
Weary grow the holidays when you miss the meals,
Through the Gate of Treason, through the gate within,
Cometh fear and greed of fame, cometh deadly sin;
If a man grow faint, master, take him ere he kneels,
Take him, break him, rend him, end him, roll him, crush him
  with the wheels.

THE SECRET PEOPLE

Smile at us, pay us, pass us; but do not quite forget.
For we are the people of England, that never have spoken
  yet.
There is many a fat farmer that drinks less cheerfully,
There is many a free French peasant who is richer and sadder
  than we.
There are no folk in the whole world so helpless or so wise.
There is hunger in our bellies, there is laughter in our eyes;
You laugh at us and love us, both mugs and eyes are wet:
Only you do not know us. For we have not spoken yet.

The fine French kings came over in a flutter of flags and
dames. *

We liked their smiles and battles, but we never could say
their names.

The blood ran red to Bosworth and the high French lords
went down;

There was naught but a naked people under a naked crown.

And the eyes of the King's Servants turned terribly every
way,

And the gold of the King's Servants rose higher every day.

They burnt the homes of the shaven men, that had been quaint
and kind,

Till there was no bed in a monk's house, nor food that man
could find.

The inns of God where no man paid, that were the wall of
the weak,

The King's Servants ate them all. And still we did not speak.

And the face of the King's Servants grew greater than the
King:

He tricked them, and they trapped him, and stood round
him in a ring.

The new grave lords closed round him, that had eaten the
abbey's fruits,

And the men of the new religion, with their Bibles in their
boots,

We saw their shoulders moving, to menace or discuss,

And some were pure and some were vile; but none took heed
of us.

We saw the King as they killed him, and his face was proud
and pale;

And a few men talked of freedom, while England talked of
ale.

A war that we understood not came over the world and woke
Americans, Frenchmen, Irish; but we knew not the things
they spoke.
They talked about rights and nature and peace and the peo-
ple's reign:
And the squires, our masters, bade us fight; and scorned us
never again.
Weak if we be for ever, could none condemn us then;
Men called us serfs and drudges; men knew that we were
men.
In foam and flame at Trafalgar, on Albuera plains,
We did and died like lions, to keep ourselves in chains
We lay in living ruins; firing and fearing not
The strange fierce face of the Frenchmen who knew for what
they fought,
And the man who seemed to be more than man we strained
against and broke;
And we broke our own rights with him. And still we never
spoke.

Our patch of glory ended; we never heard guns again.
But the squire seemed struck in the saddle; he was foolish,
as if in pain.
He leaned on a staggering lawyer, he clutched a cringing
Jew,
He was stricken; it may be, after all, he was stricken at
Waterloo.
Or perhaps the shades of the shaven men, whose spoil is in
his house,
Come back in shining shapes at last to spoil his last carouse:
We only know the last sad squires ride slowly towards the
sea,
And a new people takes the land: and still it is not we.

They have given us into the hand of new unhappy lords,
Lords without anger and honour, who dare not carry their
swords.
They fight by shuffling papers; they have bright dead alien
eyes;
They look at our labour and laughter as a tired man looks at
flies.
And the load of their loveless pity is worse than the ancient
wrongs,
Their doors are shut in the evening; and they know no songs.

We hear men speaking for us of new laws strong and sweet,
Yet is there no man speaketh as we speak in the street.
It may be we shall rise the last as Frenchmen rose the first,
Our wrath come after Russia's wrath and our wrath be the
worst.
It may be we are meant to mark with our riot and our rest
God's scorn for all men governing. It may be beer is best.
But we are the people of England; and we have not spoken
yet.
Smile at us, pay us, pass us. But do not quite forget.

LOST

So you have gained the golden crowns, so you have piled
together
The laurels and the jewels, the pearls out of the blue,
But I will beat the bounding drum and I will fly the feather
For all the glory I have lost, the good I never knew.

I saw the light of morning pale on princely human faces,
In tales irrevocably gone, in final night enfurled,
I saw the tail of flying fights, a glimpse of burning blisses,
And laughed to think what I had lost—the wealth of all
the world.

Yea, ruined in a royal game I was before my cradle;
  Was ever gambler hurling gold who lost such things as I?
The purple moth that died an hour ere I was born of woman,
    That great green sunset God shall make three days after
      I die.

When all the lights are lost and done, when all the skies are
      broken,
  Above the ruin of the stars my soul shall sit in state,
With a brain made rich, with the irrevocable sunsets.
  And a closed heart happy in the fulness of a fate.

So you have gained the golden crowns and grasped the golden
      weather,
    The kingdoms and the hemispheres that all men buy and
      sell,
But I will lash the leaping drum and swing the flaring feather,
  For the light of seven heavens that are lost to me like hell.

BALLAD OF THE SUN

O well for him that loves the sun,
That sees the heaven-race ridden or run,
The splashing seas of sunset won,
    And shouts of victory.

God made the sun to crown his head,
And when death's dart at last is sped,
At least it will not find him dead,
    And pass the carrion by.

O ill for him that loves the sun;
Shall the sun stoop for anyone?
Shall the sun weep for hearts undone
    Or heavy souls that pray?

Not less for us and everyone
Was that white web of splendour spun;
O well for him who loves the sun
    Although the sun should slay.

TRANSLATION FROM DU BELLAY

Happy, who like Ulysses or that lord
    Who raped the fleece, returning full and sage,
With usage and the world's wide reason stored,
    With his own kin can taste the end of age.
When shall I see, when shall I see, God knows!
    My little village smoke; or pass the door,
The old dear door of that unhappy house
    Which is to me a kingdom and much more?
Mightier to me the house my fathers made
    Than your audacious heads, O Halls of Rome!
More than immortal marbles undecayed,
    The thin sad slates that cover up my home;
More than your Tiber is my Loire to me,
    Than Palatine my little Lyré there;
And more than all the winds of all the sea
    The quiet kindness of the Angevin air.

THE HIGHER UNITY

"THE REV. ISAIAH BUNTER HAS DISAPPEARED INTO THE INTERIOR
OF THE SOLOMON ISLANDS, AND IT IS FEARED THAT HE MAY HAVE
BEEN DEVOURED BY THE NATIVES, AS THERE HAS BEEN A CONSIDER-
ABLE REVIVAL OF RELIGIOUS CUSTOMS AMONG THE POLYNESIANS."—
A real paragraph from a real Paper; only the names altered.

    It was Isaiah Bunter
      Who sailed to the world's end,

And spread religion in a way
  That he did not intend.

He gave, if not the gospel feast,
  At least a ritual meal;
And in a highly painful sense
  He was devoured with zeal.

And who are we (as Henson says)
  That we should close the door?
And should not Evangelicals
  All jump at shedding Gore?

And many a man will melt in man,
  Becoming one, not two,
When smacks across the startled earth
  The Kiss of Kikuyu.

When Man is the Turk, and the Atheist,
  Essene, Erastian Whig,
And the Thug and the Druse and the Catholic
  And the crew of the Captain's gig.

THE EARTH'S VIGIL

The old earth keepeth her watch the same,
  Alone in a voiceless void doth stand,
Her orange flowers in her bosom flame,
  Her gold ring in her hand,
The surfs of the long gold-crested morns
  Break evermore at her great robe's hem,
And evermore come the bleak moon-horns,
  But she keepeth not watch for them.

She keepeth her watch through the æons,
But the heart of her groweth not old,
For the peal of the bridegroom's pæans,
And the tale she once was told.

The nations shock and the cities reel,
The empires travail and rive and rend,
And she looks on havoc and smoke and steel,
And knoweth it is not the end.
The faiths may choke and the powers despair,
The powers re-arise and the faiths renew,
She is only a maiden, waiting there,
For the love whose word is true.

She keepeth her watch through the æons,
But the heart of her groweth not old,
For the peal of the bridegroom's pæans,
And the tale she once was told.

Through the cornfield's gleam and the cottage shade,
They wait unwearied, the young and old,
Mother for child and man for maid,
For love that once was told.
The hair grows grey under thatch or slates,
The eyes grow dim behind lattice panes,
The earth-race wait as the old earth waits,
And the hope in the heart remains.

She keepeth her watch through the æons,
But the heart of her groweth not old,
For the peal of the bridegroom's pæans,
And the tale she once was told.

God's gold ring on her hand is bound,
   She fires with blossom the grey hill-sides,
Her fields are quickened, her forests crowned,
   While the love of her heart abides,
And we from the fears that fret and mar
   Look up in hours and behold awhile
Her face, colossal, mid star on star,
   Still looking forth with a smile.

     She keepeth her watch through the æons,
      But the heart of her groweth not old,
     For the peal of the bridegroom's pæans,
      And the tale she once was told.

ON RIGHTEOUS INDIGNATION

When Adam went from Paradise
   He saw the sword and ran;
The dreadful shape, the new device.
The pointed end of Paradise,
And saw what Peril is and Price,
   And knew he was a man.

When Adam went from Paradise,
   He turned him back and cried
For a little flower from Paradise;
There came no flower from Paradise;
The woods were dark in Paradise,
   And not a bird replied.

For only comfort or contempt,
   For jest or great reward,
Over the walls of Paradise,

The flameless gates of Paradise,
The dumb shut doors of Paradise,
　God flung the flaming sword.

It burns the hand that holds it
　More than the skull it scars;
It doubles like a snake and stings,
Yet he in whose hand it swings
He is the most masterful of things,
　A scorner of the stars.

WHEN I CAME BACK TO FLEET STREET

When I came back to Fleet Street,
　Through a sunset nook at night,
And saw the old Green Dragon
　With the windows all alight,
And hailed the old Green Dragon
　And the Cock I used to know,
Where all good fellows were my friends
　A little while ago;

I had been long in meadows,
　And the trees took hold of me,
And the still towns in the beech-woods,
　Where men were meant to be.
But old things held; the laughter,
　The long unnatural night,
And all the truth they talk in hell,
　And all the lies they write.

For I came back to Fleet Street,
　And not in peace I came;

A cloven pride was in my heart,
  And half my love was shame.
I came to fight in fairy tale,
  Whose end shall no man know
To fight the old Green Dragon
  Until the Cock shall crow!

Under the broad bright windows
  Of men I serve no more,
The groaning of the old great wheels
  Thickened to a throttled roar:
All buried things broke upward;
  And peered from its retreat,
Ugly and silent, like an elf,
  The secret of the street.

They did not break the padlocks,
  Or clear the wall away.
The men in debt that drank of old
  Still drink in debt to-day;
Chained to the rich by ruin,
  Cheerful in chains, as then
When old unbroken Pickwick walked
  Among the broken men.

Still he that dreams and rambles
  Through his own elfin air,
Knows that the street's a prison,
  Knows that the gates are there:
Still he that scorns or struggles
  Sees, frightful and afar,
All that they leave of rebels
  Rot high on Temple Bar.

All that I loved and hated,
 All that I shunned and knew,
Clears in broad battle lightning,
 Where they, and I, and you,
Run high the barricade that breaks
 The barriers of the street,
And shout to them that shrink within,
 The Prisoners of the Fleet.

A CIDER SONG

To J. S. M.

EXTRACT FROM A ROMANCE WHICH IS NOT YET WRITTEN AND
PROBABLY NEVER WILL BE

The wine they drink in Paradise
They make in Haute Lorraine;
God brought it burning from the sod
To be a sign and signal rod
That they that drink the blood of God
Shall never thirst again.

The wine they praise in Paradise
They make in Ponterey,
The purple wine of Paradise,
But we have better at the price;
It's wine they praise on Paradise,
It's cider that they pray.

The wine they want in Paradise
They find in Plodder's End,
The apple wine of Hereford,
Of Hafod Hill and Hereford,
Where woods went down to Hereford,
And there I had a friend.

The soft feet of the blessed go
In the soft western vales,
The road the silent saints accord,
The road from heaven to Hereford,
Where the apple wood of Hereford
Goes all the way to Wales.

THE LAST HERO

The wind blew out from Bergen from the dawning to the
    day,
There was a wreck of trees and fall of towers a score of miles
    away,
And drifted like a livid leaf I go before its tide,
Spewed out of house and stable, beggared of flag and bride.
The heavens are bowed about my head, shouting like seraph
    wars,
With rains that might put out the sun and clean the sky of
    stars,
Rains like the fall of ruined seas from secret worlds above,
The roaring of the rains of God none but the lonely love.
Feast in my hall, O foemen, and eat and drink and drain,
You never loved the sun in heaven as I have loved the rain.

The chance of battle changes—so may all battle be;
I stole my lady bride from them, they stole her back from
    me.
I rent her from her red-roofed hall, I rode and saw arise
More lovely than the living flowers the hatred in her eyes.
She never loved me, never bent, never was less divine;
The sunset never loved me; the wind was never mine.
Was it all nothing that she stood imperial in duresse?
Silence itself made softer with the sweeping of her dress.

O you who drain the cup of life, O you who wear the crown,
You never loved a woman's smile as I have loved her frown.

The wind blew out from Bergen from the dawning to the
day,
They ride and run with fifty spears to break and bar my
way,
I shall not die alone, alone, but kin to all the powers,
As merry as the ancient sun and fighting like the flowers.
How white their steel, how bright their eyes! I love each
laughing knave,
Cry high and bid him welcome to the banquet of the brave.
Yea, I will bless them as they bend and love them where they
lie,
When on their skulls the sword I swing falls shattering from
the sky.
The hour when death is like a light and blood is like a rose,—
You never loved your friends, my friends, as I shall love my
foes.

Know you what earth shall lose to-night, what rich uncounted
loans,
What heavy gold of tales untold you bury with my bones?
My loves in deep dim meadows, my ships that rode at ease,
Ruffling the purple plumage of strange and secret seas.
To see this fair earth as it is to me alone was given,
The blow that breaks my brow to-night shall break the dome
of heaven.
The skies I saw, the trees I saw after no eyes shall see.
To-night I die the death of God: the stars shall die with me:
One sound shall sunder all the spears and break the trumpet's
breath:
You never laughed in all your life as I shall laugh in death.

BALLADE D'UNE GRANDE DAME

Heaven shall forgive you Bridge at dawn,
The clothes you wear—or do not wear—
And Ladies' Leap-frog on the lawn
And dyes and drugs and *petits verres.*
Your vicious things shall melt in air . . .
. . . But for the Virtuous Things you do,
The Righteous Work, the Public Care,
It shall not be forgiven you.

Because you could not even yawn
When your Committees would prepare
To have the teeth of paupers drawn
Or strip the slums of Human Hair;
Because a Doctor Otto Maehr
Spoke of "a segregated few"—
And you sat smiling in your chair—
It shall not be forgiven you.

Though your sins cried to—Father Vaughan,
These desperate you could not spare
Who steal, with nothing left to pawn;
You caged a man up like a bear
For ever in a jailer's care
Because his sins were more than *two* . . .
. . . I know a house in Hoxton where
It shall not be forgiven you.

ENVOI

Princess, you trapped a guileless Mayor
To meet some people that you knew . . .
When the last trumpet rends the air
It shall not be forgiven you.

A BALLADE OF AN ANTI-PURITAN

They spoke of Progress spiring round,
Of Light and Mrs. Humphrey Ward—
It is not true to say I frowned,
Or ran about the room and roared;
I might have simply sat and snored—
I rose politely in the club
And said, "I feel a little bored;
Will someone take me to a pub?"

The new world's wisest did surround
Me; and it pains me to record
I did not think their views profound,
Or their conclusions well assured;
The simple life I can't afford,
Besides, I do not like the grub—
I want a mash and sausage, "scored"—
Will someone take me to a pub?

I know where Men can still be found,
Anger and clamorous accord,
And virtues growing from the ground,
And fellowship of beer and board,
And song, that is a sturdy cord,
And hope, that is a hardy shrub,
And goodness, that is God's last word—
Will someone take me to a pub?

ENVOI

Prince, Bayard would have smashed his sword
To see the sort of knights you dub—
Is that the last of them—O Lord!
Will someone take me to a pub?

A BALLADE OF A BOOK-REVIEWER

I have not read a rotten page
Of "Sex-Hate" or "The Social Test,"
And here comes "Husks" and "Heritage" . . .
O Moses, give us all a rest!
"Ethics of Empire!" . . . I protest
I will not even cut the strings,
I'll read "Jack Redskin on the Quest"
And feed my brain with better things.

Somebody wants a Wiser Age
(He also wants me to invest);
Somebody likes the Finnish Stage
Because the Jesters do not jest;
And grey with dust is Dante's crest
The bell of Rabelais soundless swings;
And the winds come out of the west
And feed my brain with better things.

Lord of our laughter and our rage,
Look on us with our sins oppressed!
I, too, have trodden mine heritage,
Wickedly wearying of the best.
Burn from my brain and from my breast
Sloth, and the cowardice that clings,
And stiffness and the soul's arrest:
And feed my brain with better things.

ENVOI

Prince, you are host and I am guest,
Therefore I shrink from cavillings . . .
But I should have that fizz suppressed
And feed my brain with better things.

A BALLADE OF SUICIDE

The gallows in my garden, people say,
Is new and neat and adequately tall.
I tie the noose on in a knowing way
As one that knots his necktie for a ball;
But just as all the neighbours—on the wall—
Are drawing a long breath to shout "Hurray!"
The strangest whim has seized me. . . . After all
I think I will not hang myself to-day.

To-morrow is the time I get my pay—
My uncle's sword is hanging in the hall—
I see a little cloud all pink and grey—
Perhaps the Rector's mother will *not* call—
I fancy that I heard from Mr. Gall
That mushrooms could be cooked another way—
I never read the works of Juvenal—
I think I will not hang myself to-day.

The world will have another washing day;
The decadents decay; the pedants pall;
And H. G. Wells has found that children play,
And Bernard Shaw discovered that they squall;
Rationalists are growing rational—
And through thick woods one finds a stream astray,
So secret that the very sky seems small—
I think I will not hang myself to-day.

ENVOI

Prince, I can hear the trumpet of Germinal,
The tumbrils toiling up the terrible way;
Even to-day your royal head may fall—
I think I will not hang myself to-day.

A BALLADE OF THE FIRST RAIN

The sky is blue with summer and the sun,
The woods are brown as autumn with the tan,
It might as well be Tropics and be done,
I might as well be born a copper Khan;
I fashion me an oriental fan
Made of the wholly unreceipted bills
Brought by the ice-man, sleeping in his van
(A storm is coming on the Chiltern Hills).

I read the Young Philosophers for fun
—Fresh as our sorrow for the late Queen Anne—
The Dionysians whom a pint would stun,
The Pantheists who never heard of Pan.
—But through my hair electric needles ran,
And on my book a gout of water spills,
And on the skirts of heaven the guns began
(A storm is coming on the Chiltern Hills).

O fields of England, cracked and dry and dun,
O soul of England, sick of words, and wan!—
The clouds grow dark;—the down-rush has begun
—It comes, it comes, as holy darkness can,
Black as with banners, ban and arriere-ban;
A falling laughter all the valley fills,
Deep as God's thunder and the thirst of man:
(A storm is coming on the Chiltern Hills).

ENVOI

Prince, Prince-Elective on the modern plan,
Fulfilling such a lot of People's Wills,
You take the Chiltern Hundreds while you can—
A storm is coming on the Chiltern Hills.

Book Four
Wine, Water and Song

THE ENGLISHMAN

St. George he was for England,
And before he killed the dragon
He drank a pint of English ale
Out of an English flagon.
For though he fast right readily
In hair-shirt or in mail,
It isn't safe to give him cakes
Unless you give him ale.

St. George he was for England,
And right gallantly set free
The lady left for dragon's meat
And tied up to a tree;
But since he stood for England
And knew what England means,
Unless you give him bacon
You mustn't give him beans.

St. George he is for England,
And shall wear the shield he wore
When we go out in armour
With the battle-cross before.
But though he is jolly company
And very pleased to dine,
It isn't safe to give him nuts
Unless you give him wine.

WINE AND WATER

Old Noah he had an ostrich farm and fowls on the largest
scale,

He ate his egg with a ladle in a egg-cup big as a pail,
And the soup he took was Elephant Soup and the fish he
    took was Whale,
But they all were small to the cellar he took when he set out
    to sail,
And Noah he often said to his wife when he sat down to dine,
'I don't care where the water goes if it doesn't get into the wine.

The cataract of the cliff of heaven fell blinding off the brink
As if it would wash the stars away as suds go down a sink,
The seven heavens came roaring down for the throats of hell
    to drink,
And Noah he cocked his eye and said, 'It looks like rain, I
    think,
The water has drowned the Matterhorn as deep as a Mendip
    mine,
But I don't care where the water goes if it doesn't get into
    the wine.'

But Noah he sinned, and we have sinned; on tipsy feet we
    trod,
Till a great big black teetotaller was sent to us for a rod,
And you can't get wine at a P.S.A., or chapel, or Eisteddfod,
For the Curse of Water has come again because of the wrath
    of God,
And water is on the Bishop's board and the Higher Thinker's
    shrine,
But I don't care where the water goes if it doesn't get into
    the wine.

THE SONG AGAINST GROCERS

God made the wicked Grocer
For a mystery and a sign,

That men might shun the awful shops
And go to inns to dine;
Where the bacon's on the rafter
And the wine is in the wood,
And God that made good laughter
Has seen that they are good.

The evil-hearted Grocer
Would call his mother 'Ma'am,'
And bow at her and bob at her,
Her aged soul to damn,
And rub his horrid hands and ask
What article was next,
Though *mortis in articulo*
Should be her proper text.

His props are not his children,
But pert lads underpaid,
Who call out 'Cash!' and bang about
To work his wicked trade;
He keeps a lady in a cage
Most cruelly all day,
And makes her count and calls her 'Miss'
Until she fades away.

The righteous minds of innkeepers
Induce them now and then
To crack a bottle with a friend
Or treat unmoneyed men,
But who hath seen the Grocer
Treat housemaids to his teas
Or crack a bottle of fish-sauce
Or stand a man a cheese?

He sells us sands of Araby
As sugar for cash down;
He sweeps his shop and sells the dust
The purest salt in town,
He crams with cans of poisoned meat
Poor subjects of the King,
And when they die by thousands
Why, he laughs like anything.

The wicked Grocer groces
In spirits and in wine,
Not frankly and in fellowship
As men in inns do dine;
But packed with soap and sardines
And carried off by grooms,
For to be snatched by Duchesses
And drunk in dressing-rooms.

The hell-instructed Grocer
Has a temple made of tin,
And the ruin of good innkeepers
Is loudly urged therein;
But now the sands are running out
From sugar of a sort,
The Grocer trembles; for his time,
Just like his weight, is short.

THE ROLLING ENGLISH ROAD

Before the Roman came to Rye or out to Severn strode,
The rolling English drunkard made the rolling English road.
A reeling road, a rolling road, that rambles round the shire,
And after him the parson ran, the sexton and the squire;
A merry road, a mazy road, and such as we did tread
The night we went to Birmingham by way of Beachy Head.

I knew no harm of Bonaparte and plenty of the Squire,
And for to fight the Frenchman I did not much desire;
But I did bash their baggonets because they came arrayed
To straighten out the crooked road an English drunkard made,
Where you and I went down the lane with ale-mugs in our
     hands,
The night we went to Glastonbury by way of Goodwin Sands.

His sins they were forgiven him; or why do flowers run
Behind him; and the hedges all strengthening in the sun?
The wild thing went from left to right and knew not which
     was which,
But the wild rose was above him when they found him in the
     ditch.
God pardon us, nor harden us; we did not see so clear
The night we went to Bannockburn by way of Brighton Pier.

My friends, we will not go again or ape an ancient rage,
Or stretch the folly of our youth to be the shame of age,
But walk with clearer eyes and ears this path that wandereth,
And see undrugged in evening light the decent inn of death;
For there is good news yet to hear and fine things to be seen,
Before we go to Paradise by way of Kensal Green.

THE SONG OF QUOODLE

They haven't got no noses,
The fallen sons of Eve;
Even the smell of roses
Is not what they supposes;
But more than mind discloses
And more than men believe.

They haven't got no noses,
They cannot even tell

When door and darkness closes
The park a Jew encloses,
Where even the law of Moses
Will let you steal a smell.

The brilliant smell of water,
The brave smell of a stone,
The smell of dew and thunder,
The old bones buried under,
Are things in which they blunder
And err, if left alone.

The wind from winter forests,
The scent of scentless flowers,
The breath of brides' adorning,
The smell of snare and warning,
The smell of Sunday morning,
God gave to us for ours.

.   .   .   .

And Quoodle here discloses
All things that Quoodle can,
They haven't got no noses,
They haven't got no noses,
And goodness only knowses
The Noselessness of Man.

PIONEERS, O PIONEERS

Nebuchadnezzar the King of the Jews
Suffered from new and original views,
He crawled on his hands and knees, it's said,
With grass in his mouth and a crown on his head.
        With a wowtyiddly, etc.

Those in traditional paths that trod
Thought the thing was a curse from God,
But a Pioneer men always abuse
Like Nebuchadnezzar the King of the Jews.

Black Lord Foulon the Frenchmen slew
Thought it a Futurist thing to do.
He offered them grass instead of bread.
So they stuffed him with grass when they cut off his head.
　　　With a wowtyiddly, etc.

For the pride of his soul he perished then—
But of course it is always of Pride that men
A Man in Advance of his Age accuse,
Like Nebuchadnezzar the King of the Jews.

Simeon Scudder of Styx, in Maine,
Thought of the thing and was at it again.
He gave good grass and water in pails
To a thousand Irishmen hammering rails.
　　　With a wowtyiddly, etc.

Appetites differ; and tied to a stake
He was tarred and feathered for Conscience' Sake.
But stoning the prophets is ancient news,
Like Nebuchadnezzar the King of the Jews.

THE LOGICAL VEGETARIAN

"WHY SHOULDN'T I HAVE A PURELY VEGETARIAN DRINK? WHY SHOULDN'T I TAKE VEGETABLES IN THEIR HIGHEST FORM, SO TO SPEAK? THE MODEST VEGETARIANS OUGHT OBVIOUSLY TO STICK TO WINE OR BEER, PLAIN VEGETARIAN DRINKS, INSTEAD OF FILLING THEIR GOBLETS WITH THE BLOOD OF BULLS AND ELEPHANTS, AS ALL CONVENTIONAL MEAT-EATERS DO, I SUPPOSE."—*Dalroy.*

You will find me drinking rum,
Like a sailor in a slum,
You will find me drinking beer like a Bavarian.
You will find me drinking gin
In the lowest kind of inn,
Because I am a rigid Vegetarian.

So I cleared the inn of wine,
And I tried to climb the sign,
And I tried to hail the constable as 'Marion.'
But he said I couldn't speak,
And he bowled me to the Beak
Because I was a Happy Vegetarian.

Oh, I knew a Doctor Gluck,
And his nose it had a hook,
And his attitudes were anything but Aryan;
So I gave him all the pork
That I had, upon a fork
Because I am myself a Vegetarian.

I am silent in the Club,
I am silent in the pub.,
I am silent on a bally peak in Darien;
For I stuff away for life
Shoving peas in with a knife,
Because I am at heart a Vegetarian.

No more the milk of cows
Shall pollute my private house
Than the milk of the wild mares of the Barbarian;
I will stick to port and sherry,
For they are so very, very,
So very, very, very Vegetarian.

"THE SARACEN'S HEAD"

"The Saracen's Head" looks down the lane,
Where we shall never drink wine again,
For the wicked old women who feel well-bred
Have turned to a tea-shop "The Saracen's Head."

"The Saracen's Head" out of Araby came,
King Richard riding in arms like flame,
And where he established his folks to be fed
He set up a spear—and the Saracen's Head.

. . . .

But the "Saracen's Head" outlived the Kings,
It thought and it thought of most horrible things,
Of Health and of Soap and of Standard Bread,
And of Saracen drinks at the "Saracen's Head."

So the "Saracen's Head" fulfils its name,
They drink no wine—a ridiculous game—
And I shall wonder until I'm dead,
How it ever came into the Saracen's Head.

THE GOOD RICH MAN

Mr. Mandragon the Millionaire, he wouldn't have wine or
    wife,
He couldn't endure complexity; he lived the simple life.
He ordered his lunch by megaphone in manly, simple tones,
And used all his motors for canvassing voters, and twenty
    telephones;
Besides a dandy little machine,
Cunning and neat as ever was seen

With a hundred pulleys and cranks between,
Made of metal and kept quite clean,
To hoist him out of his healthful bed on every day of his life,
And wash him and brush him, and shave him and dress him
　　to live the Simple Life.

Mr. Mandragon was most refined and quietly, neatly dressed,
Say all the American newspapers that know refinement best;
Neat and quiet the hair and hat, and the coat quiet and neat.
A trouser worn upon either leg, while boots adorn the feet;
And not, as any one might expect,
A Tiger Skin, all striped and flecked,
And a Peacock Hat with the tail erect,
A scarlet tunic with sunflowers decked,
That might have had a more marked effect,
And pleased the pride of a weaker man that yearned for wine
　　or wife;
But fame and the flagon, for Mr. Mandragon obscured the
　　Simple Life.

Mr. Mandragon the Millionaire, I am happy to say, is dead;
He enjoyed a quiet funeral in a crematorium shed,
And he lies there fluffy and soft and grey, and certainly quite
　　refined,
When he might have rotted to flowers and fruit with Adam
　　and all mankind,
Or been eaten by wolves athirst for blood,
Or burnt on a big tall pyre of wood,
In a towering flame, as a heathen should,
Or even sat with us here at food,
Merrily taking twopenny ale and cheese with a pocket-knife;
But these were luxuries not for him who went for the Simple
　　Life.

THE SONG AGAINST SONGS

The song of the sorrow of Melisande is a weary song and a
    dreary song,
The glory of Mariana's grange had got into great decay,
The song of the Raven Never More has never been called a
    cheery song,
And the brightest things in Baudelaire are anything else but
    gay.

But who will write us a riding song
Or a hunting song or a drinking song,
Fit for them that arose and rode
When day and the wine were red?
But bring me a quart of claret out,
And I will write you a clinking song,
A song of war and a song of wine
And a song to wake the dead.

The song of the fury of Fragolette is a florid song and a torrid
    song,
The song of the sorrow of Tara is sung to a harp unstrung,
The song of the cheerful Shropshire Lad I consider a perfectly
    horrid song,
And the song of the happy Futurist is a song that can't be
    sung.

But who will write us a riding song
Or a fighting song or a drinking song,
Fit for the fathers of you and me,
That know how to think and thrive?
But the song of Beauty and Art and Love
Is simply an utterly stinking song,
To double you up and drag you down
And damn your soul alive.

ME HEART

I come from Castlepatrick, and me heart is on me sleeve,
And any sword or pistol boy can hit it with me leave,
It shines there for an epaulette, as golden as a flame,
And naked as me ancestors, as noble as me name.
For I come from Castlepatrick, and me heart is on me sleeve,
But a lady stole it from me on St. Gallowglass's Eve.

The folk that live in Liverpool, their heart is in their boots;
They go to hell like lambs, they do, because the hooter hoots.
Where men may not be dancin', though the wheels may dance
    all day;
And men may not be smokin'; but only chimneys may.
But I come from Castlepatrick, and me heart is on me sleeve,
But a lady stole it from me on St. Poleander's Eve.

The folk that live in black Belfast, their heart is in their mouth,
They set us making murders in the meadows of the South;
They think a plough's a rack, they do, and cattle-calls are
    creeds,
And they think we're burnin' witches when we're only burnin'
    weeds;
But I come from Castlepatrick, and me heart is on me sleeve,
But a lady stole it from me on St. Barnabas's Eve.

THE SONG OF THE OAK

The Druids waved their golden knives
And danced around the Oak
When they had sacrificed a man;
But though the learned search and scan
No single modern person can

Entirely see the joke.
But though they cut the throats of men
They cut not down the tree,
And from the blood the saplings sprang
Of oak-woods yet to be.
    But Ivywood, Lord Ivywood,
    He rots the tree as ivy would,
    He clings and crawls as ivy would
    About the sacred tree.

King Charles he fled from Worcester fight
And hid him in the Oak;
In convent schools no man of tact
Would trace and praise his every act,
Or argue that he was in fact
A strict and sainted bloke.
But not by him the sacred woods
Have lost their fancies free,
And though he was extremely big
    He did not break the tree.
    But Ivywood, Lord Ivywood,
    He breaks the tree as ivy would,
    And eats the woods as ivy would
    Between us and the sea.

Great Collingwood walked down the glade
And flung the acorns free,
That oaks might still be in the grove
As oaken as the beams above,
When the great Lover sailors love
Was kissed by Death at sea.
But though for him the oak-trees fell
To build the oaken ships,
The woodman worshipped what he smote

And honoured even the chips.
But Ivywood, Lord Ivywood,
He hates the tree as ivy would,
As the dragon of the ivy would
That has us in his grips.

THE ROAD TO ROUNDABOUT

Some say that Guy of Warwick,
The man that killed the Cow,
And brake the mighty Boar alive
Beyond the bridge at Slough;
Went up against a Loathly Worm
That wasted all the Downs,
And so the roads they twist and squirm
(If I may be allowed the term)
From the writhing of the stricken Worm
That died in seven towns.
I see no scientific proof
That this idea is sound,
And I should say they wound about
To find the town of Roundabout,
The merry town of Roundabout,
That makes the world go round.

Some say that Robin Goodfellow,
Whose lantern lights the meads
(To steal a phrase Sir Walter Scott
In heaven no longer needs),
Such dance around the trysting-place
The moonstruck lover leads;
Which superstition I should scout,
There is more faith in honest doubt
(As Tennyson has pointed out)

Than in those nasty creeds.
  But peace and righteousness (St. John)
  In Roundabout can kiss,
  And since that's all that's found about
  The pleasant town of Roundabout,
  The roads they simply bound about
  To find out where it is.

Some say that when Sir Lancelot
Went forth to find the Grail,
Grey Merlin wrinkled up the roads
For hope that he should fail;
All roads lead back to Lyonesse
And Camelot in the Vale,
I cannot yield assent to this
Extravagant hypothesis,
The plain, shrewd Briton will dismiss
Such rumours (*Daily Mail*).
  But in the streets of Roundabout
  Are no such factions found,
  Or theories to expound about,
  Or roll upon the ground about,
  In the happy town of Roundabout,
  That makes the world go round.

THE SONG OF THE STRANGE ASCETIC

If I had been a Heathen,
  I'd have praised the purple vine,
My slaves would dig the vineyards,
  And I would drink the wine;
But Higgins is a Heathen,
  And his slaves grow lean and grey,
That he may drink some tepid milk
  Exactly twice a day.

If I had been a Heathen,
  I'd have crowned Neæra's curls,
And filled my life with love affairs,
  My house with dancing girls;
But Higgins is a Heathen,
  And to lecture rooms is forced,
Where his aunts, who are not married,
  Demand to be divorced.

If I had been a Heathen,
  I'd have sent my armies forth,
And dragged behind my chariots
  The Chieftains of the North.
But Higgins is a Heathen,
  And he drives the dreary quill,
To lend the poor that funny cash
  That makes them poorer still.

If I had been a Heathen,
  I'd have piled my pyre on high,
And in a great red whirlwind
  Gone roaring to the sky.
But Higgins is a Heathen,
  And a richer man than I;
And they put him in an oven,
  Just as if he were a pie.

Now who that runs can read it,
  The riddle that I write,
Of why this poor old sinner,
  Should sin without delight—
But I, I cannot read it
  (Although I run and run),
Of them that do not have the faith,
  And will not have the fun.

THE SONG OF RIGHT AND WRONG

Feast on wine or fast on water
And your honour shall stand sure,
God Almighty's son and daughter
He the valiant, she the pure;
If an angel out of heaven
Brings you other things to drink,
Thank him for his kind attentions,
Go and pour them down the sink.

Tea is like the East he grows in,
A great yellow Mandarin
With urbanity of manner
And unconsciousness of sin;
All the women, like a harem,
At his pig-tail troop along;
And, like all the East he grows in,
He is Poison when he's strong.

Tea, although an Oriental,
Is a gentleman at least;
Cocoa is a cad and coward,
Cocoa is a vulgar beast,
Cocoa is a dull, disloyal,
Lying, crawling cad and clown,
And may very well be grateful
To the fool that takes him down.

As for all the windy waters,
They were rained like tempests down
When good drink had been dishonoured
By the tipplers of the town;
When red wine had brought red ruin

And the death-dance of our times,
Heaven sent us Soda Water
As a torment for our crimes.

WHO GOES HOME?

In the city set upon slime and loam
They cry in their parliament 'Who goes home?'
And there comes no answer in arch or dome,
For none in the city of graves goes home.
Yet these shall perish and understand,
For God has pity on this great land.

Men that are men again; who goes home?
Tocsin and trumpeter! Who goes home?
For there's blood on the field and blood on the foam
And blood on the body when Man goes home.
And a voice valedictory. . . . Who is for Victory?
Who is for Liberty? Who goes home?

Book Five
The Ballad of the White Horse

DEDICATION

Of great limbs gone to chaos,
  A great face turned to night—
Why bend above a shapeless shroud
Seeking in such archaic cloud
  Sight of strong lords and light?

Where seven sunken Englands
  Lie buried one by one,
Why should one idle spade, I wonder,
Shake up the dust of thanes like thunder
  To smoke and choke the sun?

In cloud of clay so cast to heaven
  What shape shall man discern?
These lords may light the mystery
Of mastery or victory,
And these ride high in history,
  But these shall not return.

Gored on the Norman gonfalon
  The Golden Dragon died;
We shall not wake with ballad strings
The good time of the smaller things,
We shall not see the holy kings
  Ride down by Severn side.

Stiff, strange, and quaintly coloured
  As the broidery of Bayeux
The England of that dawn remains,
And this of Alfred and the Danes

Seems like the tales a whole tribe feigns
   Too English to be true.

Of a good king on an island
   That ruled once on a time;
And as he walked by an apple tree
There came green devils out of the sea
With sea-plants trailing heavily
   And tracks of opal slime.

Yet Alfred is no fairy tale;
   His days as our days ran,
He also looked forth for an hour
On peopled plains and skies that lower,
From those few windows in the tower
   That is the head of a man.

But who shall look from Alfred's hood
   Or breathe his breath alive?
His century like a small dark cloud
Drifts far; it is an eyeless crowd,
Where the tortured trumpets scream aloud
   And the dense arrows drive.

Lady, by one light only
   We look from Alfred's eyes,
We know he saw athwart the wreck
The sign that hangs about your neck,
Where One more than Melchizedek
   Is dead and never dies.

Therefore I bring these rhymes to you.
   Who brought the cross to me,
Since on you flaming without flaw

I saw the sign that Guthrum saw
When he let break his ships of awe,
  And laid peace on the sea.

Do you remember when we went
  Under a dragon moon,
And 'mid volcanic tints of night
Walked where they fought the unknown fight
And saw black trees on the battle-height,
  Black thorn on Ethandune?

And I thought, "I will go with you,
  As man with God has gone,
And wander with a wandering star,
The wandering heart of things that are,
The fiery cross of love and war
  That like yourself, goes on."

O go you onward; where you are
  Shall honour and laughter be,
Past purpled forest and pearled foam,
God's winged pavilion free to roam,
Your face, that is a wandering home,
  A flying home for me.

Ride through the silent earthquake lands,
  Wide as a waste is wide,
Across these days like deserts, when
Pride and a little scratching pen
Have dried and split the hearts of men,
  Heart of the heroes, ride.

Up through an empty house of stars,
  Being what heart you are,
Up the inhuman steeps of space

As on a staircase go in grace,
Carrying the firelight on your face
    Beyond the loneliest star.

Take these: in memory of the hour
    We strayed a space from home
And saw the smoke-hued hamlets, quaint
With Westland king and Westland saint,
And watched the western glory faint
    Along the road to Frome.

BOOK I

THE VISION OF THE KING

Before the gods that made the gods
    Had seen their sunrise pass,
The White Horse of the White Horse Vale
    Was cut out of the grass.

Before the gods that made the gods
    Had drunk at dawn their fill,
The White Horse of the White Horse Vale
    Was hoary on the hill.

Age beyond age on British land,
    Æons on æons gone,
Was peace and war in western hills,
    And the White Horse looked on.

For the White Horse knew England
    When there was none to know;
He saw the first oar break or bend,
He saw heaven fall and the world end,
    O God, how long ago.

For the end of the world was long ago—
   And all we dwell to-day
As children of some second birth,
Like a strange people left on earth
   After a judgment day.

For the end of the world was long ago,
   When the ends of the world waxed free,
When Rome was sunk in a waste of slaves,
   And the sun drowned in the sea.

When Cæsar's sun fell out of the sky
   And whoso hearkened right
Could only hear the plunging
   Of the nations in the night.

When the ends of the earth came marching in
   To torch and cresset gleam.
And the roads of the world that lead to Rome
Were filled with faces that moved like foam,
   Like faces in a dream.

And men rode out of the eastern lands,
   Broad river and burning plain;
Trees that are Titan flowers to see,
And tiger skies, striped horribly,
   With tints of tropic rain.

Where Ind's enamelled peaks arise
   Around that inmost one,
Where ancient eagles on its brink,
Vast as archangels, gather and drink
   The sacrament of the sun.

And men brake out of the northern lands,
　Enormous lands alone,
Where a spell is laid upon life and lust
And the rain is changed to a silver dust
　And the sea to a great green stone.

And a Shape that moveth murkily
　In mirrors of ice and night,
Hath blanched with fear all beasts and birds,
As death and a shock of evil words
　Blast a man's hair with white.

And the cry of the palms and the purple moons,
　Or the cry of the frost and foam,
Swept ever around an inmost place,
And the din of distant race on race
　Cried and replied round Rome.

And there was death on the Emperor
　And night upon the Pope:
And Alfred, hiding in deep grass,
　Hardened his heart with hope.

A sea-folk blinder than the sea
　Broke all about his land,
But Alfred up against them bare
And gripped the ground and grasped the air,
　Staggered, and strove to stand.

He bent them back with spear and spade,
　With desperate dyke and wall,
With foemen leaning on his shield
And roaring on him when he reeled;
　And no help came at all.

He broke them with a broken sword
  A little towards the sea,
And for one hour of panting peace,
Ringed with a roar that would not cease,
With golden crown and girded fleece
  Made laws under a tree.

*   *   *   *   *   *   *   *   *

The Northmen came about our land
  A Christless chivalry:
Who knew not of the arch or pen,
Great, beautiful half-witted men
  From the sunrise and the sea.

Misshapen ships stood on the deep
  Full of strange gold and fire,
And hairy men, as huge as sin
With hornèd heads, came wading in
  Through the long, low sea-mire.

Our towns were shaken of tall kings
  With scarlet beards like blood:
The world turned empty where they trod,
They took the kindly cross of God
  And cut it up for wood.

Their souls were drifting as the sea,
  And all good towns and lands
They only saw with heavy eyes,
  And broke with heavy hands.

Their gods were sadder than the sea,
  Gods of a wandering will,
Who cried for blood like beasts at night,
  Sadly, from hill to hill.

They seemed as trees walking the earth,
  As witless and as tall,
Yet they took hold upon the heavens
  And no help came at all.

They bred like birds in English woods,
  They rooted like the rose,
When Alfred came to Athelney
  To hide him from their bows.

There was not English armour left,
  Nor any English thing,
When Alfred came to Athelney
  To be an English king.

For earthquake swallowing earthquake
  Uprent the Wessex tree;
The whirlpool of the pagan sway
Had swirled his sires as sticks away
  When a flood smites the sea.

And the great kings of Wessex
  Wearied and sank in gore,
And even their ghosts in that great stress
Grew greyer and greyer, less and less,
With the lords that died in Lyonesse
  And the king that comes no more.

And the God of the Golden Dragon
  Was dumb upon his throne,
And the lord of the Golden Dragon
  Ran in the woods alone.

And if ever he climbed the crest of luck
  And set the flag before,
Returning as a wheel returns,
Came ruin and the rain that burns,
  And all began once more.

And naught was left King Alfred
  But shameful tears of rage,
In the island in the river
  In the end of all his age.

In the island in the river
  He was broken to his knee:
And he read, writ with an iron pen,
That God had wearied of Wessex men
And given their country, field and fen,
  To the devils of the sea.

And he saw in a little picture,
  Tiny and far away,
His mother sitting in Egbert's hall,
And a book she showed him, very small,
Where a sapphire Mary sat in stall
  With a golden Christ at play.

It was wrought in the monk's slow manner,
  From silver and sanguine shell,
Where the scenes are little and terrible,
  Keyholes of heaven and hell.

In the river island of Athelney,
  With the river running past,
In colours of such simple creed

All things sprang at him, sun and weed,
Till the grass grew to be grass indeed
  And the tree was a tree at last.

Fearfully plain the flowers grew,
  Like the child's book to read,
Or like a friend's face seen in a glass;
He looked; and there Our Lady was,
She stood and stroked the tall live grass
  As a man strokes his steed.

Her face was like an open word
  When brave men speak and choose,
The very colours of her coat
  Were better than good news.

She spoke not, nor turned not,
  Nor any sign she cast,
Only she stood up straight and free,
Between the flowers in Athelney,
  And the river running past.

One dim ancestral jewel hung
  On his ruined armour grey,
He rent and cast it at her feet:
Where, after centuries, with slow feet,
Men came from hall and school and street
  And found it where it lay.

"Mother of God," the wanderer said,
  "I am but a common king,
Nor will I ask what saints may ask,
  To see a secret thing.

"The gates of heaven are fearful gates
  Worse than the gates of hell;
Not I would break the splendours barred
Or seek to know the thing they guard,
  Which is too good to tell.

"But for this earth most pitiful,
  This little land I know,
If that which is for ever is,
Or if our hearts shall break with bliss,
  Seeing the stranger go?

"When our last bow is broken, Queen,
  And our last javelin cast,
Under some sad, green evening sky,
Holding a ruined cross on high,
Under warm westland grass to lie,
  Shall we come home at last?"

And a voice came human but high up,
  Like a cottage climbed among
The clouds; or a serf of hut and croft
That sits by his hovel fire as oft,
But hears on his old bare roof aloft
  A belfry burst in song.

"The gates of heaven are lightly locked,
  We do not guard our gain,
The heaviest hind may easily
Come silently and suddenly
  Upon me in a lane.

"And any little maid that walks
  In good thoughts apart,

May break the guard of the Three Kings
And see the dear and dreadful things
  I hid within my heart.

"The meanest man in grey fields gone
  Behind the set of sun,
Heareth between star and other star,
Through the door of the darkness fallen ajar,
The council, eldest of things that are,
  The talk of the Three in One.

"The gates of heaven are lightly locked,
  We do not guard our gold,
Men may uproot where worlds begin,
Or read the name of the nameless sin;
But if he fail or if he win
  To no good man is told.

"The men of the East may spell the stars,
  And times and triumphs mark,
But the men signed of the cross of Christ
  Go gaily in the dark.

"The men of the East may search the scrolls
  For sure fates and fame,
But the men that drink the blood of God
  Go singing to their shame.

"The wise men know what wicked things
  Are written on the sky,
They trim sad lamps, they touch sad strings,
Hearing the heavy purple wings,
Where the forgotten seraph kings
  Still plot how God shall die.

"The wise men know all evil things
    Under the twisted trees,
Where the perverse in pleasure pine
And men are weary of green wine
    And sick of crimson seas.

"But you and all the kind of Christ
    Are ignorant and brave,
And you have wars you hardly win
    And souls you hardly save.

"I tell you naught for your comfort,
    Yea, naught for your desire,
Save that the sky grows darker yet
    And the sea rises higher.

"Night shall be thrice night over you,
    And heaven an iron cope.
Do you have joy without a cause,
    Yea, faith without a hope?"

Even as she spoke she was not,
    Nor any word said he,
He only heard, still as he stood
Under the old night's nodding hood,
The sea-folk breaking down the wood
    Like a high tide from sea.

He only heard the heathen men,
    Whose eyes are blue and bleak,
Singing about some cruel thing
Done by a great and smiling king
    In daylight on a deck.

He only heard the heathen men,
  Whose eyes are blue and blind,
Singing what shameful things are done
Between the sunlit sea and the sun
  When the land is left behind.

BOOK II

THE GATHERING OF THE CHIEFS

Up across windy wastes and up
  Went Alfred over the shaws,
Shaken of the joy of giants,
  The joy without a cause.

In the slopes away to the western bays,
  Where blows not ever a tree,
He washed his soul in the west wind
  And his body in the sea.

And he set to rhyme his ale-measures,
  And he sang aloud his laws,
Because of the joy of the giants,
  The joy without a cause.

For the King went gathering Wessex men,
  As grain out of the chaff,
The few that were alive to die,
Laughing, as littered skulls that lie
After lost battles turn to the sky
  An everlasting laugh.

The King went gathering Christian men,
  As wheat out of the husk;

Eldred, the Franklin by the sea,
And Mark, the man from Italy,
And Colan of the Sacred Tree,
  From the old tribe on Usk.

The rook croaked homeward heavily,
  The west was clear and warm,
The smoke of evening food and ease
Rose like a blue tree in the trees
  When he came to Eldred's farm.

But Eldred's farm was fallen awry,
  Like an old cripple's bones,
And Eldred's tools were red with rust,
And on his well was a green crust,
And purple thistles upward thrust,
  Between the kitchen stones.

But smoke of some good feasting
  Went upwards evermore,
And Eldred's doors stood wide apart
For loitering foot or labouring cart,
And Eldred's great and foolish heart
  Stood open like his door.

A mighty man was Eldred,
  A bulk for casks to fill,
His face a dreaming furnace,
  His body a walking hill.

In the old wars of Wessex
  His sword had sunken deep,
But all his friends, he sighed and said,
Were broken about Ethelred;

And between the deep drink and the dead
  He had fallen upon sleep.

"Come not to me, King Alfred,
  Save always for the ale:
Why should my harmless hands be slain
Because the chiefs cry once again,
As in all fights, that we shall gain,
  And in all fights we fail?

"Your scalds still thunder and prophesy
  That crown that never comes;
Friend, I will watch the certain things,
Swine, and slow moons like silver rings,
  And the ripening of the plums."

And Alfred answered, drinking,
  And gravely, without blame,
"Nor bear I boast of scald or king,
The thing I bear is a lesser thing,
  But comes in a better name.

"Out of the mouth of the Mother of God,
  More than the doors of doom,
I call the muster of Wessex men
From grassy hamlet or ditch or den,
To break and be broken, God knows when,
  But I have seen for whom.

"Out of the mouth of the Mother of God
  Like a little word come I;
For I go gathering Christian men
From sunken paving and ford and fen,
To die in a battle, God knows when,
  By God, but I know why.

And this is the word of Mary,
  The word of the world's desire:
'No more of comfort shall ye get,
Save that the sky grows darker yet
  And the sea rises higher.' "

Then silence sank. And slowly
  Arose the sea-land lord,
Like some vast beast for mystery,
He filled the room and porch and sky,
And from a cobwebbed nail on high
  Unhooked his heavy sword.

Up on the shrill sea-downs and up
  Went Alfred all alone,
Turning but once e'er the door was shut,
Shouting to Eldred over his butt,
That he bring all spears to the woodman's hut
  Hewn under Egbert's Stone.

And he turned his back and broke the fern,
  And fought the moths of dusk,
And went on his way for other friends,
Friends fallen of all the wide world's ends,
From Rome that wrath and pardon sends
  And the grey tribes on Usk.

He saw gigantic tracks of death
  And many a shape of doom,
Good steadings to grey ashes gone
And a monk's house white like a skeleton
  In the green crypt of the combe.

And in many a Roman villa
  Earth and her ivies eat,

Saw coloured pavements sink and fade
In flowers, and the windy colonnade
  Like the spectre of a street.

But the cold stars clustered
  Among the cold pines
Ere he was half on his pilgrimage
  Over the western lines.

And the white dawn widened
  Ere he came to the last pine,
Where Mark, the man from Italy,
  Still made the Christian sign.

The long farm lay on the large hill-side,
  Flat like a painted plan,
And by the side the low white house,
  Where dwelt the southland man.

A bronzed man, with a bird's bright eye,
  And a strong bird's beak and brow,
His skin was brown like buried gold,
And of certain of his sires was told
That they came in the shining ship of old,
  With Cæsar in the prow.

His fruit trees stood like soldiers
  Drilled in a straight line,
His strange, stiff olives did not fail,
And all the kings of the earth drank ale,
  But he drank wine.

Wide over wasted British plains
  Stood never an arch or dome,

Only the trees to toss and reel,
The tribes to bicker, the beasts to squeal;
But the eyes in his head were strong like steel,
  And his soul remembered Rome.

Then Alfred of the lonely spear
  Lifted his lion head;
And fronted with the Italian's eye,
Asking him of his whence and why,
  King Alfred stood and said:

"I am that oft-defeated King
  Whose failure fills the land,
Who fled before the Danes of old,
Who chaffered with the Danes with gold,
Who now upon the Wessex wold
  Hardly has feet to stand.

"But out of the mouth of the Mother of God
  I have seen the truth like fire,
This—that the sky grows darker yet
  And the sea rises higher."

Long looked the Roman on the land;
  The trees as golden crowns
Blazed, drenched with dawn and dew-empearled,
While faintlier coloured, freshlier curled,
The clouds from underneath the world
  Stood up over the downs.

"These vines be ropes that drag me hard,"
  He said. "I go not far;
Where would you meet? For you must hold
Half Wiltshire and the White Horse wold,

And the Thames bank to Owsenfold,
  If Wessex goes to war.

"Guthrum sits strong on either bank
  And you must press his lines
Inwards, and eastward drive him down;
I doubt if you shall take the crown
Till you have taken London town.
  For me, I have the vines."

"If each man on the Judgment Day
  Meet God on a plain alone,"
Said Alfred, "I will speak for you
As for myself, and call it true
That you brought all fighting folk you knew
  Lined under Egbert's Stone.

"Though I be in the dust ere then,
  I know where you will be."
And shouldering suddenly his spear
He faded like some elfin fear,
Where the tall pines ran up, tier on tier,
  Tree overtoppling tree.

He shouldered his spear at morning
  And laughed to lay it on,
But he leaned on his spear as on a staff,
With might and little mood to laugh,
Or ever he sighted chick or calf
  Of Colan of Caerleon.

For the man dwelt in a lost land
  Of boulders and broken men,
In a great grey cave far off to the south

Where a thick green forest stopped the mouth,
  Giving darkness in his den.

And the man was come like a shadow,
  From the shadow of Druid trees,
Where Usk, with mighty murmurings,
Past Caerleon of the fallen kings,
  Goes out to ghostly seas.

Last of a race in ruin—
  He spoke the speech of the Gaels;
His kin were in holy Ireland,
  Or up in the crags of Wales.

But his soul stood with his mother's folk,
  That were of the rain-wrapped isle,
Where Patrick and Brandan westerly
Looked out at last on a landless sea
  And the sun's last smile.

His harp was carved and cunning,
  As the Celtic craftsman makes,
Graven all over with twisting shapes
  Like many headless snakes.

His harp was carved and cunning,
  His sword prompt and sharp,
And he was gay when he held the sword,
  Sad when he held the harp.

For the great Gaels of Ireland
  Are the men that God made mad,
For all their wars are merry,
  And all their songs are sad.

He kept the Roman order,
  He made the Christian sign;
But his eyes grew often blind and bright,
And the sea that rose in the rocks at night
  Rose to his head like wine.

He made the sign of the cross of God,
  He knew the Roman prayer,
But he had unreason in his heart
  Because of the gods that were.

Even they that walked on the high cliffs,
  High as the clouds were then,
Gods of unbearable beauty
  That broke the hearts of men.

And whether in seat or saddle,
  Whether with frown or smile,
Whether at feast or fight was he,
He heard the noise of a nameless sea
  On an undiscovered isle.

Lifting the great green ivy
  And the great spear lowering,
One said, "I am Alfred of Wessex,
  And I am a conquered king."

And the man of the cave made answer,
  And his eyes were stars of scorn,
"And better kings were conquered
  Or ever your sires were born.

"What goddess was your mother,
  What fay your breed begot,

That you should not die with Uther
  And Arthur and Lancelot?

"But when you win you brag and blow,
  And when you lose you rail,
Army of eastland yokels
  Not strong enough to fail."

"I bring not boast or railing,"
  Spake Alfred not in ire,
"I bring of Our Lady a lesson set,
This—that the sky grows darker yet
  And the sea rises higher."

Then Colan of the Sacred Tree
  Tossed his black mane on high,
And cried, as rigidly he rose,
"And if the sea and sky be foes,
  We will tame the sea and sky."

Smiled Alfred, "Seek ye a fable
  More dizzy and more dread
Than all your mad barbarian tales
  Where the sky stands on its head?

"A tale where a man looks down on the sky
  That has long looked down on him;
A tale where a man can swallow a sea
  That might swallow the seraphim.

"Bring to the hut by Egbert's Stone
  All bills and bows ye have."
And Alfred strode off rapidly,
And Colan of the Sacred Tree
  Went slowly to his cave.

BOOK III

THE HARP OF ALFRED

In a tree that yawned and twisted
  The King's few goods were flung,
A mass-book mildewed, line by line,
And weapons and a skin of wine,
  And an old harp unstrung.

By the yawning tree in the twilight
  The King unbound his sword,
Severed the harp of all his goods,
And there in the cool and soundless woods
  Sounded a single chord.

Then laughed; and watched the finches flash,
  The sullen flies in swarm,
And went unarmed over the hills,
  With the harp upon his arm,

Until he came to the White Horse Vale
  And saw across the plains,
In the twilight high and far and fell,
Like the fiery terraces of hell,
  The camp fires of the Danes—

The fires of the Great Army
  That was made of iron men,
Whose lights of sacrilege and scorn
Ran around England red as morn,
Fires over Glastonbury Thorn—
  Fires out on Ely Fen.

And as he went by White Horse Vale
  He saw lie wan and wide
The old horse graven, God knows when,
By gods or beasts or what things then
Walked a new world instead of men
  And scrawled on the hill-side.

And when he came to White Horse Down
  The great White Horse was grey,
For it was ill scoured of the weed,
And lichen and thorn could crawl and feed,
Since the foes of settled house and creed
  Had swept old works away.

King Alfred gazed all sorrowful
  At thistle and mosses grey,
Till a rally of Danes with shield and bill
Rolled drunk over the dome of the hill,
And, hearing of his harp and skill,
  They dragged him to their play.

And as they went through the high green grass
  They roared like the great green sea;
But when they came to the red camp fire
  They were silent suddenly.

And as they went up the wastes away
  They went reeling to and fro;
But when they came to the red camp fire
  They stood all in a row.

For golden in the firelight,
  With a smile carved on his lips,

And a beard curled right cunningly,
Was Guthrum of the Northern Sea,
  The emperor of the ships—

With three great earls King Guthrum
  Went the rounds from fire to fire,
With Harold, nephew of the King,
And Ogier of the Stone and Sling,
And Elf, whose gold lute had a string
  That sighed like all desire.

The Earls of the Great Army
  That no men born could tire,
Whose flames anear him or aloof
Took hold of towers or walls of proof,
Fire over Glastonbury roof
  And out on Ely, fire.

And Guthrum heard the soldiers' tale
  And bade the stranger play;
Not harshly, but as one on high,
On a marble pillar in the sky,
Who sees all folk that live and die—
  Pigmy and far away.

And Alfred, King of Wessex,
  Looked on his conqueror—
And his hands hardened; but he played,
And leaving all later hates unsaid,
He sang of some old British raid
  On the wild west march of yore.

He sang of war in the warm wet shires,
  Where rain nor fruitage fails,

Where England of the motley states
Deepens like a garden to the gates
    In the purple walls of Wales.

He sang of the seas of savage heads
    And the seas and seas of spears,
Boiling all over Offa's Dyke,
What time a Wessex club could strike
    The kings of the mountaineers.

Till Harold laughed and snatched the harp,
    The kinsman of the King,
A big youth, beardless like a child,
Whom the new wine of war sent wild,
    Smote, and began to sing—

And he cried of the ships as eagles
    That circle fiercely and fly,
And sweep the seas and strike the towns
    From Cyprus round to Skye.

How swiftly and with peril
    They gather all good things,
The high horns of the forest beasts,
    Or the secret stones of kings.

"For Rome was given to rule the world,
    And gat of it little joy—
But we, but we shall enjoy the world,
    The whole huge world a toy.

"Great wine like blood from Burgundy,
    Cloaks like the clouds from Tyre,
And marble like solid moonlight,
    And gold like frozen fire.

"Smells that a man might swill in a cup,
    Stones that a man might eat,
And the great smooth women like ivory
    That the Turks sell in the street."

He sang the song of the thief of the world,
    And the gods that love the thief;
And he yelled aloud at the cloister-yards,
    Where men go gathering grief.

"Well have you sung, O stranger,
    Of death on the dyke in Wales,
Your chief was a bracelet-giver;
But the red unbroken river
Of a race runs not for ever,
    But suddenly it fails.

"Doubtless your sires were sword-swingers
    When they waded fresh from foam,
Before they were turned to women
    By the god of the nails from Rome;

"But since you bent to the shaven men,
    Who neither lust nor smite,
Thunder of Thor, we hunt you
    A hare on the mountain height."

King Guthrum smiled a little,
    And said, "It is enough,
Nephew, let Elf retune the string;
A boy must needs like bellowing,
But the old ears of a careful king
    Are glad of songs less rough."

Blue-eyed was Elf the minstrel,
  With womanish hair and ring,
Yet heavy was his hand on sword,
  Though light upon the string.

And as he stirred the strings of the harp
  To notes but four or five,
The heart of each man moved in him
  Like a babe buried alive.

And they felt the land of the folk-songs
  Spread southward of the Dane,
And they heard the good Rhine flowing
  In the heart of all Allemagne.

They felt the land of the folk-songs,
  Where the gifts hang on the tree,
Where the girls give ale at morning
  And the tears come easily.

The mighty people, womanlike,
  That have pleasure in their pain
As he sang of Balder beautiful,
  Whom the heavens loved in vain.

As he sang of Balder beautiful,
  Whom the heavens could not save,
Till the world was like a sea of tears
  And every soul a wave.

"There is always a thing forgotten
  When all the world goes well;
A thing forgotten, as long ago,
When the gods forgot the mistletoe,

And soundless as an arrow of snow
  The arrow of anguish fell.

"The thing on the blind side of the heart,
  On the wrong side of the door,
The green plant groweth, menacing
Almighty lovers in the spring;
There is always a forgotten thing,
  And love is not secure."

And all that sat by the fire were sad,
  Save Ogier, who was stern,
And his eyes hardened, even to stones,
  As he took the harp in turn;

Earl Ogier of the Stone and Sling
  Was odd to ear and sight,
Old he was, but his locks were red,
And jests were all the words he said,
Yet he was sad at board and bed
  And savage in the fight.

"You sing of the young gods easily
  In the days when you are young;
But I go smelling yew and sods,
And I know there are gods behind the gods,
  Gods that are best unsung.

"And a man grows ugly for women,
  And a man grows dull with ale,
Well if he find in his soul at last
  Fury, that does not fail.

"The wrath of the gods behind the gods
  Who would rend all gods and men,

Well if the old man's heart hath still
Wheels sped of rage and roaring will,
Like cataracts to break down and kill,
  Well for the old man then—

"While there is one tall shrine to shake,
  Or one live man to rend;
For the wrath of the gods behind the gods
  Who are weary to make an end.

"There lives one moment for a man
  When the door at his shoulder shakes,
When the taut rope parts under the pull,
And the barest branch is beautiful
  One moment, while it breaks.

"So rides my soul upon the sea
  That drinks the howling ships,
Though in black jest it bows and nods
Under the moons with silver rods,
I know it is roaring at the gods,
  Waiting the last eclipse.

"And in the last eclipse the sea
  Shall stand up like a tower,
Above all moons made dark and riven,
Hold up its foaming head in heaven,
  And laugh, knowing its hour.

"And the high ones in the happy town
  Propped of the planets seven,
Shall know a new light in the mind,
A noise about them and behind,
Shall hear an awful voice, and find
  Foam in the courts of heaven.

"And you that sit by the fire are young,
  And true love waits for you;
But the king and I grow old, grow old,
  And hate alone is true."

And Guthrum shook his head but smiled,
  For he was a mighty clerk,
And had read lines in the Latin books
  When all the north was dark.

He said, "I am older than you, Ogier;
  Not all things would I rend,
For whether life be bad or good
  It is best to abide the end."

He took the great harp wearily,
  Even Guthrum of the Danes,
With wide eyes bright as the one long day
  On the long polar plains.

For he sang of a wheel returning,
  And the mire trod back to mire,
And how red hells and golden heavens
  Are castles in the fire.

"It is good to sit where the good tales go,
  To sit as our fathers sat;
But the hour shall come after his youth,
When a man shall know not tales but truth,
  And his heart fail thereat.

"When he shall read what is written
  So plain in clouds and clods,

When he shall hunger without hope
  Even for evil gods.

"For this is a heavy matter,
  And the truth is cold to tell;
Do we not know, have we not heard,
The soul is like a lost bird,
  The body a broken shell.

"And a man hopes, being ignorant,
  Till in white woods apart
He finds at last the lost bird dead:
And a man may still lift up his head
  But never more his heart.

"There comes no noise but weeping
  Out of the ancient sky,
And a tear is in the tiniest flower
  Because the gods must die.

"The little brooks are very sweet,
  Like a girl's ribbons curled,
But the great sea is bitter
  That washes all the world.

"Strong are the Roman roses,
  Or the free flowers of the heath,
But every flower, like a flower of the sea,
  Smelleth with the salt of death.

"And the heart of the locked battle
  Is the happiest place for men;
When shrieking souls as shafts go by
And many have died and all may die;

Though this word be a mystery,
  Death is most distant then.

"Death blazes bright above the cup,
  And clear above the crown;
But in that dream of battle
  We seem to tread it down.

"Wherefore I am a great king,
  And waste the world in vain,
Because man hath not other power,
Save that in dealing death for dower,
He may forget it for an hour
  To remember it again."

And slowly his hands and thoughtfully
  Fell from the lifted lyre,
And the owls moaned from the mighty trees
Till Alfred caught it to his knees
  And smote it as in ire.

He heaved the head of the harp on high
  And swept the framework barred,
And his stroke had all the rattle and spark
  Of horses flying hard.

"When God put man in a garden
  He girt him with a sword,
And sent him forth a free knight
  That might betray his lord;

"He brake Him and betrayed Him,
  And fast and far he fell,
Till you and I may stretch our necks
  And burn our beards in hell.

"But though I lie on the floor of the world,
    With the seven sins for rods,
I would rather fall with Adam
    Then rise with all your gods.

"What have the strong gods given?
    Where have the glad gods led?
When Guthrum sits on a hero's throne
    And asks if he is dead?

"Sirs, I am but a nameless man,
    A rhymester without home,
Yet since I come of the Wessex clay
    And carry the cross of Rome,

"I will even answer the mighty earl
    That asked of Wessex men
Why they be meek and monkish folk,
And bow to the White Lord's broken yoke;
What sign have we save blood and smoke?
    Here is my answer then.

"That on you is fallen the shadow,
    And not upon the Name;
That though we scatter and though we fly,
And you hang over us like the sky,
You are more tired of victory,
    Than we are tired of shame.

"That though you hunt the Christian man
    Like a hare on the hill-side,
The hare has still more heart to run
    Than you have heart to ride.

"That though all lances split on you,
All swords be heaved in vain,
We have more lust again to lose
Than you to win again.

"Your lord sits high in the saddle,
A broken-hearted king,
But our king Alfred, lost from fame,
Fallen among foes or bonds of shame,
In I know not what mean trade or name,
Has still some song to sing;

"Our monks go robed in rain and snow,
But the heart of flame therein,
But you go clothed in feasts and flames,
When all is ice within;

"Nor shall all iron dooms make dumb
Men wondering ceaselessly,
If it be not better to fast for joy
Than feast for misery.

"Nor monkish order only
Slides down, as field to fen,
All things achieved and chosen pass,
As the White Horse fades in the grass,
No work of Christian men.

"Ere the sad gods that made your gods
Saw their sad sunrise pass,
The White Horse of the White Horse Vale,
That you have left to darken and fail,
Was cut out of the grass.

"Therefore your end is on you,
  Is on you and your kings,
Not for a fire in Ely fen,
Not that your gods are nine or ten,
But because it is only Christian men
  Guard even heathen things.

"For our God hath blessed creation,
  Calling it good. I know
What spirit with whom you blindly band
Hath blessed destruction with his hand;
Yet by God's death the stars shall stand
  And the small apples grow."

And the King, with harp on shoulder,
  Stood up and ceased his song;
And the owls moaned from the mighty trees,
  And the Danes laughed loud and long.

BOOK IV

THE WOMAN IN THE FOREST

Thick thunder of the snorting swine,
  Enormous in the gloam,
Rending among all roots that cling,
And the wild horses whinnying,
Were the night's noises when the King,
  Shouldering his harp, went home.

With eyes of owl and feet of fox,
  Full of all thoughts he went;
He marked the tilt of the pagan camp,
The paling of pine, the sentries' tramp,

And the one great stolen altar-lamp
  Over Guthrum in his tent.

By scrub and thorn in Ethandune
  That night the foe had lain;
Whence ran across the heather grey
The old stones of a Roman way;
And in a wood not far away
  The pale road split in twain.

He marked the wood and the cloven ways
  With an old captain's eyes,
And he thought how many a time had he
Sought to see Doom he could not see;
How ruin had come and victory,
  And both were a surprise.

Even so he had watched and wondered
  Under Ashdown from the plains;
With Ethelred praying in his tent,
Till the white hawthorn swung and bent,
As Alfred rushed his spears and rent
  The shield-wall of the Danes.

Even so he had watched and wondered,
  Knowing neither less nor more,
Till all his lords lay dying,
And axes on axes plying,
Flung him, and drove him flying
  Like a pirate to the shore.

Wise he had been before defeat,
  And wise before success;
Wise in both hours and ignorant,
  Knowing neither more nor less.

As he went down to the river-hut
  He knew a night-shade scent,
Owls did as evil cherubs rise,
With little wings and lantern eyes,
As though he sank through the under-skies;
  But down and down he went.

As he went down to the river-hut
  He went as one that fell;
Seeing the high forest domes and spars.
Dim green or torn with golden scars,
As the proud look up at the evil stars,
  In the red heavens of hell.

For he must meet by the river-hut
  Them he had bidden to arm,
Mark from the towers of Italy,
And Colan of the Sacred Tree,
And Eldred who beside the sea
  Held heavily his farm.

The roof leaned gaping to the grass,
  As a monstrous mushroom lies;
Echoing and empty seemed the place;
But opened in a little space
A great grey woman with scarred face
  And strong and humbled eyes.

King Alfred was but a meagre man,
  Bright eyed, but lean and pale:
And swordless, with his harp and rags,
He seemed a beggar, such as lags
  Looking for crusts and ale.

And the woman, with a woman's eyes
  Of pity at once and ire,
Said, when that she had glared a span,
"There is a cake for any man
  If he will watch the fire."

And Alfred, bowing heavily,
  Sat down the fire to stir,
And even as the woman pitied him
  So did he pity her.

Saying, "O great heart in the night,
  O best cast forth for worst,
Twilight shall melt and morning stir,
And no kind thing shall come to her,
Till God shall turn the world over
  And all the last are first.

"And well may God with the serving-folk
  Cast in His dreadful lot;
Is not He too a servant,
  And is not He forgot?

"For was not God my gardener
  And silent like a slave;
That opened oaks on the uplands
  Or thicket in graveyard gave?

"And was not God my armourer,
  All patient and unpaid,
That sealed my skull as a helmet,
  And ribs for hauberk made?

"Did not a great grey servant
  Of all my sires and me,

Build this pavilion of the pines,
And herd the fowls and fill the vines,
And labour and pass and leave no signs
  Save mercy and mystery?

"For God is a great servant,
  And rose before the day,
From some primordial slumber torn;
But all we living later born
Sleep on, and rise after the morn,
  And the Lord has gone away.

"On things half sprung from sleeping,
  All sleepy suns have shone,
They stretch stiff arms, the yawning trees,
The beasts blink upon hands and knees,
Man is awake and does and sees—
  But Heaven has done and gone.

"For who shall guess the good riddle
  Or speak of the Holiest,
Save in faint figures and failing words,
Who loves, yet laughs among the swords,
  Labours, and is at rest?

"But some see God like Guthrum,
  Crowned, with a great beard curled,
But I see God like a good giant,
  That, labouring, lifts the world.

"Wherefore was God in Golgotha,
  Slain as a serf is slain;
And hate He had of prince and peer,
And love He had and made good cheer,

Of them that, like this woman here,
  Go powerfully in pain.

"But in this grey morn of man's life,
  Cometh sometime to the mind
A little light that leaps and flies,
  Like a star blown on the wind.

"A star of nowhere, a nameless star,
  A light that spins and swirls,
And cries that even in hedge and hill,
Even on earth, it may go ill
  At last with the evil earls.

"A dancing sparkle, a doubtful star,
  On the waste wind whirled and driven;
But it seems to sing of a wilder worth,
A time discrowned of doom and birth,
And the kingdom of the poor on earth
  Come, as it is in heaven.

"But even though such days endure,
  How shall it profit her?
Who shall go groaning to the grave,
With many a meek and mighty slave,
Field-breaker and fisher on the wave,
  And woodman and waggoner.

"Bake ye the big world all again
  A cake with kinder leaven;
Yet these are sorry evermore—
Unless there be a little door,
  A little door in heaven."

And as he wept for the woman
    He let her business be,
And like his royal oath and rash
The good food fell upon the ash
    And blackened instantly.

Screaming, the woman caught a cake
    Yet burning from the bar,
And struck him suddenly on the face,
    Leaving a scarlet scar.

King Alfred stood up wordless,
    A man dead with surprise,
And torture stood and the evil things
That are in the childish hearts of kings
    An instant in his eyes.

And even as he stood and stared
    Drew round him in the dusk
Those friends creeping from far-off farms,
Marcus with all his slaves in arms,
And the strange spears hung with ancient charms
    Of Colan of the Usk.

With one whole farm marching afoot
    The trampled road resounds,
Farm-hands and farm-beasts blundering by
And jars of mead and stores of rye,
Where Eldred strode above his high
    And thunder-throated hounds.

And grey cattle and silver lowed
    Against the unlifted morn,
And straw clung to the spear-shafts tall.

And a boy went before them all
　　Blowing a ram's horn.

As mocking such rude revelry,
　　The dim clan of the Gael
Came like a bad king's burial-end,
With dismal robes that drop and rend
　　And demon pipes that wail—

In long, outlandish garments,
　　Torn, though of antique worth,
With Druid beards and Druid spears,
As a resurrected race appears
　　Out of an elder earth.

And though the King had called them forth
　　And knew them for his own,
So still each eye stood like a gem,
So spectral hung each broidered hem,
Grey carven men he fancied them,
　　Hewn in an age of stone.

And the two wild peoples of the north
　　Stood fronting in the gloam,
And heard and knew each in its mind
The third great thunder on the wind,
The living walls that hedge mankind,
　　The walking walls of Rome.

Mark's were the mixed tribes of the west,
　　Of many a hue and strain,
Gurth, with rank hair like yellow grass,
And the Cornish fisher, Gorlias,
And Halmer, come from his first mass,
　　Lately baptized, a Dane.

But like one man in armour
  Those hundreds trod the field,
From red Arabia to the Tyne
The earth had heard that marching line,
Since the cry on the hill Capitoline,
  And the fall of the golden shield.

And the earth shook and the King stood still
  Under the greenwood bough,
And the smoking cake lay at his feet
  And the blow was on his brow.

Then Alfred laughed out suddenly,
  Like thunder in the spring,
Till shook aloud the lintel-beams,
And the squirrels stirred in dusty dreams,
And the startled birds went up in streams,
  For the laughter of the King.

And the beasts of the earth and the birds looked down,
  In a wild solemnity,
On a stranger sight than a sylph or elf,
On one man laughing at himself
  Under the greenwood tree—

The giant laughter of Christian men
  That roars through a thousand tales,
Where greed is an ape and pride is an ass,
And Jack's away with his master's lass,
And the miser is banged with all his brass,
  The farmer with all his flails;

Tales that tumble and tales that trick,
  Yet end not all in scorning—

Of kings and clowns in a merry plight,
And the clock gone wrong and the world gone right,
That the mummers sing upon Christmas night
   And Christmas Day in the morning.

"Now here is a good warrant,"
   Cried Alfred, "by my sword;
For he that is struck for an ill servant
   Should be a kind lord.

"He that has been a servant
   Knows more than priests and kings,
But he that has been an ill servant,
   He knows all earthly things.

"Pride flings frail palaces at the sky,
   As a man flings up sand,
But the firm feet of humility
   Take hold of heavy land.

"Pride juggles with her toppling towers,
   They strike the sun and cease,
But the firm feet of humility
   They grip the ground like trees.

"He that hath failed in a little thing
   Hath a sign upon the brow;
And the Earls of the Great Army
   Have no such seal to show.

"The red print on my forehead,
   Small flame for a red star,
In the van of the violent marching, then
When the sky is torn of the trumpets ten,

And the hands of the happy howling men
  Fling wide the gates of war.

"This blow that I return not
  Ten times will I return
On kings and earls of all degree,
And armies wide as empires be
Shall slide like landslips to the sea
  If the red star burn.

"One man shall drive a hundred,
  As the dead kings drave;
Before me rocking hosts be riven,
And battering cohorts backwards driven,
For I am the first king known of heaven
  That has been struck like a slave.

"Up on the old white road, brothers,
  Up on the Roman walls!
For this is the night of the drawing of swords,
And the tainted tower of the heathen hordes
Leans to our hammers, fires and cords,
  Leans a little and falls.

"Follow the star that lives and leaps,
  Follow the sword that sings,
For we go gathering heathen men,
A terrible harvest, ten by ten,
As the wrath of the last red autumn—then
  When Christ reaps down the kings.

"Follow a light that leaps and spins,
  Follow the fire unfurled!
For riseth up against realm and rod,

A thing forgotten, a thing downtrod,
The last lost giant, even God,
  Is risen against the world."

Roaring they went o'er the Roman wall,
  And roaring up the lane,
Their torches tossed, a ladder of fire,
Higher their hymn was heard and higher,
More sweet for hate and for heart's desire,
And up in the northern scrub and brier
  They fell upon the Dane.

BOOK V

ETHANDUNE: THE FIRST STROKE

King Guthrum was a dread king,
  Like death out of the north;
Shrines without name or number
He rent and rolled as lumber,
From Chester to the Humber
  He drove his foemen forth.

The Roman villas heard him
  In the valley of the Thames,
Come over the hills roaring
Above their roofs, and pouring
On spire and stair and flooring
  Brimstone and pitch and flames.

Sheer o'er the great chalk uplands
  And the hill of the Horse went he,
Till high on Hampshire beacons
  He saw the southern sea.

High on the heights of Wessex
  He saw the southern brine,
And turned him to a conquered land,
And where the northern thornwoods stand,
And the road parts on either hand,
  There came to him a sign.

King Guthrum was a war-chief,
  A wise man in the field,
And though he prospered well, and knew
How Alfred's folk were sad and few,
Not less with weighty care he drew
  Long lines for pike and shield.

King Guthrum lay on the upper land,
  On a single road at gaze,
And his foe must come with lean array,
Up the left arm of the cloven way,
  To the meeting of the ways.

And long ere the noise of armour,
  An hour ere the break of light,
The woods awoke with crash and cry,
And the birds sprang clamouring harsh and high,
And the rabbits ran like an elves' army
  Ere Alfred came in sight.

The live wood came at Guthrum,
  On foot and claw and wing,
The nests were noisy overhead,
For Alfred and the star of red,
All life went forth, and the forest fled
  Before the face of the King.

But halted in the woodways
　　Christ's few were grim and grey,
And each with a small, far, bird-like sight
Saw the high folly of the fight;
And though strange joys had grown in the night,
　　Despair grew with the day.

And when white dawn crawled through the wood,
　　Like cold foam of a flood,
Then weakened every warrior's mood,
In hope, though not in hardihood;
And each man sorrowed as he stood
　　In the fashion of his blood.

For the Saxon Franklin sorrowed
　　For the things that had been fair;
For the dear dead woman, crimson-clad,
And the great feasts and the friends he had;
But the Celtic prince's soul was sad
　　For the things that never were.

In the eyes Italian all things
　　But a black laughter died;
And Alfred flung his shield to earth
　　And smote his breast and cried—

"I wronged a man to his slaying,
　　And a woman to her shame,
And once I looked on a sworn maid
　　That was wed to the Holy Name.

"And once I took my neighbour's wife,
　　That was bound to an eastland man,
In the starkness of my evil youth,
　　Before my griefs began.

"People, if you have any prayers,
   Say prayers for me:
And lay me under a Christian stone
In that lost land I thought my own,
To wait till the holy horn is blown,
   And all poor men are free."

Then Eldred of the idle farm
   Leaned on his ancient sword,
As fell his heavy words and few;
And his eyes were of such alien blue
As gleams where the Northman saileth new
   Into an unknown fiord.

"I was a fool and wasted ale—
   My slaves found it sweet;
I was a fool and wasted bread,
   And the birds had bread to eat.

"The kings go up and the kings go down,
   And who knows who shall rule;
Next night a king may starve or sleep,
But men and birds and beasts shall weep
   At the burial of a fool.

"O, drunkards in my cellar,
   Boys in my apple tree,
The world grows stern and strange and new,
And wise men shall govern you,
   And you shall weep for me.

"But yoke me my own oxen,
   Down to my own farm;
My own dog will whine for me,

My own friends will bend the knee,
And the foes I slew openly
  Have never wished me harm."

And all were moved a little,
  But Colan stood apart,
Having first pity, and after
Hearing, like rat in rafter,
That little worm of laughter
  That eats the Irish heart.

And his grey-green eyes were cruel,
  And the smile of his mouth waxed hard,
And he said, "And when did Britain
  Become your burying-yard?

"Before the Romans lit the land,
  When schools and monks were none,
We reared such stones to the sun-god
  As might put out the sun.

"The tall trees of Britain
  We worshipped and were wise,
But you shall raid the whole land through
And never a tree shall talk to you,
Though every leaf is a tongue taught true
  And the forest is full of eyes.

"On one round hill to the seaward
  The trees grow tall and grey
And the trees talk together
  When all men are away.

"O'er a few round hills forgotten
  The trees grow tall in rings,

And the trees talk together
Of many pagan things.

"Yet I could lie and listen
With a cross upon my clay,
And hear unhurt for ever
What the trees of Britain say."

A proud man was the Roman,
His speech a single one,
But his eyes were like an eagle's eyes
That is staring at the sun.

"Dig for me where I die," he said,
"If first or last I fall—
Dead on the fell at the first charge,
Or dead by Wantage wall;

"Lift not my head from bloody ground,
Bear not my body home,
For all the earth is Roman earth
And I shall die in Rome."

Then Alfred, King of England,
Bade blow the horns of war,
And fling the Golden Dragon out,
With crackle and acclaim and shout,
Scrolled and aflame and far.

And under the Golden Dragon
Went Wessex all along,
Past the sharp point of the cloven ways,
Out from the black wood into the blaze
Of sun and steel and song.

And when they came to the open land
  They wheeled, deployed, and stood;
Midmost were Marcus and the King,
And Eldred on the right-hand wing,
And leftwards Colan darkling,
  In the last shade of the wood.

But the Earls of the Great Army
  Lay like a long half moon,
Ten poles before their palisades,
With wide-winged helms and runic blades
Red giants of an age of raids,
  In the thornland of Ethandune.

Midmost the saddles rose and swayed,
  And a stir of horses' manes,
Where Guthrum and a few rode high
On horses seized in victory;
But Ogier went on foot to die,
  In the old way of the Danes.

Far to the King's left Elf the bard
  Led on the eastern wing
With songs and spells that change the blood;
And on the King's right Harold stood,
  The kinsman of the King.

Young Harold, coarse, with colours gay,
  Smoking with oil and musk,
And the pleasant violence of the young,
Pushed through his people, giving tongue
Foewards, where, grey as cobwebs hung,
  The banners of the Usk.

But as he came before his line
  A little space along,
His beardless face broke into mirth,
And he cried: "What broken bits of earth
Are here? For what their clothes are worth
  I would sell them for a song."

For Colan was hung with raiment
  Tattered like autumn leaves,
And his men were all as thin as saints,
  And all as poor as thieves.

No bows nor slings nor bolts they bore,
  But bills and pikes ill-made;
And none but Colan bore a sword,
  And rusty was its blade.

And Colan's eyes with mystery
  And iron laughter stirred,
And he spoke aloud, but lightly
  Not labouring to be heard.

"Oh, truly we be broken hearts,
  For that cause, it is said,
We light our candles to that Lord
  That broke Himself for bread.

"But though we hold but bitterly
  What land the Saxon leaves,
Though Ireland be but a land of saints,
  And Wales a land of thieves,

"I say you yet shall weary
  Of the working of your word,

That stricken spirits never strike
  Nor lean hands hold a sword.

"And if ever ye ride in Ireland,
  The jest may yet be said,
There is the land of broken hearts,
  And the land of broken heads."

Not less barbarian laughter
  Choked Harold like a flood,
"And shall I fight with scarecrows
  That am of Guthrum's blood?

"Meeting may be of war-men,
  Where the best war-man wins;
But all this carrion a man shoots
  Before the fight begins."

And stopping in his onward strides,
  He snatched a bow in scorn
From some mean slave, and bent it on
Colan, whose doom grew dark; and shone
Stars evil over Caerleon,
  In the place where he was born.

For Colan had not bow nor sling,
  On a lonely sword leaned he,
Like Arthur on Excalibur
  In the battle by the sea.

To his great gold ear-ring Harold
  Tugged back the feathered tail,
And swift had sprung the arrow,
  But swifter sprang the Gael.

Whirling the one sword round his head,
  A great wheel in the sun,
He sent it splendid through the sky,
Flying before the shaft could fly—
It smote Earl Harold over the eye,
  And blood began to run.

Colan stood bare and weaponless,
  Earl Harold, as in pain,
Strove for a smile, put hand to head,
Stumbled and suddenly fell dead;
And the small white daisies all waxed red
  With blood out of his brain.

And all at that marvel of the sword,
  Cast like a stone to slay,
Cried out. Said Alfred: "Who would see
Signs, must give all things. Verily
Man shall not taste of victory
  Till he throws his sword away."

Then Alfred, prince of England,
  And all the Christian earls,
Unhooked their swords and held them up,
Each offered to Colan, like a cup
  Of chrysolite and pearls.

And the King said, "Do thou take my sword
  Who have done this deed of fire,
For this is the manner of Christian men,
Whether of steel or priestly pen,
That they cast their hearts out of their ken
  To get their heart's desire.

"And whether ye swear a hive of monks,
　　Or one fair wife to friend,
This is the manner of Christian men,
　　That their oath endures the end.

"For love, our Lord, at the end of the world,
　　Sits a red horse like a throne,
With a brazen helm and an iron bow,
　　But one arrow alone.

"Love with the shield of the Broken Heart
　　Ever his bow doth bend,
With a single shaft for a single prize,
And the ultimate bolt that parts and flies
Comes with a thunder of split skies,
　　And a sound of souls that rend.

"So shall you earn a king's sword,
　　Who cast your sword away."
And the King took, with a random eye,
A rude axe from a hind hard by
　　And turned him to the fray.

For the swords of the Earls of Daneland
　　Flamed round the fallen lord.
The first blood woke the trumpet-tune,
As in monk's rhyme or wizard's rune,
Beginneth the battle of Ethandune
　　With the throwing of the sword.

BOOK VI

ETHANDUNE: THE SLAYING OF THE CHIEFS

As the sea flooding the flat sands
　　Flew on the sea-born horde,

The two hosts shocked with dust and din,
Left of the Latian paladin,
Clanged all Prince Harold's howling kin
  On Colan and the sword.

Crashed in the midst on Marcus,
  Ogier with Guthrum by,
And eastward of such central stir,
Far to the right and faintlier,
The house of Elf the harp-player,
  Struck Eldred's with a cry.

The centre swat for weariness,
  Stemming the screaming horde,
And wearily went Colan's hands
  That swung King Alfred's sword.

But like a cloud of morning
  To eastward easily,
Tall Eldred broke the sea of spears
  As a tall ship breaks the sea.

His face like a sanguine sunset,
  His shoulder a Wessex down,
His hand like a windy hammer-stroke;
Men could not count the crests he broke,
  So fast the crests went down.

As the tall white devil of the Plague
  Moves out of Asian skies,
With his foot on a waste of cities
  And his head in a cloud of flies;

Or purple and peacock skies grow dark
  With a moving locust-tower;

Or tawny sand-winds tall and dry,
Like hell's red banners beat and fly,
When death comes out of Araby,
  Was Eldred in his hour.

But while he moved like a massacre
  He murmured as in sleep,
And his words were all of low hedges
  And little fields and sheep.

Even as he strode like a pestilence,
  That strides from Rhine to Rome,
He thought how tall his beans might be
  If ever he went home.

Spoke some stiff piece of childish prayer,
  Dull as the distant chimes,
That thanked our God for good eating
  And corn and quiet times—

Till on the helm of a high chief
  Fell shatteringly his brand,
And the helm broke and the bone broke
  And the sword broke in his hand.

Then from the yelling Northmen
  Driven splintering on him ran
Full seven spears, and the seventh
  Was never made by man.

Seven spears, and the seventh
  Was wrought as the faerie blades,
And given to Elf the minstrel
  By the monstrous water-maids;

By them that dwell where luridly
  Lost waters of the Rhine
Move among roots of nations,
  Being sunken for a sign.

Under all graves they murmur,
  They murmur and rebel,
Down to the buried kingdoms creep,
And like a lost rain roar and weep
  O'er the red heavens of hell.

Thrice drowned was Elf the minstrel,
  And washed as dead on sand;
And the third time men found him
  The spear was in his hand.

Seven spears went about Eldred,
  Like stays about a mast;
But there was sorrow by the sea
  For the driving of the last.

Six spears thrust upon Eldred
  Were splintered while he laughed;
One spear thrust into Eldred,
  Three feet of blade and shaft.

And from the great heart grievously
  Came forth the shaft and blade,
And he stood with the face of a dead man,
  Stood a little, and swayed—

Then fell, as falls a battle-tower,
  On smashed and struggling spears.
Cast down from some unconquered town

That, rushing earthward, carries down
Loads of live men of all renown—
    Archers and engineers.

And a great clamour of Christian men
    Went up in agony,
Crying, "Fallen is the tower of Wessex
    That stood beside the sea."

Centre and right the Wessex guard
    Grew pale for doubt and fear,
And the flank failed at the advance,
For the death-light on the wizard lance—
    The star of the evil spear.

"Stand like an oak," cried Marcus,
    "Stand like a Roman wall!
Eldred the Good is fallen—
    Are you too good to fall?

"When we were wan and bloodless
    He gave you ale enow;
The pirates deal with him as dung,
    God! are you bloodless now?"

"Grip, Wulf and Gorlias, grip the ash!
    Slaves, and I make you free!
Stamp, Hildred, hard in English land,
Stand Gurth, stand Gorlias, Gawen stand!
Hold, Halfgar, with the other hand,
    Halmer, hold up on knee!

"The lamps are dying in your homes,
    The fruits upon your bough;

Even now your old thatch smoulders, Gurth,
Now is the judgment of the earth,
  Now is the death-grip, now!"

For thunder of the captain,
  Not less the Wessex line,
Leaned back and reeled a space to rear
As Elf charged with the Rhine maids' spear,
  And roaring like the Rhine.

For the men were borne by the waving walls
  Of woods and clouds that pass,
By dizzy plains and drifting sea,
And they mixed God with glamoury,
God with the gods of the burning tree
  And the wizard's tower and glass.

But Mark was come of the glittering towns
  Where hot white details show,
Where men can number and expound,
And his faith grew in a hard ground
Of doubt and reason and falsehood found,
  Where no faith else could grow.

Belief that grew of all beliefs
  One moment back was blown
And belief that stood on unbelief
  Stood up iron and alone.

The Wessex crescent backwards
  Crushed, as with bloody spear
Went Elf roaring and routing,
And Mark against Elf yet shouting,
  Shocked, in his mid-career.

Right on the Roman shield and sword
  Did spear of the Rhine maids run;
But the shield shifted never,
The sword rang down to sever,
The great Rhine sang for ever,
  And the songs of Elf were done.

And a great thunder of Christian men
  Went up against the sky,
Saying, "God hath broken the evil spear
  Ere the good man's blood was dry."

"Spears at the charge!" yelled Mark amain,
  "Death on the gods of death!
Over the thrones of doom and blood
Goeth God that is a craftsman good,
And gold and iron, earth and wood,
  Loveth and laboureth.

"The fruits leap up in all your farms,
  The lamps in each abode;
God of all good things done on earth,
All wheels or webs of any worth,
The God that makes the roof, Gurth,
  The God that makes the road.

"The God that heweth kings in oak
  Writeth songs on vellum,
God of gold and flaming glass,
Confregit potentias
Arcuum, scutum, Gorlias,
  Gladium et bellum."

Steel and lightning broke about him,
  Battle-bays and palm,

All the sea-kings swayed among
Woods of the Wessex arms upflung,
The trumpet of the Roman tongue,
  The thunder of the psalm.

And midmost of that rolling field
  Ran Ogier ragingly,
Lashing at Mark, who turned his blow,
And brake the helm about his brow,
  And broke him to his knee.

Then Ogier heaved over his head
  His huge round shield of proof;
But Mark set one foot on the shield,
One on some sundered rock upheeled,
And towered above the tossing field,
  A statue on a roof.

Dealing far blows about the fight,
  Like thunder-bolts a-roam,
Like birds about the battle-field,
While Ogier writhed under his shield
  Like a tortoise in his dome.

But hate in the buried Ogier
  Was strong as pain in hell,
With bare brute hand from the inside
He burst the shield of brass and hide,
And a death-stroke to the Roman's side
  Sent suddenly and well.

Then the great statue on the shield
  Looked his last look around
With level and imperial eye;

And Mark, the man from Italy,
Fell in the sea of agony,
   And died without a sound.

And Ogier, leaping up alive,
   Hurled his huge shield away
Flying, as when a juggler flings
   A whizzing plate in play.

And held two arms up rigidly,
   And roared to all the Danes:
"Fallen is Rome, yea, fallen
   The city of the plains!

"Shall no man born remember,
   That breaketh wood or weald,
How long she stood on the roof of the world
   As he stood on my shield.

"The new wild world forgetteth her
   As foam fades on the sea,
How long she stood with her foot on Man
   As he with his foot on me.

"No more shall the brown men of the south
   Move like the ants in lines,
To quiet men with olives
   Or madden men with vines.

"No more shall the white towns of the south,
   Where Tiber and Nilus run,
Sitting around a secret sea
   Worship a secret sun.

"The blind gods roar for Rome fallen,
  And forum and garland gone,
For the ice of the north is broken,
  And the sea of the north comes on.

"The blind gods roar and rave and dream
  Of all cities under the sea,
For the heart of the north is broken,
  And the blood of the north is free.

"Down from the dome of the world we come,
  Rivers on rivers down,
Under us swirl the sects and hordes
  And the high dooms we drown.

"Down from the dome of the world and down,
  Struck flying as a skiff
On a river in spate is spun and swirled
Until we come to the end of the world
  That breaks short, like a cliff.

"And when we come to the end of the world
  For me, I count it fit
To take the leap like a good river,
  Shot shrieking over it.

"But whatso hap at the end of the world,
  Where Nothing is struck and sounds,
It is not, by Thor, these monkish men
  These humbled Wessex hounds—

"Not this pale line of Christian hinds,
  This one white string of men,
Shall keep us back from the end of the world,
  And the things that happen then.

"It is not Alfred's dwarfish sword,
  Nor Egbert's pigmy crown,
Shall stay us now that descend in thunder,
Rending the realms and the realms thereunder,
  Down through the world and down."

There was that in the wild men back of him,
  There was that in his own wild song,
A dizzy throbbing, a drunkard smoke,
That dazed to death all Wessex folk,
  And swept their spears along.

Vainly the sword of Colan
  And the axe of Alfred plied—
The Danes poured in like a brainless plague,
  And knew not when they died.

Prince Colan slew a score of them,
  And was stricken to his knee;
King Alfred slew a score and seven
  And was borne back on a tree.

Back to the black gate of the woods,
  Back up the single way,
Back by the place of the parting ways
  Christ's knights were whirled away.

And when they came to the parting ways
  Doom's heaviest hammer fell,
For the King was beaten, blind, at bay,
Down the right lane with his array,
But Colan swept the other way,
  Where he smote great strokes and fell.

The thornwoods over Ethandune
　Stand sharp and thick as spears,
By night and furze and forest-harms
Far sundered were the friends in arms;
The loud lost blows, the last alarms,
　Came not to Alfred's ears.

The thornwoods over Ethandune
　Stand stiff as spikes in mail;
As to the Haut King came at morn
Dead Roland on a doubtful horn,
Seemed unto Alfred lightly borne
　The last cry of the Gael.

BOOK VII

ETHANDUNE: THE LAST CHARGE

Away in the waste of White Horse Down
　An idle child alone
Played some small game through hours that pass,
And patiently would pluck the grass,
　Patiently push the stone.

On the lean, green edge for ever,
　Where the blank chalk touched the turf,
The child played on, alone, divine,
As a child plays on the last line
　That sunders sand and surf.

For he dwelleth in high divisions
　Too simple to understand,
Seeing on what morn of mystery
The Uncreated rent the sea
　With roarings, from the land.

Through the long infant hours like days
  He built one tower in vain—
Piled up small stones to make a town,
And evermore the stones fell down,
  And he piled them up again.

And crimson kings on battle-towers,
  And saints on Gothic spires,
And hermits on their peaks of snow,
  And heroes on their pyres, '

And patriots riding royally,
  That rush the rocking town,
Stretch hands, and hunger and aspire,
Seeking to mount where high and higher,
The child whom Time can never tire,
  Sings over White Horse Down.

And this was the might of Alfred,
  At the ending of the way;
That of such smiters, wise or wild,
He was least distant from the child,
  Piling the stones all day.

For Eldred fought like a frank hunter
  That killeth and goeth home;
And Mark had fought because all arms
  Rang like the name of Rome.

And Colan fought with a double mind,
  Moody and madly gay;
But Alfred fought as gravely
  As a good child at play.

He saw wheels break and work run back
  And all things as they were;
And his heart was orbed like victory
  And simple like despair.

Therefore is Mark forgotten,
  That was wise with his tongue and brave;
And the cairn over Colan crumbled,
  And the cross on Eldred's grave.

Their great souls went on a wind away,
  And they have not tale or tomb;
And Alfred born in Wantage
  Rules England till the doom.

Because in the forest of all fears
  Like a strange fresh gust from sea,
Struck him that ancient innocence
  That is more than mastery.

And as a child whose bricks fall down
  Re-piles them o'er and o'er,
Came ruin and the rain that burns,
Returning as a wheel returns,
And crouching in the furze and ferns
  He began his life once more.

He took his ivory horn unslung
  And smiled, but not in scorn:
"Endeth the Battle of Ethandune
  With the blowing of a horn."

On a dark horse at the double way
  He saw great Guthrum ride,

Heard roar of brass and ring of steel,
The laughter and the trumpet peal,
    The pagan in his pride.

And Ogier's red and hated head
    Moved in some talk or task;
But the men seemed scattered in the brier,
And some of them had lit a fire,
    And one had broached a cask.

And waggons one or two stood up,
    Like tall ships in sight,
As if an outpost were encamped
    At the cloven ways for night.

And joyous of the sudden stay
    Of Alfred's routed few,
Sat one upon a stone to sigh,
And some slipped up the road to fly,
Till Alfred in the fern hard by
    Set horn to mouth and blew.

And they all abode like statues—
    One sitting on the stone,
One half-way through the thorn hedge tall,
One with a leg across a wall,
And one looked backwards, very small,
    Far up the road, alone.

Grey twilight and a yellow star
    Hung over thorn and hill;
Two spears and a cloven war-shield lay
Loose on the road as cast away,
The horn died faint in the forest grey,
    And the fleeing men stood still.

"Brothers at arms," said Alfred,
   "On this side lies the foe;
Are slavery and starvation flowers,
   That you should pluck them so?

"For whether is it better
   To be prodded with Danish poles,
Having hewn a chamber in a ditch,
And hounded like a howling witch,
   Or smoked to death in holes?

"Or that before the red cock crow
   All we, a thousand strong,
Go down the dark road to God's house,
   Singing a Wessex song?

"To sweat a slave to a race of slaves,
   To drink up infamy?
No, brothers, by your leave, I think
Death is a better ale to drink,
And by all the stars of Christ that sink,
   The Danes shall drink with me.

"To grow old cowed in a conquered land,
   With the sun itself discrowned,
To see trees crouch and cattle slink—
Death is a better ale to drink,
And by high Death on the fell brink,
   That flagon shall go round.

"Though dead are all the paladins
   Whom glory had in ken,
Though all your thunder-sworded thanes
With proud hearts died among the Danes,

While a man remains, great war remains:
  Now is a war of men.

"The men that tear the furrows,
  The men that fell the trees,
When all their lords be lost and dead
The bondsmen of the earth shall tread
  The tyrants of the seas.

"The wheel of the roaring stillness
  Of all labours under the sun,
Speed the wild work as well at least
  As the whole world's work is done.

"Let Hildred hack the shield-wall
  Clean as he hacks the hedge;
Let Gurth the fowler stand as cool
  As he stands on the chasm's edge;

"Let Gorlias ride the sea-kings
  As Gorlias rides the sea,
Then let all hell and Denmark drive,
Yelling to all its fiends alive,
  And not a rag care we."

When Alfred's word was ended
  Stood firm that feeble line,
Each in his place with club or spear,
And fury deeper than deep fear,
  And smiles as sour as brine.

And the King held up the horn and said,
  "See ye my father's horn,
That Egbert blew in his empery,

Once, when he rode out commonly,
Twice when he rode for venery,
  And thrice on the battle-morn.

"But heavier fates have fallen
  The horn of the Wessex kings,
And I blew once, the riding sign,
To call you to the fighting line
  And glory and all good things.

"And now two blasts, the hunting sign,
  Because we turn to bay;
But I will not blow the three blasts,
  Till we be lost or they.

"And now I blow the hunting sign,
  Charge some, by rule and rod;
But when I blow the battle sign,
  Charge all and go to God."

Wild stared the Danes at the double ways
  Where they loitered, all at large,
As that dark line for the last time
  Doubled the knee to charge—

And caught their weapons clumsily,
  And marvelled how and why—
In such degree, by rule and rod,
The people of the peace of God
  Went roaring down to die.

And when the last arrow
  Was fitted and was flown,
When the broken shield hung on the breast,

And the hopeless lance was laid in rest,
  And the hopeless horn blown,

The King looked up, and what he saw
  Was a great light like death,
For Our Lady stood on the standards rent,
As lonely and as innocent
As when between white walls she went
  And the lilies of Nazareth.

One instant in a still light
  He saw Our Lady then,
Her dress was soft as western sky,
And she was a queen most womanly—
  But she was a queen of men.

Over the iron forest
  He saw Our Lady stand,
Her eyes were sad withouten art,
And seven swords were in her heart—
  But one was in her hand.

Then the last charge went blindly,
  And all too lost for fear:
The Danes closed round, a roaring ring,
And twenty clubs rose o'er the King,
Four Danes hewed at him, halloing,
And Ogier of the Stone and Sling
  Drove at him with a spear.

But the Danes were wild with laughter,
  And the great spear swung wide,
The point stuck to a straggling tree,
And either host cried suddenly,
  As Alfred leapt aside.

Short time had shaggy Ogier
  To pull his lance in line—
He knew King Alfred's axe on high,
  He heard it rushing through the sky,

He cowered beneath it with a cry—
  It split him to the spine:
And Alfred sprang over him dead,
  And blew the battle sign.

Then bursting all and blasting
  Came Christendom like death,
Kicked of such catapults of will,
The staves shiver, the barrels spill,
The waggons waver and crash and kill
  The waggoners beneath.

Barriers go backwards, banners rend,
  Great shields groan like a gong—
Horses like horns of nightmare
  Neigh horribly and long.

Horses ramp high and rock and boil
  And break their golden reins,
And slide on carnage clamorously,
Down where the bitter blood doth lie,
Where Ogier went on foot to die,
  In the old way of the Danes.

"The high tide!" King Alfred cried.
  "The high tide and the turn!
As a tide turns on the tall grey seas,
See how they waver in the trees,
How stray their spears, how knock their knees,
  How wild their watchfires burn!

"The Mother of God goes over them,
  Walking on wind and flame,
And the storm-cloud drifts from city and dale,
And the White Horse stamps in the White Horse Vale,
And we all shall yet drink Christian ale
  In the village of our name.

"The Mother of God goes over them,
  On dreadful cherubs borne;
And the psalm is roaring above the rune,
And the Cross goes over the sun and moon,
Endeth the battle of Ethandune
  With the blowing of a horn."

For back indeed disorderly
  The Danes went clamouring,
Too worn to take anew the tale,
Or dazed with insolence and ale,
Or stunned of heaven, or stricken pale
  Before the face of the King.

For dire was Alfred in his hour
  The pale scribe witnesseth,
More mighty in defeat was he
Then all men else in victory,
And behind, his men came murderously,
  Dry-throated, drinking death.

And Edgar of the Golden Ship
  He slew with his own hand,
Took Ludwig from his lady's bower,
And smote down Harmar in his hour,
And vain and lonely stood the tower—
  The tower in Guelderland.

And Torr out of his tiny boat,
　Whose eyes beheld the Nile,
Wulf with his war-cry on his lips,
And Harco born in the eclipse,
Who blocked the Seine with battleships
　Round Paris on the Isle.

And Hacon of the Harvest-Song,
　And Dirck from the Elbe he slew,
And Cnut that melted Durham bell
And Fulk and fiery Oscar fell,
And Goderic and Sigael,
　And Uriel of the Yew.

And highest sang the slaughter,
　And fastest fell the slain,
When from the wood-road's blackening throat
A crowning and crashing wonder smote
　The rear-guard of the Dane.

For the dregs of Colan's company—
　Lost down the other road—
Had gathered and grown and heard the din,
And with wild yells came pouring in,
Naked as their old British kin,
　And bright with blood for woad.

And bare and bloody and aloft
　They bore before their band
The body of their mighty lord,
Colan of Caerleon and its horde,
That bore King Alfred's battle-sword
　Broken in his left hand.

And a strange music went with him,
  Loud and yet strangely far;
The wild pipes of the western land,
Too keen for the ear to understand,
Sang high and deathly on each hand
  When the dead man went to war.

Blocked between ghost and buccaneer,
  Brave men have dropped and died;
And the wild sea-lords well might quail
As the ghastly war-pipes of the Gael
Called to the horns of White Horse Vale,
And all the horns replied.

And Hildred the poor hedger
  Cut down four captains dead,
And Halmar laid three others low,
And the great earls wavered to and fro
  For the living and the dead.

And Gorlias grasped the great flag,
  The Raven of Odin, torn;
And the eyes of Guthrum altered,
  For the first time since morn.

As a turn of the wheel of tempest
  Tilts up the whole sky tall,
And cliffs of wan cloud luminous
Lean out like great walls over us,
  As if the heavens might fall.

As such a tall and tilted sky
  Sends certain snow or light,
So did the eyes of Guthrum change,

And the turn was more certain and more strange
   Than a thousand men in flight.

For not till the floor of the skies is split,
   And hell-fire shines through the sea,
Or the stars look up through the rent earth's knees,
Cometh such rending of certainties,
As when one wise man truly sees
   What is more wise than he.

He set his horse in the battle-breech
   Even Guthrum of the Dane,
And as ever had fallen fell his brand,
A falling tower o'er many a land,
But Gurth the fowler laid one hand
   Upon this bridle rein.

King Guthrum was a great lord,
   And higher than his gods—
He put the popes to laughter,
   He chid the saints with rods,

He took this hollow world of ours
   For a cup to hold his wine;
In the parting of the woodways
   There came to him a sign.

In Wessex in the forest,
   In the breaking of the spears,
We set a sign on Guthrum
   To blaze a thousand years.

Where the high saddles jostle
   And the horse-tails toss,

There rose to the birds flying
A roar of dead and dying;
In deafness and strong crying
    We signed him with the cross.

Far out to the winding river
    The blood ran down for days,
When we put the cross on Guthrum
    In the parting of the ways.

BOOK VIII

THE SCOURING OF THE HORSE

In the years of the peace of Wessex,
    When the good King sat at home;
Years following on that bloody boon
When she that stands above the moon
Stood above death at Ethandune
    And saw his kingdom come—

When the pagan people of the sea
    Fled to their palisades,
Nailed there with javelins to cling
And wonder smote the pirate king,
And brought him to his christening
    And the end of all his raids.

(For not till the night's blue slate is wiped
    Of its last star utterly,
And fierce new signs writ there to read,
Shall eyes with such amazement heed,
As when a great man knows indeed
    A greater thing than he.)

And there came to his chrism-loosing
  Lords of all lands afar,
And a line was drawn north-westerly
That set King Egbert's empire free,
Giving all lands by the northern sea
  To the sons of the northern star.

In the days of the rest of Alfred,
  When all these things were done,
And Wessex lay in a patch of peace,
  Like a dog in a patch of sun—

The King sat in his orchard,
  Among apples green and red,
With the little book in his bosom
  And the sunshine on his head.

And he gathered the songs of simple men
  That swing with helm and hod,
And the alms he gave as a Christian
Like a river alive with fishes ran;
And he made gifts to a beggar man
  As to a wandering god.

And he gat good laws of the ancient kings,
  Like treasure out of the tombs;
And many a thief in thorny nook,
Or noble in sea-stained turret shook,
For the opening of his iron book,
  And the gathering of the dooms.

Then men would come from the ends of the earth,
  Whom the King sat welcoming,

And men would go to the ends of the earth
   Because of the word of the King.

For folk came in to Alfred's face
   Whose javelins had been hurled
On monsters that make boil the sea,
Crakens and coils of mystery.
Or thrust in ancient snows that be
   The white hair of the world.

And some had knocked at the northern gates
   Of the ultimate icy floor,
Where the fish freeze and the foam turns black,
And the wide world narrows to a track,
And the other sea at the world's back
   Cries through a closed door.

And men went forth from Alfred's face,
   Even great gift-bearing lords,
Not to Rome only, but more bold,
Out to the high hot courts of old,
Of negroes clad in cloth of gold,
   Silence, and crooked swords,

Scrawled screens and secret gardens
   And insect-laden skies—
Where fiery plains stretch on and on
To the purple country of Prester John
   And the walls of Paradise.

And he knew the might of the Terre Majeure,
   Where kings began to reign;
Where in a night-rout, without name,
Of gloomy Goths and Gauls there came

White, above candles all aflame,
  Like a vision, Charlemagne.

And men, seeing such embassies,
  Spake with the King and said:
"The steel that sang so sweet a tune
On Ashdown and on Ethandune,
Why hangs it scabbarded so soon,
  All heavily like lead?

"Why dwell the Danes in North England,
  And up to the river ride?
Three more such marches like thine own
Would end them; and the Pict should own
Our sway; and our feet climb the throne
  In the mountains of Strathclyde."

And Alfred in the orchard,
  Among apples green and red,
With the little book in his bosom,
  Looked at green leaves and said:

"When all philosophies shall fail,
  This word alone shall fit;
That a sage feels too small for life,
  And a fool too large for it.

"Asia and all imperial plains
  Are too little for a fool;
But for one man whose eyes can see
The little island of Athelney
  Is too large a land to rule.

"Haply it had been better
  When I built my fortress there,

Out in the reedy waters wide,
I had stood on my mud wall and cried:
'Take England all, from tide to tide—
 Be Athelney my share.'

"Those madmen of the throne-scramble—
 Oppressors and oppressed—
Had lined the banks by Athelney,
And waved and wailed unceasingly,
Where the river turned to the broad sea,
 By an island of the blest.

"An island like a little book
 Full of a hundred tales,
Like the gilt page the good monks pen,
That is all smaller than a wren,
Yet hath high towns, meteors, and men,
 And suns and spouting whales;

"A land having a light on it
 In the river dark and fast,
An isle with utter clearness lit,
Because a saint had stood in it;
Where flowers are flowers indeed and fit,
 And trees are trees at last.

"So were the island of a saint;
 But I am a common king,
And I will make my fences tough
From Wantage Town to Plymouth Bluff,
Because I am not wise enough
 To rule so small a thing."

And it fell in the days of Alfred,
 In the days of his repose,

That as old customs in his sight
Were a straight road and a steady light,
He bade them keep the White Horse white
  As the first plume of the snows.

And right to the red torchlight,
  From the trouble of morning grey,
They stripped the White Horse of the grass
  As they strip it to this day.

And under the red torchlight
  He went dreaming as though dull,
Of his old companions slain like kings,
And the rich irrevocable things
Of a heart that hath not openings,
  But is shut fast, being full.

And the torchlight touched the pale hair
  Where silver clouded gold,
And the frame of his face was made of cords,
And a young lord turned among the lords
  And said: "The King is old."

And even as he said it
  A post ran in amain,
Crying: "Arm, Lord King, the hamlets arm,
In the horror and the shade of harm,
They have burnt Brand of Aynger's farm—
  The Danes are come again!

"Danes drive the white East Angles
  In six fights on the plains,
Danes waste the world about the Thames,
  Danes to the eastward—Danes!"

And as he stumbled on one knee,
　The thanes broke out in ire,
Crying: "Ill the watchmen watch, and ill
　The sheriffs keep the shire."

But the young earl said: "Ill the saints,
　The saints of England, guard
The land wherein we pledge them gold;
The dykes decay, the King grows old,
　And surely this is hard.

"That we be never quit of them;
　That when his head is hoar
He cannot say to them he smote,
And spared with a hand hard at the throat,
　'Go, and return no more.'"

Then Alfred smiled. And the smile of him
　Was like the sun for power.
But he only pointed: bade them heed
Those peasants of the Berkshire breed,
Who plucked the old Horse of the weed
　As they pluck it to this hour.

"Will ye part with the weeds for ever?
　Or show daisies to the door?
Or will you bid the bold grass
　Go, and return no more?

"So ceaseless and so secret
　Thrive terror and theft set free;
Treason and shame shall come to pass
While one weed flowers in a morass;

And like the stillness of stiff grass
  The stillness of tyranny.

"Over our white souls also
  Wild heresies and high
Wave prouder than the plumes of grass,
  And sadder than their sigh.

"And I go riding against the raid,
  And ye know not where I am;
But ye shall know in a day or year,
When one green star of grass grows here;
Chaos has charged you, charger and spear,
  Battle-axe and battering-ram.

"And though skies alter and empires melt,
  This word shall still be true:
If we would have the horse of old,
  Scour ye the horse anew.

"One time I followed a dancing star
  That seemed to sing and nod,
And ring upon earth all evil's knell;
But now I wot if ye scour not well
Red rust shall grow on God's great bell
  And grass in the streets of God."

Ceased Alfred; and above his head
  The grand green domes, the Downs,
Showed the first legions of the press,
Marching in haste and bitterness
  For Christ's sake and the crown's.

Beyond the cavern of Colan,
  Past Eldred's by the sea,

Rose men that owned King Alfred's rod,
From the windy wastes of Exe untrod,
Or where the thorn of the grave of God
   Burns over Glastonbury.

Far northward and far westward
   The distant tribes drew nigh,
Plains beyond plains, fell beyond fell,
That a man at sunset sees so well,
And the tiny coloured towns that dwell
   In the corners of the sky.

But dark and thick as thronged the host,
   With drum and torch and blade,
The still-eyed King sat pondering,
As one that watches a live thing,
   The scoured chalk; and he said,

"Though I give this land to Our Lady,
   That helped me in Athelney,
Though lordlier trees and lustier sod
And happier hills hath no flesh trod
Than the garden of the Mother of God
   Between Thames side and the sea,

"I know that weeds shall grow in it
   Faster than men can burn;
And though they scatter now and go,
In some far century, sad and slow,
I have a vision, and I know
   The heathen shall return.

"They shall not come with warships,
   They shall not waste with brands,

But books be all their eating,
And ink be on their hands.

"Not with the humour of hunters
Or savage skill in war,
But ordering all things with dead words,
Strings shall they make of beasts and birds,
And wheels of wind and star.

"They shall come mild as monkish clerks,
With many a scroll and pen;
And backward shall ye turn and gaze,
Desiring one of Alfred's days,
When pagans still were men.

"The dear sun dwarfed of dreadful suns,
Like fiercer flowers on stalk,
Earth lost and little like a pea
In high heaven's towering forestry,
—These be the small weeds ye shall see
Crawl, covering the chalk.

"But though they bridge St. Mary's sea,
Or steal St. Michael's wing—
Though they rear marvels over us,
Greater than great Vergilius
Wrought for the Roman king;

"By this sign you shall know them,
The breaking of the sword,
And man no more a free knight,
That loves or hates his lord.

"Yea, this shall be the sign of them,
The sign of the dying fire;

And Man made like a half-wit,
   That knows not of his sire.

"What though they come with scroll and pen,
   And grave as a shaven clerk,
By this sign you shall know them,
   That they ruin and make dark;

"By all men bond to Nothing,
   Being slaves without a lord,
By one blind idiot world obeyed,
   Too blind to be abhorred;

"By terror and the cruel tales
   Of curse in bone and kin,
By weird and weakness winning,
Accursed from the beginning,
By detail of the sinning,
   And denial of the sin;

"By thought a crawling ruin,
   By life a leaping mire,
By a broken heart in the breast of the world,
   And the end of the world's desire;

"By God and man dishonoured,
   By death and life made vain,
Know ye the old barbarian,
   The barbarian come again—

"When is great talk of trend and tide,
   And wisdom and destiny,
Hail that undying heathen
   That is sadder than the sea.

"In what wise men shall smite him,
　Or the Cross stand up again,
Or charity or chivalry,
My vision saith not; and I see
No more; but now ride doubtfully
　To the battle of the plain."

And the grass-edge of the great down
　Was cut clean as a lawn,
While the levies thronged from near and far,
From the warm woods of the western star,
And the King went out to his last war
　On a tall grey horse at dawn.

And news of his far-off fighting
　Came slowly and brokenly
From the land of the East Saxons,
　From the sunrise and the sea.

From the plains of the white sunrise,
　And sad St. Edmund's crown,
Where the pools of Essex pale and gleam
　Out beyond London Town—

In mighty and doubtful fragments,
　Like faint or fabled wars,
Climbed the old hills of his renown,
Where the bald brow of White Horse Down
　Is close to the cold stars.

But away in the eastern places
　The wind of death walked high,
And a raid was driven athwart the raid,
The sky reddened and the smoke swayed,
　And the tall grey horse went by.

The gates of the great river
  Were breached as with a barge,
The walls sank crowded, say the scribes,
And high towers populous with tribes
  Seemed leaning from the charge.

Smoke like rebellious heavens rolled
  Curled over coloured flames,
Mirrored in monstrous purple dreams
  In the mighty pools of Thames.

Loud was the war on London wall,
  And loud in London gates,
And loud the sea-kings in the cloud
Broke through their dreaming gods, and loud
  Cried on their dreadful Fates.

And all the while on White Horse Hill
  The horse lay long and wan,
The turf crawled and the fungus crept,
And the little sorrel, while all men slept,
  Unwrought the work of man.

With velvet finger, velvet foot,
  The fierce soft mosses then
Crept on the large white commonweal
All folk had striven to strip and peel,
And the grass, like a great green witch's wheel,
  Unwound the toils of men.

And clover and silent thistle throve,
  And buds burst silently,
With little care for the Thames Valley
  Or what things there might be—

That away on the widening river,
  In the eastern plains for crown
Stood up in the pale purple sky
One turret of smoke like ivory;
And the smoke changed and the wind went by,
  And the King took London Town.

Book Six
The Wild Knight

Note to second edition of The Wild Knight:

I leave these verses as they stand, although they contain innumerable examples of what I now see to be errors of literature, and one or two examples of what I have come to think errors of opinion. But they never had any great merit beyond genuineness, and I do not wish to spoil that by mixing up two periods of my life. It will be seen that the philosophy is not wholly that of my later years, though perhaps a foundation for it. On two special points embodied in verse I have altered my opinion; and if I mention what they are I really do not mean it for egoism, but only for honesty.

In the matter of the "Anglo-American Alliance," [1] I have come to see that our hopes of brotherhood with America are the same in kind as our hopes of brotherhood with any other of the great independent nations of Christendom. And a very small study of history was sufficient to show me that the American nation, which is a hundred years old, is at least fifty years older than the Anglo-Saxon race.

And in the matter of the Dreyfus [2] case, while not having been able to reach any final conclusion about the proper verdict on the individual, I have come largely to attribute the difficulty of doing so to the acrid and irrational unanimity of the English press. My position may be roughly stated thus: There may have been a fog of injustice in the French courts; I know that there was a fog of injustice in the English newspapers. For the rest, there are verses which I cannot take so seriously as to alter them. The man who wrote them was honest; and he had the same basic views as myself. Besides, nobody need read the book: I certainly beg to be excused.

G. K. C.

Battersea. 1905.

[1] An Alliance.
[2] To A Certain Nation.

BY THE BABE UNBORN

If trees were tall and grasses short,
    As in some crazy tale,
If here and there a sea were blue
    Beyond the breaking pale,

If a fixed fire hung in the air
    To warm me one day through,
If deep green hair grew on great hills,
    I know what I should do.

In dark I lie: dreaming that there
    Are great eyes cold or kind,
And twisted streets and silent doors,
    And living men behind.

Let storm-clouds come: better an hour,
    And leave to weep and fight,
Than all the ages I have ruled
    The empires of the night.

I think that if they gave me leave
    Within the world to stand,
I would be good through all the day
    I spent in fairyland.

They should not hear a word from me
    Of selfishness or scorn,
If only I could find the door,
    If only I were born.

THE WORLD'S LOVER

My eyes are full of lonely mirth:
 Reeling with want and worn with scars,
For pride of every stone on earth,
 I shake my spear at all the stars.

A live bat beats my crest above,
 Lean foxes nose where I have trod,
And on my naked face the love
 Which is the loneliness of God.

Outlawed: since that great day gone by—
 When before prince and pope and queen
I stood and spoke a blasphemy—
 'Behold the summer leaves are green.'

They cursed me: what was that to me
 Who in that summer darkness furled,
With but an owl and snail to see,
 Had blessed and conquered all the world?

They bound me to the scourging-stake,
 They laid their whips of thorn on me;
I wept to see the green rods break,
 Though blood be beautiful to see.

Beneath the gallows' foot abhorred
 The crowds cry 'Crucify!' and 'Kill!'
Higher the priests sing, 'Praise the Lord,
 The warlock dies'; and higher still

Shall heaven and earth hear one cry sent
 Even from the hideous gibbet height,

'Praise to the Lord Omnipotent,
  The vultures have a feast to-night.'

THE SKELETON

Chattering finch and water-fly
Are not merrier than I;
Here among the flowers I lie
Laughing everlastingly.
No: I may not tell the best;
Surely, friends, I might have guessed
Death was but the good King's jest,
  It was hid so carefully.

A CHORD OF COLOUR

My Lady clad herself in grey,
  That caught and clung about her throat;
Then all the long grey winter day
  On me a living splendour smote;
And why grey palmers holy are,
  And why grey minsters great in story,
And grey skies ring the morning star,
  And grey hairs are a crown of glory.

My Lady clad herself in green,
  Like meadows where the wind-waves pass;
Then round my spirit spread, I ween,
  A splendour of forgotten grass.
Then all that dropped of stem or sod,
  Hoarded as emeralds might be,
I bowed to every bush, and trod
  Amid the live grass fearfully.

My Lady clad herself in blue,
  Then on me, like the seer long gone,
The likeness of a sapphire grew,
  The throne of him that sat thereon.
Then knew I why the Fashioner
  Splashed reckless blue on sky and sea;
And ere 'twas good enough for her,
  He tried it on Eternity.

Beneath the gnarled old Knowledge-tree
  Sat, like an owl, the evil sage:
'The World's a bubble,' solemnly
  He read, and turned a second page.
'A bubble, then, old crow,' I cried,
  'God keep you in your weary wit!
'A bubble—have you ever spied
  The colours I have seen on it?'

THE HAPPY MAN

To teach the grey earth like a child,
  To bid the heavens repent,
I only ask from Fate the gift
  Of one man well content.

Him will I find: though when in vain
  I search the feast and mart,
The fading flowers of liberty,
  The painted masks of art,

I only find him at the last,
  On one old hill where nod
Golgotha's ghastly trinity—
  Three persons and one god.

THE UNPARDONABLE SIN

I do not cry, beloved, neither curse.
   Silence and strength, these two at least are good.
   He gave me sun and stars and aught He could,
But not a woman's love; for that is hers.

He sealed her heart from sage and questioner—
   Yea, with seven seals, as he has sealed the grave.
   And if she give it to a drunken slave,
The Day of Judgment shall not challenge her.

Only this much: if one, deserving well,
   Touching your thin young hands and making suit,
   Feel not himself a crawling thing, a brute,
Buried and bricked in a forgotten hell.

Prophet and poet be he over sod,
   Prince among angels in the highest place,
   God help me, I will smite him on the face,
Before the glory of the face of God.

A NOVELTY

Why should I care for the Ages
   Because they are old and grey?
To me, like sudden laughter,
   The stars are fresh and gay;
The world is a daring fancy,
   And finished yesterday.

Why should I bow to the Ages
   Because they were drear and dry?
Slow trees and ripening meadows
   For me go roaring by,

A living charge, a struggle
    To escalade the sky.

The eternal suns and systems,
    Solid and silent all,
To me are stars of an instant,
    Only the fires that fall
From God's good rocket, rising
    On this night of carnival.

ULTIMATE

The vision of a haloed host
    That weep around an empty throne;
And, aureoles dark and angels dead,
    Man with his own life stands alone.

'I am,' he says his bankrupt creed;
    'I am,' and is again a clod:
The sparrow starts, the grasses stir,
    For he has said the name of God.

THE DONKEY

When fishes flew and forests walked
    And figs grew upon thorn,
Some moment when the moon was blood
    Then surely I was born.

With monstrous head and sickening cry
    And ears like errant wings,
The devil's walking parody
    On all four-footed things.

The tattered outlaw of the earth,
  Of ancient crooked will;
Starve, scourge, deride me: I am dumb,
  I keep my secret still.

Fools! For I also had my hour;
  One far fierce hour and sweet:
There was a shout about my ears,
  And palms before my feet.

THE BEATIFIC VISION

Through what fierce incarnations, furled
  In fire and darkness, did I go,
Ere I was worthy in the world
  To see a dandelion grow?

Well, if in any woes or wars
  I bought my naked right to be,
Grew worthy of the grass, nor gave
  The wren, my brother, shame for me.

But what shall God not ask of him
  In the last time when all is told,
Who saw her stand beside the hearth,
  The firelight garbing her in gold?

THE HOPE OF THE STREETS

The still sweet meadows shimmered: and I stood
  And cursed them, bloom of hedge and bird of tree,
And bright and high beyond the hunch-backed wood
  The thunder and the splendour of the sea.

Give back the Babylon where I was born,
  The lips that gape give back, the hands that grope,
And noise and blood and suffocating scorn
  An eddy of fierce faces—and a hope

That 'mid those myriad heads one head find place,
  With brown hair curled like breakers of the sea,
And two eyes set so strangely in the face
  That all things else are nothing suddenly.

ECCLESIASTES

There is one sin: to call a green leaf grey,
  Whereat the sun in heaven shuddereth.
There is one blasphemy: for death to pray,
  For God alone knoweth the praise of death.

There is one creed: 'neath no world-terror's wing
  Apples forget to grow on apple-trees.
There is one thing is needful—everything—
  The rest is vanity of vanities.

THE SONG OF THE CHILDREN

The world is ours till sunset,
  Holly and fire and snow;
And the name of our dead brother
  Who loved us long ago.

The grown folk mighty and cunning,
  They write his name in gold;
But we can tell a little
  Of the million tales he told.

He taught them laws and watchwords,
　To preach and struggle and pray;
But he taught us deep in the hayfield
　The games that the angels play.

Had he stayed here for ever,
　Their world would be wise as ours—
And the king be cutting capers,
　And the priest be picking flowers.

But the dark day came: they gathered:
　On their faces we could see
They had taken and slain our brother,
　And hanged him on a tree.

THE FISH

Dark the sea was: but I saw him,
　One great head with goggle eyes,
Like a diabolic cherub
　Flying in those fallen skies.

I have heard the hoarse deniers,
　I have known the wordy wars;
I have seen a man, by shouting,
　Seek to orphan all the stars.

I have seen a fool half-fashioned
　Borrow from the heavens a tongue,
So to curse them more at leisure—
　—And I trod him not as dung.

For I saw that finny goblin
　Hidden in the abyss untrod;

And I knew there can be laughter
  On the secret face of God.

Blow the trumpets, crown the sages,
  Bring the age by reason fed!
('He that sitteth in the heavens,
  'He shall laugh'—the prophet said).

GOLD LEAVES

Lo! I am come to autumn,
  When all the leaves are gold;
Grey hairs and golden leaves cry out
  The year and I are old.

In youth I sought the prince of men,
  Captain in cosmic wars,
Our Titan, even the weeds would show
  Defiant, to the stars.

But now a great thing in the street
  Seems any human nod,
Where shift in strange democracy
  The million masks of God.

In youth I sought the golden flower
  Hidden in wood or wold,
But I am come to autumn,
  When all the leaves are gold.

THOU SHALT NOT KILL

I had grown weary of him; of his breath
And hands and features I was sick to death.

Each day I heard the same dull voice and tread;
I did not hate him: but I wished him dead.
And he must with his blank face fill my life—
Then my brain blackened, and I snatched a knife.

But ere I struck, my soul's grey deserts through
A voice cried, 'Know at least what thing you do.
'This is a common man: knowest thou, O soul,
'What this thing is? somewhere where seasons roll
'There is some living thing for whom this man
'Is as seven heavens girt into a span,
'For some one soul you take the world away—
'Now know you well your deed and purpose. Slay!'
Then I cast down the knife upon the ground
And saw that mean man for one moment crowned.
I turned and laughed: for there was no one by—
The man that I had sought to slay was I.

A CERTAIN EVENING

That night the whole world mingled,
    The souls were babes at play,
And angel danced with devil,
    And God cried, 'Holiday!'

The sea had climbed the mountain peaks
    And shouted to the stars
To come to play: and down they came
    Splashing in happy wars.

The pine grew apples for a whim,
    The cart-horse built a nest;
The oxen flew, the flowers sang,
    The sun rose in the west.

And 'neath the load of many worlds,
   The lowest life God made
Lifted his huge and heavy limbs
   And into heaven strayed.

To where the highest life God made
   Before His presence stands;
But God Himself cried, 'Holiday!'
   And she gave me both her hands.

A MAN AND HIS IMAGE

All day the nations climb and crawl and pray
   In one long pilgrimage to one white shrine,
Where sleeps a saint whose pardon, like his peace,
   Is wide as death, as common, as divine.

His statue in an aureole fills the shrine,
   The reckless nightingale, the roaming fawn,
Share the broad blessing of his lifted hands,
   Under the canopy, above the lawn.

But one strange night, a night of gale and flood,
   A sound came louder than the wild wind's tone;
The grave-gates shook and opened: and one stood
   Blue in the moonlight, rotten to the bone.

Then on the statue, graven with holy smiles,
   There came another smile—tremendous—one
Of an Egyptian god. 'Why should you rise?'
   Do I not guard your secret from the sun?

'The nations come; they kneel among the flowers
   Sprung from your blood, blossoms of May and June

Which do not poison them—is it not strange?
  Speak!' And the dead man shuddered in the moon.

'Shall I not cry the truth?'—the dead man cowered—
  'Is it not sad, with life so tame and cold,
That earth should fade into the sun's white fires
  With the best jest in all its tales untold?

'If I should cry that in this shrine lie hid
  Stories that Satan from his mouth would spew;
Wild tales that men in hell tell hoarsely—speak!
  Saint and Deliverer! Should I slander you?'

Slowly the cowering corse reared up its head,
  'Nay, I am vile . . . but when for all to see,
You stand there, pure and painless—death of life!
  Let the stars fall—I say you slander me!

'You make me perfect, public, colourless;
  You make my virtues sit at ease—you lie!
For mine were never easy—lost or saved,
  I had a soul—I was. And where am I?

'Where is my good? the little real hoard,
  The secret tears, the sudden chivalries;
The tragic love, the futile triumph—where?
  Thief, dog, and son of devils—where are these?

'I will lift up my head: in leprous loves
  Lost, and the soul's dishonourable scars—
By God, I was a better man than This
  That stands and slanders me to all the stars.

'Come down!' And with an awful cry, the corse
  Sprang on the sacred tomb of many tales,

And stone and bone, locked in a loathsome strife,
    Swayed to the singing of the nightingales.

Then one was thrown: and where the statue stood
    Under the canopy, above the lawn.
The corse stood; grey and lean, with lifted hands
    Raised in tremendous welcome to the dawn.

'Now let all nations climb and crawl and pray;
    Though I be basest of my old red clan,
They shall not scale, with cries or sacrifice,
    The stature of the spirit of a man.'

THE MARINER

The violet scent is sacred
    Like dreams of angels bright;
The hawthorn smells of passion
    Told in a moonless night.

But the smell is in my nostrils,
    Through blossoms red or gold,
Of my own green flower unfading,
    A bitter smell and bold.

The lily smells of pardon,
    The rose of mirth; but mine
Smells shrewd of death and honour,
    And the doom of Adam's line.

The heavy scent of wine-shops
    Floats as I pass them by,
But never a cup I quaff from,
    And never a house have I.

Till dropped down forty fathoms,
  I lie eternally;
And drink from God's own goblet
  The green wine of the sea.

THE TRIUMPH OF MAN

I plod and peer amid mean sounds and shapes,
  I hunt for dusty gain and dreary praise,
  And slowly pass the dismal grinning days,
Monkeying each other like a line of apes.

What care? There was one hour amid all these
  When I had stripped off like a tawdry glove
  My starriest hopes and wants, for very love
Of time and desolate eternities.

Yea, for one great hour's triumph, not in me
  Nor any hope of mine did I rejoice,
  But in a meadow game of girls and boys
Some sunset in the centuries to be.

CYCLOPEAN

A mountainous and mystic brute
No rein can curb, no arrow shoot,
Upon whose doomed deformèd back
I sweep the planets' scorching track.

Old is the elf, and wise, men say,
His hair grows green as ours grows grey;
He mocks the stars with myriad hands,
High as that swinging forest stands.

But though in pigmy wanderings dull
I scour the deserts of his skull,
I never find the face, eyes, teeth,
Lowering or laughing underneath.

I met my foe in an empty dell,
His face in the sun was naked hell.
I thought, 'One silent, bloody blow,
No priest would curse, no crowd would know.'

Then cowered: a daisy, half concealed,
Watched for the fame of that poor field;
And in that flower and suddenly
Earth opened its one eye on me.

JOSEPH

If the stars fell; night's nameless dreams
   Of bliss and blasphemy came true,
If skies were green and snow were gold,
   And you loved me as I love you;

O long light hands and curled brown hair,
   And eyes where sits a naked soul;
Dare I even then draw near and burn
   My fingers in the aureole?

Yes, in the one wise foolish hour
   God gives this strange strength to a man.
He can demand, though not deserve,
   Where ask he cannot, seize he can.

But once the blood's wild wedding o'er,
   Were not dread his, half dark desire,

To see the Christ-child in the cot,
   The Virgin Mary by the fire?

MODERN ELFLAND

I cut a staff in a churchyard copse,
   I clad myself in ragged things,
I set a feather in my cap
   That fell out of an angel's wings.

I filled my wallet with white stones,
   I·took three foxgloves in my hand,
I slung my shoes across my back,
   And so I went to fairyland.

But lo, within that ancient place
   Science had reared her iron crown,
And the great cloud of steam went up
   That telleth where she takes a town.

But cowled with smoke and starred with lamps,
   That strange land's light was still its own;
The word that witched the woods and hills
   Spoke in the iron and the stone.

Not Nature's hand had ever curved
   That mute unearthly porter's spine.
Like sleeping dragon's sudden eyes
   The signals leered along the line.

The chimneys thronging crooked or straight
   Were fingers signalling the sky;
The dog that strayed across the street
   Seemed four-legged by monstrosity.

'In vain,' I cried, 'though you too touch
  The new time's desecrating hand,
Through all the noises of a town
  I hear the heart of fairyland.'

I read the name above a door,
  Then through my spirit pealed and passed:
'This is the town of thine own home,
  And thou hast lookéd on it at last.'

ETERNITIES

I cannot count the pebbles in the brook.
  Well hath He spoken: 'Swear not by thy head,
  Thou knowest not the hairs,' though He, we read,
Writes that wild number in His own strange book.

I cannot count the sands or search the seas,
  Death cometh, and I leave so much untrod.
  Grant my immortal aureole, O my God,
And I will name the leaves upon the trees.

In heaven I shall stand on gold and glass,
  Still brooding earth's arithmetic to spell;
  Or see the fading of the fires of hell
Ere I have thanked my God for all the grass.

A CHRISTMAS CAROL

The Christ-child lay on Mary's lap,
  His hair was like a light.
(O weary, weary were the world,
  But here is all aright.)

The Christ-child lay on Mary's breast,
   His hair was like a star.
(O stern and cunning are the kings,
   But here the true hearts are.)

The Christ-child lay on Mary's heart,
   His hair was like a fire.
(O weary, weary is the world,
   But here the world's desire.)

The Christ-child stood at Mary's knee,
   His hair was like a crown,
And all the flowers looked up at Him,
   And all the stars looked down.

ALONE

Blessings there are of cradle and of clan,
   Blessings that fall of priests' and princes' hands;
   But never blessing full of lives and lands,
Broad as the blessing of a lonely man.

Though that old king fell from his primal throne,
   And ate among the cattle, yet this pride
   Had found him in the deepest grass, and cried
And 'Ecce Homo' with the trumpets blown.

And no mad tyrant, with almighty ban,
   Who in strong madness dreams himself divine,
   But hears through fumes of flattery and of wine
The thunder of this blessing name him man.

Let all earth rot past saints' and seraphs' plea,
   Yet shall a Voice cry through its last lost war,

'This is the world, this red wreck of a star,
That a man blessed beneath an alder-tree.'

KING'S CROSS STATION

This circled cosmos whereof man is god
  Has suns and stars of green and gold and red,
And cloudlands of great smoke, that range o'er range
  Far floating, hide its iron heavens o'erhead.

God! shall we ever honour what we are,
  And see one moment ere the age expire,
The vision of man shouting and erect,
  Whirled by the shrieking steeds of flood and fire?

Or must Fate act the same grey farce again,
  And wait, till one, amid Time's wrecks and scars,
Speaks to a ruin here, 'What poet-race
  Shot such cyclopean arches at the stars?'

THE HUMAN TREE

Many have Earth's lovers been
Tried in seas and wars, I ween;
Yet the mightiest have I seen
  Yea, the best saw I.
One that in a field alone
Stood up stiller than a stone
  Lest a moth should fly.

Birds had nested in his hair,
On his shoon were mosses rare,
Insect empires flourished there,
  Worms in ancient wars;

But his eyes burn like a glass,
Hearing a great sea of grass
   Roar towards the stars.

From them to the human tree
Rose a cry continually,
'Thou art still, our Father, we
   Fain would have thee nod.
Make the skies as blood below thee,
Though thou slay us, we shall know thee
   Answer us, O God!

'Show thine ancient fame and thunder,
Split the stillness once asunder,
Lest we whisper, lest we wonder
   Art thou there at all?'
But I saw him there alone,
Standing stiller than a stone
   Lest a moth should fall.

TO THEM THAT MOURN

(W. E. G. 1898)

Lift up your heads: in life, in death,
   God knoweth his head was high.
Quit we the coward's broken breath
   Who watched a strong man die.

If we must say, 'No more his peer
   Cometh; the flag is furled.'
Stand not too near him, lest he hear
   That slander on the world.

The good green earth he loved and trod
  Is still, with many a scar,
Writ in the chronicles of God,
  A giant-bearing star.

He fell: but Britain's banner swings
  Above his sunken crown.
Black death shall have his toll of kings
  Before that cross goes down.

Once more shall move with mighty things
  His house of ancient tale,
Where kings whose hands were kissed of kings
  Went in: and came out pale.

O young ones of a darker day,
  In art's wan colours clad,
Whose very love and hate are grey—
  Whose very sin is sad,

Pass on: one agony long-drawn
  Was merrier than your mirth,
When hand-in-hand came death and dawn,
  And spring was on the earth.

THE OUTLAW

Priest, is any song-bird stricken
  Is one leaf less on the tree?
Is this wine less red and royal
  That the hangman waits for me?

He upon your cross that hangeth,
  It is writ of priestly pen,

On the night they built His gibbet,
    Drank red wine among His men.

Quaff, like a brave man, as He did,
    Wine and death as heaven pours—
This is my fate: O ye rulers,
    O ye pontiffs, what is yours?

To wait trembling, lest yon loathly
    Gallows-shape whereon I die,
In strange temples yet unbuilded,
    Blaze upon an altar high.

BEHIND

I saw an old man like a child,
His blue eyes bright, his white hair wild,
Who turned for ever, and might not stop,
Round and round like an urchin's top.

'Fool,' I cried, 'while you spin round,
'Others grow wise, are praised, are crowned.'
Ever the same round road he trod,
'This is better: I seek for God.'

'We see the whole world, left and right,
'Yet at the blind back hides from sight
'The unseen Master that drives us forth
'To East and West, to South and North.

'Over my shoulder for eighty years
I have looked for the gleam of the sphere of spheres.'
'In all your turning, what have you found?'
'At least, I know why the world goes round.'

THE END OF FEAR

Though the whole heaven be one-eyed with the moon,
  Though the dead landscape seem a thing possessed,
  Yet I go singing through that land oppressed
As one that singeth through the flowers of June.

No more, with forest-fingers crawling free
  O'er dark flint wall that seems a wall of eyes,
  Shall evil break my soul with mysteries
Of some world-poison maddening bush and tree.

No more shall leering ghosts of pimp and king
  With bloody secrets veiled before me stand.
  Last night I held all evil in my hand
Closed; and behold it was a little thing.

I broke the infernal gates and looked on him
  Who fronts the strong creation with a curse;
  Even the gods of a lost universe,
Smiling above his hideous cherubim.

And pierced far down in his soul's crypt unriven
  The last black crooked sympathy and shame,
  And hailed him with that ringing rainbow name
Erased upon the oldest book in heaven.

Like emptied idiot masks, sin's loves and wars
  Stare at me now: for in the night I broke
  The bubble of a great world's jest, and woke
Laughing with laughter such as shakes the stars.

THE HOLY OF HOLIES

'Elder father, though thine eyes
Shine with hoary mysteries,
Canst thou tell me what in the heart
Of a cowslip blossom lies?

'Smaller than all lives that be,
Secret as the deepest sea,
Stands a little house of seeds,
Like an elfin's granary.

'Speller of the stones and weeds,
Skilled in Nature's crafts and creeds,
Tell me what is in the heart
Of the smallest of the seeds.'

'God Almighty, and with Him
Cherubim and Seraphim,
Filling all eternity—
Adonai Elohim.'

THE MIRROR OF MADMEN

I dreamed a dream of heaven, white as frost,
The splendid stillness of a living host;
Vast choirs of upturned faces, line o'er line.
Then my blood froze; for every face was mine.

Spirits with sunset plumage throng and pass,
Glassed darkly in the sea of gold and glass.
But still on every side, in every spot,
I saw a million selves, who saw me not.

I fled to quiet wastes, where on a stone,
Perchance, I found a saint, who sat alone;
I came behind: he turned with slow, sweet grace,
And faced me with my happy, hateful face.

I cowered like one that in a tower doth bide,
Shut in by mirrors upon every side;
Then I saw, islanded in skies alone
And silent, one that sat upon a throne.

His robe was bordered with rich rose and gold,
Green, purple, silver out of sunsets old;
But o'er his face a great cloud edged with fire,
Because it covereth a world's desire.

But as I gazed, a silent worshipper,
Methought the cloud began to faintly stir;
Then I fell flat, and screamed with grovelling head,
'If thou hast any lightning, strike me dead!

'But spare a brow where the clean sunlight fell,
The crown of a new sin that sickens hell.
Let me not look aloft and see mine own
Feature and form upon the Judgment-throne.'

Then my dream snapped: and with a heart that leapt
I saw across the tavern where I slept,
The sight of all my life most full of grace,
A gin-damned drunkard's wan half-witted face.

E. C. B.

Before the grass grew over me,
   I knew one good man through and through

And knew a soul and body joined
    Are stronger than the heavens are blue.

A wisdom worthy of thy joy,
    O great heart, read I as I ran;
Now, though men smite me on the face,
    I cannot curse the face of man.

I loved the man I saw yestreen
    Hanged with his babe's blood on his palms.
I loved the man I saw to-day
    Who knocked not when he came with alms.

Hush!—for thy sake I even faced
    The knowledge that is worse than hell;
And loved the man I saw but now
    Hanging head downwards in the well.

THE DESECRATERS

Witness all: that unrepenting,
    Feathers flying, music high,
I go down to death unshaken
    By your mean philosophy.

For your wages, take my body,
    That at least to you I leave;
Set the sulky plumes upon it,
    Bid the grinning mummers grieve.

Stand in silence, steep your raiment
    In the night that hath no star;
Don the mortal dress of devils,
    Blacker than their spirits are.

Since ye may not, of your mercy,
　Ere I lie on such a hearse,
Hurl me to the living jackals
　God hath built for sepulchres.

AN ALLIANCE

This is the weird of a world-old folk,
　That not till the last link breaks,
Not till the night is blackest,
　The blood of Hengist wakes.
When the sun is black in heaven,
　The moon as blood above,
And the earth is full of hatred,
　This people tells its love.

In change, eclipse, and peril,
　Under the whole world's scorn,
By blood and death and darkness
　The Saxon peace is sworn;
That all our fruit be gathered
　And all our race take hands,
And the sea be a Saxon river
　That runs through Saxon lands.

Lo! not in vain we bore him;
　Behold it! not in vain,
Four centuries' doom of torture
　Choked in the throat of Spain,
Ere priest or tyrant triumph—
　We know how well—we know—
Bone of that bone can whiten,
　Blood of that blood can flow.

Deep grows the hate of kindred,
  Its roots take hold on hell;
No peace or praise can heal it,
  But a stranger heals it well.
Seas shall be red as sunsets,
  And kings' bones float as foam,
And heaven be dark with vultures,
  The night our son comes home.

THE ANCIENT OF DAYS

A child sits in a sunny place,
  Too happy for a smile,
And plays through one long holiday
  With balls to roll and pile;
A painted wind-mill by his side,
  Runs like a merry tune,
But the sails are the four great winds of heaven,
  And the balls are the sun and moon.

A staring doll's-house shows to him
  Green floors and starry rafter,
And many-coloured graven dolls
  Live for his lonely laughter.
The dolls have crowns and aureoles,
  Helmets and horns and wings,
For they are the saints and seraphim,
  The prophets and the kings.

THE LAST MASQUERADE

A wan new garment of young green,
  Touched, as you turned your soft brown hair;
  And in me surged the strangest prayer
Ever in lover's heart hath been.

That I who saw your youth's bright page,
  A rainbow change from robe to robe,
  Might see you on this earthly globe,
Crowned with the silver crown of age.

Your dear hair powdered in strange guise,
  Your dear face touched with colours pale,
  And gazing through the mask and veil
The mirth of your immortal eyes.

THE EARTH'S SHAME

Name not his deed: in shuddering and in haste
  We dragged him darkly o'er the windy fell:
That night there was a gibbet in the waste,
  And a new sin in hell.

Be his deed hid from commonwealths and kings,
  By all men born be one true tale forgot;
But three things, braver than all earthly things,
  Faced him and feared him not.

Above his head and sunken secret face
  Nested the sparrow's young and dropped not dead.
From the red blood and slime of that lost place
  Grew daisies white, not red.

And from high heaven looking upon him,
  Slowly upon the face of God did come
A smile the cherubim and seraphim
  Hid all their faces from.

VANITY

A wan sky greener than the lawn,
  A wan lawn paler than the sky.

She gave a flower into my hand,
   And all the hours of eve went by.

Who knows what round the corner waits
   To smite? If shipwreck, snare, or slur
Shall leave me with a head to lift,
   Worthy of him that spoke with her.

A wan sky greener than the lawn,
   A wan lawn paler than the sky.
She gave a flower into my hand,
   And all the days of life went by.

Live ill or well, this thing is mine,
   From all I guard it, ill or well.
One tawdry, tattered, faded flower
   To show the jealous kings in hell.

THE LAMP POST

Laugh your best, O blazoned forests,
   Me you shall not shift or shame
With your beauty: here among you
   Man hath set his spear of flame.

Lamp to lamp we send the signal,
   For our lord goes forth to war;
Since a voice, ere stars were builded,
   Bade him colonise a star.

Laugh ye, cruel as the morning,
   Deck your heads with fruit and flower,
Though our souls be sick with pity,
   Yet our hands are hard with power.

We have read your evil stories,
  We have heard the tiny yell
Through the voiceless conflagration
  Of your green and shining hell.

And when men, with fires and shouting,
  Break your old tyrannic pales;
And where ruled a single spider
  Laugh and weep a million tales.

This shall be your best of boasting:
  That some poet, poor of spine,
Full and sated with our wisdom,
  Full and fiery with our wine,

Shall steal out and make a treaty
  With the grasses and the showers,
Rail against the grey town-mother,
  Fawn upon the scornful flowers;

Rest his head among the roses,
  Where a quiet song-bird sounds,
And no sword made sharp for traitors,
  Hack him into meat for hounds.

THE PESSIMIST

You that have snarled through the ages, take your answer and
  go—
I know your hoary question, the riddle that all men know.
You have weighed the stars in the balance, and grasped the
  skies in a span:
Take, if you must have answer, the word of a common man.

Deep in my life lies buried one love unhealed, unshriven,
One hunger still shall haunt me—yea, in the streets of heaven;
This is the burden, babbler, this is the curse shall cling,
This is the thing I bring you; this is the pleasant thing.

'Gainst you and all your sages, no joy of mine shall strive,
This one dead self shall shatter the men you call alive.
My grief I send to smite you, no pleasure, no belief,
Lord of the battered grievance, what do you know of grief?

I only know the praises to heaven that one man gave,
That he came on earth for an instant, to stand beside a grave,
The peace of a field of battle, where flowers are born of blood.
I only know one evil that makes the whole world good.

Beneath this single sorrow the globe of moon and sphere
Turns to a single jewel, so bright and brittle and dear
That I dread lest God should drop it, to be dashed into stars
    below.

.   .   .   .

You that have snarled through the ages, take your answer
    and go.

A FAIRY TALE

All things grew upwards, foul and fair:
The great trees fought and beat the air
With monstrous wings that would have flown;
But the old earth clung to her own,
Holding them back from heavenly wars,
Though every flower sprang at the stars.

But he broke free: while all things ceased,
Some hour increasing, he increased.
The town beneath him seemed a map,
Above the church he cocked his cap,
Above the cross his feather flew,
Above the birds: and still he grew.

The trees turned grass; the clouds were riven;
His feet were mountains lost in heaven;
Through strange new skies he rose alone,
The earth fell from him like a stone,
And his own limbs beneath him far
Seemed tapering down to touch a star.

He reared his head, shaggy and grim,
Staring among the cherubim;
The seven celestial floors he rent,
One crystal dome still o'er him bent:
Above his head, more clear than hope,
All heaven was a microscope.

A PORTRAIT

Fair faces crowd on Christmas night
  Like seven suns a-row,
But all beyond is the wolfish wind
  And the crafty feet of the snow.

But through the rout one figure goes
  With quick and quiet tread;
Her robe is plain, her form is frail—
  Wait if she turn her head.

I say no word of line or hue,
  But if that face you see,

Your soul shall know the smile of faith's
    Awful frivolity.

Know that in this grotesque old masque
    Too loud we cannot sing,
Or dance too wild, or speak too wide
    To praise a hidden thing.

That though the jest be old as night,
    Still shaketh sun and sphere
An everlasting laughter
    Too loud for us to hear.

FEMINA CONTRA MUNDUM

The sun was black with judgment, and the moon
    Blood: but between
I saw a man stand, saying, 'To me at least
    The grass is green.

'There was no star that I forgot to fear
    With love and wonder.
The birds have loved me'; but no answer came—
    Only the thunder.

Once more the man stood, saying, 'A cottage door,
    Wherethrough I gazed
That instant as I turned—yea, I am vile;
    Yet my eyes blazed.

'For I had weighed the mountains in a balance,
    And the skies in a scale,
I come to sell the stars—old lamps for new—
    Old stars for sale.'

Then a calm voice fell all the thunder through,
  A tone less rough:
'Thou hast begun to love one of my works
  Almost enough.'

TO A CERTAIN NATION

We will not let thee be, for thou art ours.
  We thank thee still, though thou forget these things,
For that hour's sake when thou didst wake all powers
  With a great cry that God was sick of kings.

Leave thee there grovelling at their rusted greaves,
  These hulking cowards on a painted stage,
Who, with imperial pomp and laurel leaves,
  Show their Marengo—one man in a cage.

These, for whom stands no type or title given
  In all the squalid tales of gore and pelf;
Though cowed by crashing thunders from all heaven,
  Cain never said, 'My brother slew himself.'

Tear you the truth out of your drivelling spy,
  The maniac whom you set to swing death's scythe.
Nay; torture not the torturer—let him lie:
  What need of racks to teach a worm to writhe?

Bear with us, O our sister, not in pride,
  Nor any scorn we see thee spoiled of knaves,
But only shame to hear, where Danton died,
  Thy foul dead kings all laughing in their graves.

Thou has a right to rule thyself; to be
  The thing thou wilt; to grin, to fawn, to creep;

To crown these clumsy liars; ay, and we
Who knew thee once, we have a right to weep.

THE PRAISE OF DUST

'What of vile dust?' the preacher said.
    Methought the whole world woke,
The dead stone lived beneath my foot,
    And my whole body spoke.

'You, that play tyrant to the dust,
    And stamp its wrinkled face,
This patient star that flings you not
    Far into homeless space.

'Come down out of your dusty shrine
    The living dust to see,
The flowers that at your sermon's end
    Stand blazing silently.

'Rich white and blood-red blossom; stones,
    Lichens like fire encrust;
A gleam of blue, a glare of gold,
    The vision of the dust.

'Pass them all by: till, as you come
    Where, at a city's edge,
Under a tree—I know it well—
    Under a lattice ledge,

'The sunshine falls on one brown head.
    You, too, O cold of clay,
Eater of stones, may haply hear
    The trumpets of that day.

'When God to all his paladins
　　By his own splendour swore
To make a fairer face than heaven,
　　Of dust and nothing more.'

THE BALLAD OF THE BATTLE OF GIBEON

Five kings ruled o'er the Amorite,
Mighty as fear and old as night;
Swathed with unguent and gold and jewel,
Waxed they merry and fat and cruel.
Zedek of Salem, a terror and glory,
Whose face was hid while his robes were gory;
And Hoham of Hebron, whose loathly face is
Heavy and dark o'er the ruin of races;
And Piram of Jarmuth, drunk with strange wine,
Who dreamed he had fashioned all stars that shine;
And Debir of Eglon wild, without pity,
Who raged like a plague in the midst of his city;
And Japhia of Lachish, a fire that flameth,
Who did in the daylight what no man nameth.

These five kings said one to another,
'King unto king o'er the world is brother,
Seeing that now, for a sign and a wonder,
A red eclipse and a tongue of thunder,
A shape and a finger of desolation,
Is come against us a kingless nation.
Gibeon hath failed us: it were not good
That a man remember where Gibeon stood.'
Then Gibeon sent to our captain, crying,
'Son of Nun, let a shaft be flying,
For unclean birds are gathering greedily;
Slack not thy hand, but come thou speedily.

Yea, we are lost save thou maintain'st us,
For the kings of the mountains are gathered against us.'

Then to our people spake the Deliverer,
'Gibeon is high, yet a host may shiver her;
Gibeon hath sent to me crying for pity,
For the lords of the cities encompass the city
With chariot and banner and bowman and lancer,
And I swear by the living God I will answer.
Gird you, O Israel, quiver and javelin,
Shield and sword for the road we travel in;
Verily, as I have promised, pay I
Life unto Gibeon, death unto Ai.'

Sudden and still as a bolt shot right
Up on the city we went by night.
Never a bird of the air could say,
'This was the children of Israel's way.'
Only the hosts sprang up from sleeping,
Saw from the heights a dark stream sweeping;
Sprang up straight as a great shout stung them
And heard the Deliverer's war-cry among them,
Heard under cupola, turret, and steeple
The awful cry of the kingless people.

Started the weak of them, shouted the strong of them,
Crashed we a thunderbolt into the throng of them,
Blindly with heads bent, and shields forced before us,
We heard the dense roar of the strife closing o'er us.
And drunk with the crash of the song that it sung them,
We drove the great spear-blade in God's name among them.

Redder and redder the sword-flash fell,
Our eyes and our nostrils were hotter than hell;

Till full all the crest of the spear-surge shocking us,
Hoham of Hebron cried out mocking us,
'Nay, what need of the war-sword's plying,
Out of the desert the dust comes flying.
A little red dust, if the wind be blowing—
Who shall reck of its coming or going?'
Back the Deliverer spake as a clarion,
'Mock at thy slaves, thou eater of carrion!
Laughest thou at us, in thy kingly clowning,
We, that laughed upon Ramases frowning,
We that stood up, proud, unpardoned,
When his face was dark, and his heart was hardened?
Pharoah we knew and his steeds, not faster
Than the word of the Lord in thine ear, O master.'
Sheer through the turban his wantons wove him,
Clean to the skull the Deliverer clove him;
And the two hosts reeled at the sign appalling,
As the great king fell like a great house falling.

Loudly we shouted, and living, and dying,
Bore them all backward with strength and strong crying;
And Caleb struck Zedek hard at the throat,
And Japhia of Lachish Zebulon smote.
The war-swords and axes were clashing and groaning,
The fallen were fighting and foaming and moaning,
The war spears were breaking, the war-horns were braying,
Ere the hands of the slayers were sated with slaying.
And deep in the grasses grown gory and sodden,
The treaders of all men were trampled and trodden;
And over them, routed and reeled like cattle,
High over the turn of the tide of the battle,
High over noises that deafen and cover us,
Rang the Deliverer's voice out over us.

'Stand thou still, thou sun upon Gibeon,
Stand thou, moon, in the valley of Ajalon!
Shout thou, people, a cry like thunder,
For the kings of the earth are broken asunder.
Now we have said as the thunder says it,
Something is stronger than strength and slays it.
Now we have written for all time later,
Five kings are great, yet a law is greater.
Stare, O sun! in thine own great glory,
This is the turn of the whole world's story.
Stand thou still, thou sun upon Gibeon,
Stand thou, moon, in the valley of Ajalon!

'Smite! amid spear-blades blazing and breaking,
More than we know of is rising and making.
Stab with the javelin, crash with the car!
Cry! for we know not the thing that we are.
Stand, O sun! that in horrible patience
Smiled on the smoke and the slaughter of nations.
Thou shalt grow sad for a little crying,
Thou shalt be darkened for one man's dying—
Stand thou still, thou sun of Gibeon,
Stand thou, moon, in the valley of Ajalon!'

After the battle was broken and spent
Up to the hill the Deliverer went,
Flung up his arms to the storm-clouds flying,
And cried unto Israel, mightily crying,
'Come up, O warriors! come up, O brothers!
Tribesmen and herdsmen, maidens and mothers;
The bondman's son and the bondman's daughter,
The hewer of wood and the drawer of water,
He that carries and he that brings,
And set your foot on the neck of kings.'

This is the story of Gibeon fight—
Where we smote the lords of the Amorite;
Where the banners of princes with slaughter were sodden,
And the beards of seers in the rank grass trodden;
Where the trees were wrecked by the wreck of cars,
And the reek of the red field blotted the stars;
Where the dead heads dropp'd from the swords that sever,
Because His mercy endureth for ever.

"VULGARISED"

All round they murmur, 'O profane,
   Keep thy heart's secret hid as gold';
But I, by God, would sooner be
   Some knight in shattering wars of old,

In brown outlandish arms to ride,
   And shout my love to every star
With lungs to make a poor maid's name
   Deafen the iron ears of war.

Here, where these subtle cowards crowd,
   To stand and so to speak of love,
That the four corners of the world
   Should hear it and take heed thereof.

That to this shrine obscure there be
   One witness before all men given,
As naked as the hanging Christ,
   As shameless as the sun in heaven.

These whimperers—have they spared to us
   One dripping woe, one reeking sin?
These thieves that shatter their own graves
   To prove the soul is dead within.

They talk; by God, is it not time
  Some of Love's chosen broke the girth,
And told the good all men have known
  Since the first morning of the earth?

THE BALLAD OF GOD-MAKERS

A bird flew out at the break of day
  From the nest where it had curled,
And ere the eve the bird had set
  Fear on the kings of the world.

The first tree it lit upon
  Was green with leaves unshed;
The second tree it lit upon
  Was red with apples red;

The third tree it lit upon
  Was barren and was brown,
Save for a dead man nailed thereon
  On a hill above a town.

That night the kings of the earth were gay
  And filled the cup and can;
Last night the kings of the earth were chill
  For dread of a naked man.

'If he speak two more words,' they said,
  'The slave is more than the free:
'If he speak three more words,' they said,
  'The stars are under the sea.'

Said the King of the East to the King of the West,
  I wot his frown was set,

'Lo, let us slay him and make him as dung,
  It is well that the world forget.'

Said the King of the West to the King of the East,
  I wot his smile was dread,
'Nay, let us slay him and make him a god,
  It is well that our god be dead.'

They set the young man on a hill,
  They nailed him to a rod;
And there in darkness and in blood
  They made themselves a god.

And the mightiest word was left unsaid,
  And the world had never a mark,
And the strongest man of the sons of men
  Went dumb into the dark.

Then hymns and harps of praise they brought,
  Incense and gold and myrrh,
And they throned above the seraphim,
  The poor dead carpenter.

'Thou art the prince of all,' they sang,
  'Ocean and earth and air,'
Then the bird flew on to the cruel cross,
  And hid in the dead man's hair.

'Thou art the sun of the world,' they cried,
  'Speak if our prayers be heard.'
And the brown bird stirred in the dead man's hair,
  And it seemed that the dead man stirred.

Then a shriek went up like the world's last cry
  From all nations under heaven,

And a master fell before a slave
  And begged to be forgiven.

They cowered, for dread in his wakened eyes
  The ancient wrath to see;
And a bird flew out of the dead Christ's hair,
  And lit on a lemon-tree.

AT NIGHT

How many million stars there be,
That only God hath numberéd;
  But this one only chosen for me
In time before her face was fled.
Shall not one mortal man alive
  Hold up his head?

THE WOOD-CUTTER

We came behind him by the wall,
  My brethren drew their brands,
And they had strength to strike him down—
  And I to bind his hands.

Only once, to a lantern gleam,
  He turned his face from the wall,
And it was as the accusing angel's face
  On the day when the stars shall fall.

I grasped the axe with shaking hands,
  I stared at the grass I trod;
For I feared to see the whole bare heavens
  Filled with the face of God.

I struck: the serpentine slow blood
 In four arms soaked the moss—
Before me, by the living Christ,
 The blood ran in a cross.

Therefore I toil in forests here
 And pile the wood in stacks,
And take no fee from the shivering folk
 Till I have cleansed the axe.

But for a curse God cleared my sight,
 And where each tree doth grow
I see a life with awful eyes,
 And I must lay it low.

ART COLOURS

On must we go: we search dead leaves,
 We chase the sunset's saddest flames,
The nameless hues that o'er and o'er
 In lawless weddings lost their names.

God of the daybreak! Better be
 Black savages; and grin to gird
Our limbs in gaudy rags of red,
 The laughing-stock of brute and bird.

And feel again the fierce old feast,
 Blue for seven heavens that had sufficed,
A gold like shining hoards, a red
 Like roses from the blood of Christ.

THE TWO WOMEN

Lo! very fair is she who knows the ways
  Of joy: in pleasure's mocking wisdom old,
The eyes that might be cold to flattery, kind;
  The hair that might be grey with knowledge, gold.

But thou art more than these things, O my queen,
  For thou art clad in ancient wars and tears.
And looking forth, framed in the crown of thorns,
  I saw the youngest face in all the spheres.

THE WILD KNIGHT

The wasting thistle whitens on my crest,
The barren grasses blow upon my spear,
A green, pale pennon: blazon of wild faith
And love of fruitless things: yea, of my love,
Among the golden loves of all the knights,
Alone: most hopeless, sweet, and blasphemous,
The love of God:
              I hear the crumbling creeds
Like cliffs washed down by water, change, and pass;
I hear a noise of words, age after age,
A new cold wind that blows across the plains,
And all the shrines stand empty; and to me
All these are nothing: priests and schools may doubt
Who never have believed; but I have loved.
Ah friends, I know it passing well, the love
Wherewith I love; it shall not bring to me
Return or hire or any pleasant thing—
Ay, I have tried it: Ay, I know its roots.

Earthquake and plague have burst on it in vain
And rolled back shattered—
                              Babbling neophytes!

Blind, startled fools—think you I know it not?
Think you to teach me? Know I not His ways?
Strange-visaged blunders, mystic cruelties.
All! all! I know Him, for I love Him. Go!

So, with the wan waste grasses on my spear,
I ride for ever, seeking after God,
My hair grows whiter than my thistle plume,
And all my limbs are loose; but in my eyes
The star of an unconquerable praise:
For in my soul one hope for ever sings,
That at the next white corner of a road
My eyes may look on Him. . . .
                              Hush—I shall know
The place when it is found: a twisted path
Under a twisted pear-tree—this I saw
In the first dream I had ere I was born,
Wherein He spoke. . . .
                              But the grey clouds come down
In hail upon the icy plains: I ride,
Burning for ever in consuming fire.

*A dark manor-house shuttered and unlighted, outlined against
   a pale sunset: in front a large, but neglected, garden. To the
   right, in the foreground, the porch of a chapel, with coloured
   windows lighted. Hymns within.*
*Above the porch a grotesque carved bracket, supporting a lan-
   tern. Astride of it sits* CAPTAIN REDFEATHER, *a flagon in his
   hand.*

REDFEATHER

I have drunk to all I know of,
To every leaf on the tree,
To the highest bird of the heavens,
To the lowest fish of the sea.
What toast, what toast remaineth,
Drunk down in the same good wine,
By the tippler's cup in the tavern,
And the priest's cup at the shrine?
  [*A Priest comes out, stick in hand and looks right and left.*]

VOICES WITHIN

The brawler . . .

PRIEST

He has vanished

REDFEATHER

To the stars.
  [*The Priest looks up.*]

PRIEST [*angrily*]

What would you there, sir?

REDFEATHER

Give you all a toast.
  [*Lifts his flagon. More priests come out.*]
I see my life behind me: bad enough—
Drink, duels, madness, beggary, and pride,
The life of the unfit: yet ere I drop
On Nature's rubbish heap, I weigh it all,
And give you all a toast—
  [*Reels to his feet and stands.*]
The health of God!
  [*They all recoil from him.*]

Let's give the Devil of the Heavens His due!
He that made grass so green, and wine so red,
Is not so black as you have painted Him.

[*Drinks.*]

PRIEST

Blaspheming profligate!

REDFEATHER [*hurls the flagon among them.*]
Howl! ye dumb dogs,
I named your king— let me have one great shout,
Flutter the seraphim like startled birds;
Make God recall the good days of His youth
Ere saints had saddened Him: when He came back
Conqueror of Chaos in a six days' war,
With all the sons of God shouting for joy . . .

PRIEST

And you—what is your right, and who are you,
To praise God?

REDFEATHER

A lost soul. In earth or heaven
What has a better right?

PRIEST

Go, pagan, go!
Drink, dice, and dance: take no more thought than blind
Beasts of the field. . . .

REDFEATHER

Or . . . lilies of the field,
To quote a pagan sage. I go my way.

PRIEST [*solemnly*]

And when Death comes . . .

REDFEATHER

He shall not find me dead.
[*Puts on his plumed hat. The priests go out.*]

REDFEATHER

These frozen fools . . .
[*The Lady Olive comes out of the chapel. He sees her.*]
Oh, they were right enough,
Where shall I hide my carrion from the sun?
[*Buries his face. His hat drops to the ground.*]

OLIVE [*looking up*]
Captain, are you from church? I saw you not.

REDFEATHER

No, I am here.
[*Lays his hand on a gargoyle.*]
I, too, am a grotesque,
And dance with all the devils on the roof.

OLIVE [*with a strange smile*]
For Satan, also, I have often prayed.

REDFEATHER [*roughly*]
Satan may worry women if he will.
For he was but an angel ere he fell.
But I—before I fell—I was a man.

OLIVE

He, too, my Master, was a man: too strong
To fear a strong man's sins: 'tis written He
Descended into hell.

REDFEATHER

Write, then, that I
                    [*Leaps to the ground before her.*]
Descended into heaven . . .

                    You are ill?

OLIVE

No, well . . .

REDFEATHER

          You speak the truth—you are the Truth—
Lady, say once again then, 'I am *well.*'

OLIVE

I—ah! God give me grace—I am nigh dead.

REDFEATHER [*quietly*]

Lord Orm?

OLIVE

     Yes—yes.

REDFEATHER

          Is in your father's house—
Having the title-deeds—would drive you forth,
Homeless, and with your father sick to death,
Into this winter, save on a condition
Named . . .

OLIVE

          And unnameable. Even so; Lord Orm—
Ah! do you know him?

REDFEATHER

          Ay, I saw him once.
The sun shone on his face, that smiled and smiled
A sight not wholesome to the eyes of man.

OLIVE

Captain, I tell you God once fell asleep,
And in that hour the world went as it would;
Dogs brought forth cats, and poison grew in grapes,
And Orm was born . . .

REDFEATHER

Why, curse him! can he not

Be kicked or paid?

OLIVE [*feverishly*]

Hush! He is just behind
There in the house—see how the great house glares,
Glares like an ogre's mask—the whole dead house
Possessed with bestial meaning. . . .

[*Screams.*]

Ah! the face
The whole great grinning house—his face! his face!
His face!

REDFEATHER [*in a voice of thunder, pointing away from the house*]

Look there—look there!

OLIVE

What is it? What?

REDFEATHER

I think it was a bird.

OLIVE

What thought you, truly?

REDFEATHER

I think a mighty thought is drawing near.

[*Enter* THE WILD KNIGHT.]

THE WILD KNIGHT

That house . . .

[*Points.*]

OLIVE

Ah Christ! [*Shudders.*] I had forgotten it.

THE WILD KNIGHT [*still pointing*]

That house! the house at last, the house of God,
Wherein God makes an evening feast for me.
The house at last: I know the twisted path
Under the twisted pear-tree: this I saw
In the first dream I had ere I was born.
It is the house of God. He welcomes me.

[*Strides forward.*]

REDFEATHER

That house. God's blood!

OLIVE [*hysterically*]

Is not this hell's own wit?

THE WILD KNIGHT

God grows impatient, and His wine is poured,
His bread is broken.

[*Rushes forward.*]

REDFEATHER [*leaps between*]

Stand away, great fool,

There is a devil there!

THE WILD KNIGHT [*draws his sword, and waves it as he rushes*]

God's house!—God's house!

REDFEATHER [*plucks out his own sword*]

Better my hand than his.

[*The blades clash.*]

God alone knows

What That within might do to you, poor fool
I can but kill you.

[*They fight.* Olive *tries to part them.*]

REDFEATHER

Olive, stand away!

OLIVE

I will not stand away!

[*Steps between the swords.*]

Stranger, a word,

Yes—you are right—God is within that house.

REDFEATHER

Olive!

OLIVE

But He is all too beautiful

For us who only know of stars and flowers
The thing within is all too pure and fair,

[*Shudders.*]

Too awful in its ancient innocence,
For men to look upon it and not die;
Ourselves would fade into those still white fires
Of peace and mercy.

[*Struggles with her voice.*]

There . . . enough . . . the law—

No flesh shall look upon the Lord and live.

REDFEATHER [*sticking his sword in the ground*]

You are the bravest lady in the world.

THE WILD KNIGHT [*dazed*]

May I not go within?

REDFEATHER
Keep you the law—
No flesh shall look upon the Lord and live.

THE WILD KNIGHT [*sadly*]
Then I will go and lay me in the flowers,
For He may haply, as in ancient time,
Walk in the garden in the cool of day.

[*He goes out.*]
[OLIVE *reels.* REDFEATHER *catches her.*]

REDFEATHER
You are the strongest woman upon earth.
The weakest woman than the strongest man
Is stronger in her hour: this is the law.
When the hour passes—then may we be strong.

OLIVE [*wildly*]
The House . . . the Face.

REDFEATHER [*fiercely*]
I love you. Look at me!

OLIVE [*turns her face to him*]
I hear six birds sing in that little tree,
Say, is the old earth laughing at my fears?
I think I love you also . . .

REDFEATHER
What I am
You know. But I will never curse a man,
Even in a mirror.

OLIVE [*smiling at him*]
And the Devil's dance?

REDFEATHER

The Devil plotted since the world was young
With alchemies of fire and witches' oil
And magic. But he never made a man.

OLIVE

No, not a man.

REDFEATHER

Not even my Lord Orm
Look at the house now—

　　　　　　　　　　[*She starts and looks.*]
　　　　　Honest brick and tiles.

OLIVE

You have a strange strength in this hour.

REDFEATHER

　　　　　　　　This hour
I see with mortal eyes as in one flash
The whole divine democracy of things,
And dare the stars to scorn a scavenge-heap.
Olive, I tell you every soul is great.
Weave we green crowns—how noble and how high;
Fling we white flowers—how radiant and how pure
Is he, whoe'er he be, who next shall cross
This scrap of grass . . .

　　　　　　　　　　　[*Enter* LORD ORM.]

　　　　OLIVE [*screams*]
　　　　　Ah!

　　REDFEATHER [*pointing to the chapel*]
　　　　　Olive, go and pray

For a man soon to die. Good day, my Lord.

                                        [*She goes in.*]

LORD ORM

Good day.

REDFEATHER
I am a friend to Lady Olive.

LORD ORM

Sir, you are fortunate.

REDFEATHER
                Most fortunate
In finding, sword on thigh and ready, one
Who is a villain and a gentleman.

        LORD ORM [*picks up the flagon*]

Empty, I see.

REDFEATHER
        Oh sir, you never drink
You dread to lose yourself before the stars—
Do you not dread to sleep?

                LORD ORM [*violently*]
                        What would you here?

REDFEATHER
Receive from you the title-deeds you hold.

LORD ORM

You entertain me.

REDFEATHER
With a bout at foils?

LORD ORM

Evil, be thou my good;
Let the sun blacken and the moon be blood:
I have said the words.

REDFEATHER [*studying him*]

And if I struck you dead,
You would turn to daisies!

LORD ORM

And you do not strike.

REDFEATHER [*dreamily*]

Indeed, poor soul, such magic would be kind
And full of pity as a fairy-tale:
One touch of this bright wand [*Lifts his sword*] and down
    would drop
The dark abortive blunder that is you,
And you would change, forgiven, into flowers.

LORD ORM

And yet—and yet you do not strike me dead.
I do not draw: the sword is in your hand —
Drive the blade through me where I stand.

REDFEATHER

Lord Orm,

You asked the Lady Olive (I can speak
As to a toad to you, my lord)—you asked
Olive to be your paramour: and she—

LORD ORM

Refused.

REDFEATHER

And yet her father was at stake,
And she is soft and kind. Now look at me,

Lord Orm

I will not fight.

Redfeather

I know you better, then.
I have seen men grow mangier than the beasts,
Eat bread with blood upon their fingers, grin
While women burned: but one last law they served.
When I say 'Coward,' is the law awake?

Lord Orm

Hear me, then too: I have seen robbers rule,
And thieves go clad in gold— age after age—
Because, though sordid, ragged, rude, and mean,
They saw, like gods, no law above their heads.
But when they fell—then for this cause they fell,
This last mean cobweb of the fairy tales
Of good and ill: that they must stand and fight
When a man bade, though they had chose to stand
And fight not, I am stronger than the world.

[Folds his arms.]

Redfeather *[lifts his hand]*

If in your body be the blood of a man,

[Strikes him.

Now let it rush to the face—

God! Have you sunk
Lower than anger?

Lord Orm
How I triumph now.

Redfeather *[stamps wildly]*

Damned, whimpering dog! vile, snivelling sick poltroon!
Are you alive?

Ragged and ruined, soaked in bestial sins:
My lord, I too have my virginity—
Turn the thing round, my lord, and topside down,
You cannot spell it. Be the fact enough,
I use no sword upon a swordless man.

LORD ORM

For her?

REDFEATHER

I too have my virginity.

LORD ORM

Now look on me: I am the lord of earth,
For I have broken the last bond of man.
I stand erect, crowned with the stars—and why?
Because I stand a coward—because you
Have mercy—on a coward. Do I win?

REDFEATHER

Though there you stand with moving mouth and eyes,
I think, my lord, you are not possible—
God keep you from my dreams.

[*Goes out.*]

LORD ORM

                    Alone and free.
Since first in flowery meads a child I ran,
My one long thirst—to be alone and free.
Free of all laws, creeds, codes, and common tests,
Shameless, anarchic, infinite.
                    Why, then,
I might have done in that dark liberty—
If I should say 'a good deed,' men would laugh,
But here are none to laugh.

The godless world

Be thanked there is no God to spy on me,
Catch me and crown me with a vulgar crown
For what I do: if I should once believe
The horror of that ancient Eavesdropper
Behind the starry arras of the skies,
I should—well, well, enough of menaces—
I should not do the thing I come to do.
What do I come to do? Let me but try
To spell it to my soul.

Suppose a man

Perfectly free and utterly alone,
Free of all love of law, equally free
Of all the love of mutiny it breeds,
Free of the love of heaven, and also free
Of all the love of hell it drives us to;
Not merely void of rules, unconscious of them;
So strong that naught alive could do him hurt,
So wise that he knew all things, and so great
That none knew what he was or what he did—
A lawless giant.   [*A pause: then in a low voice.*]

Would he not be good?

Hate is the weakness of a thwarted thing,
Pride is the weakness of a thing unpraised.
But he, this man . . .

He would be like a child

Girt with the tomes of some vast library,
Who reads romance after romance, and smiles
When every tale ends well: impersonal
As God he grows—melted in suns and stars;
So would this boundless man, whom none could spy,
Taunt him with virtue, censure him with vice,
Rejoice in all men's joys; with golden pen

Write all the live romances of the earth
To a triumphant close . . .
                              Alone and free—
In this grey, cool, clean garden, washed with winds,
What do I come to do among the grass,
The daisies, and the dews? An awful thing,
To prove I am that man.
                              That while these saints
Taunt me with trembling, dare me to revenge,
I breathe an upper air of ancient good
And strong eternal laughter; send my sun
And rain upon the evil and the just,
Turn my left cheek unto the smiter. He
That told me, sword in hand, that I had fallen
Lower than anger, knew not I had risen
Higher than pride . . .
                              Enough the deeds are mine.
                    [*Takes out the title-deeds.*]
I come to write the end of a romance.
A good romance: the characters—Lord Orm,
Type of the starvéd heart and storéd brain,
Who strives to hate and cannot; fronting him —
Redfeather, rake in process of reform,
At root a poet: I have hopes of him:
He can love virtue, for he still loves vice.
He is not all burnt out. He beats me there
(How I beat him in owning it!); in love
He is still young, and has the joy of shame.
And for the Lady Olive—who shall speak?
A man may weigh the courage of a man,
But if there be a bottomless abyss
It is a woman's valour: such as I
Can only bow the knee and hide the face

(Thank God there is no God to spy on me
And bring his curséd crowns).
                              No, there is none:
The old incurable hunger of the world
Surges in wolfish wars, age after age.
There was no God before me: none sees where
Between the brute-womb and the deaf, dead grave,
Unhoping, unrecorded, unrepaid,
I make with smoke, fire, and burnt-offering
This sacrifice to Chaos. [*Lights the paper.*] None behold
Me write in fire the end of the romance.
Burn! I am God, and crown myself with stars
Upon creation day: before was night
And chaos of a blind and cruel world.
I am the first God; I will trample hell,
Fight, conquer, make the story of the stars,
Like this poor story, end like a romance:
                                    [*The paper burns.*]
Before was brainless night: but I am God
In this black world I rend. Let there be light!
            [*The paper blazes up, illuminating the garden.*]
I, God . . .

            THE WILD KNIGHT [*rushes forward*]
            God's Light! God's voice; yes it is He
Walking in Eden in the cool of the day!

                LORD ORM [*screams*]
Tricked! Caught!
Damned screeching rat in a hole!
    [*Stabs him again and again with his sword; stamps on his
      face.*]

                THE WILD KNIGHT [*faintly*]
Earth grows too beautiful around me: shapes

And colours fearfully wax fair and clear,
For I have heard, as thro' a door ajar,
Scraps of the huge soliloquy of God
That moveth as a mask the lips of man,
If man be very silent: they were right,
No flesh shall look upon the Lord and live.

[*Dies.*]

LORD ORM [*staggers back laughing*]
Saved, saved, my secret.

REDFEATHER [*rushing in, sword in hand*]
The drawn sword at last!
Guard, son of hell!
[*They fight.* ORM *falls.* OLIVE *comes in.*]
He too can die. Keep back!
Olive, keep back from him! I did not fear
Him living, and he fell before my sword;
But dead I fear him. All is ended now;
A man's whole life tied in a bundle there,
And no good deed. I fear him. Come away.

GOOD NEWS

Between a meadow and a cloud that sped
    In rain and twilight, in desire and fear,
    I heard a secret—hearken in your ear,
'Behold the daisy has a ring of red.'

That hour, with half of blessing, half of ban,
    A great voice went through heaven and earth and hell,
    Crying, 'We are tricked, my great ones, is it well?
Now is the secret stolen by a man.'

Then waxed I like the wind because of this,
  And ran, like gospel and apocalypse,
  From door to door, with new anarchic lips,
Crying the very blasphemy of bliss.

In the last wreck of Nature, dark and dread,
  Shall in eclipse's hideous hieroglyph,
  One wild form reel on the last rocking cliff,
And shout, 'The daisy has a ring of red.'

Book Seven
Miscellaneous

A SONG OF SELF-ESTEEM

The Simple Social Lifer is a harmless sort of elf,
He feeds a dog on mutton that he mustn't eat himself.
I tolerate his sandals and his tresses long and lank,
I reverence his madness but I deprecate his Swank.

    O the Swank of the Crank in the future's foremost rank,
    And the child of all the ages there was nobody to spank.
    He has told us all he means by his water and his beans
    In a style that might be pardoned on the theory that he
        drank.

The Banker is an expert on economy and strikes,
He uses all your money to do anything he likes;
And the usurer who uses it you're called upon to thank.
I do not mind the swindle but I do not like the swank.

    O the Swank of the Bank and the cheque you give it
    For the cryptic explanations when the rate of wages sank.
    But I hope to see the fun when a Frenchman with a gun
    Shall ask him what the devil he is doing with the Franc.

The Yankee is a dab at electricity and crime,
He tells you how he hustles and it takes him quite a time,
I like his hospitality that's cordial and frank,
I do not mind his money but I do not like his swank.

    O the Swank of the Yank on the Prohibition Plank,
    O take the water-waggoner and drown him in the tank.
    Since the Faith of Tennessee has wafted o'er the sea,
    The odour of its sanctity—and Golly how it stank!

A SONG OF MODERATION

They have said, the good and wise,
That it pays to advertise,
　　And it's only right to speak with Moderation
Of a truth that stands so high,
Simply written on the sky,
　　Though perhaps with just a touch of ostentation.

The beers that are best known
Are not arsenic alone,
　　It is modified by salt and other things.
If you tell a waiter "Please
Will you bring some Gruyere cheese,"
　　You can trifle with the substance that he brings.

There's a Port that you can drink,
And distinguish it from ink
　　By a something that's not easy to define,
But not only from the poster
Of an after-dinner toaster
　　Who has drunk enough to talk of it as wine.

The Yankee car is slick,
Put together very quick.
　　When it comes apart with similar rapidity,
It will comfort you to know
It would take an hour or so
　　To make it with Victorian solidity.

For it pays to advertise,
And when the engine lies
　　On your stomach and the petrol's in a blaze,
And the car lies round you wrecked,

You'll have leisure to reflect
Upon whom it is exactly that it pays.

THE NEGLECTED CHILD

(Dedicated, in a glow of Christmas charity, to a philanthropic
society)

The Teachers in the Temple
They did not lift their eyes
For the blazing star on Bethlehem
Or the Wise Men grown wise.

They heeded jot and tittle,
They heeded not a jot
The rending voice of Ramah
And the children that were not.

Or how the panic of the poor
Choked all the field with flight,
Or how the red sword of the rich
Ran ravening through the night.

They made their notes; while naked
And monstrous and obscene
A tyrant bathed in all the blood
Of men that might have been.

But they did chide Our Lady
And tax her for this thing,
That she had lost Him for a time
And sought Him sorrowing.

TO A TURK

Warrior by warriors smitten,
Gambler whose luck has turned,

Read not the small words written,
  Who know what love you earned:
You know, and none shall tell you,
  What and how long and how
They did endure in silence
  That smite in silence now.

A Liberal may belabour
  With rods your reckless dead,
As the Tory licked your sabre
  For the blood he dared not shed;
Since from the creedless chapel
  And the cushioned prize-ring came
The men that feared your glory
  And they that praised your shame.

With us too rage against the rood
  Your devils and your swine;
A colder scorn of womanhood,
  A baser fear of wine.
And lust without the harem,
  And Doom without the God.
Go. It is not this rabble
  Sayeth to you 'Ichabod.'

Because our sorrow has sufficed
  And what we know we know;
And because you were great, Lord Antichrist,
  In the name of Christ you go;
But you shall not turn your turban
  For the little dogs that yell,
When a man rides out of a city
  In the name of God; farewell.

THE ARISTOCRAT

The Devil is a gentleman, and asks you down to stay
At his little place at What'sitsname (it isn't far away).
They say the sport is splendid; there is always something new,
And fairy scenes, and fearful feats that none but he can do;
He can shoot the feathered cherubs if they fly on the estate,
Or fish for Father Neptune with the mermaids for a bait;
He scaled amid the staggering stars that precipice, the sky,
And blew his trumpet above heaven, and got by mastery
The starry crown of God Himself, and shoved it on the shelf;
But the Devil is a gentleman, and doesn't brag himself.

O blind your eyes and break your heart and hack your hand
    away,
And lose your love and shave your head; but do not go to stay
At the little place in What'sitsname where folks are rich and
    clever;
The golden and the goodly house, where things grow worse
    for ever;
There are things you need not know of, though you live and
    die in vain,
There are souls more sick of pleasure than you are sick of pain;
There is a game of April Fool that's played behind its door,
Where the fool remains for ever and the April comes no more,

Where the splendour of the daylight grows drearier than the
    dark,
And life droops like a vulture that once was such a lark:
And that is the Blue Devil that once was the Blue Bird;
For the Devil is a gentleman, and doesn't keep his word.

INDEX OF TITLES

INDEX OF FIRST LINES